JAMES

VOLUME 1

JAMES

A Young Man with An Unplanned Future

ELEANOR LIGGENS

JAMES: A Young Man with an Unplanned Future

Copyright © 2025 by Eleanor Liggens. All rights reserved.

No part of this publication may be reproduced, distributed, or transmitted in any form or by any means, including photocopying, recording, or other electronic or mechanical methods, without the prior written permission of the author, except in the case of brief quotations embodied in critical reviews and certain other noncommercial uses permitted by copyright law.

The contents of this work, including, but not limited to, the accuracy of events, people, and places depicted; opinions expressed; permission to use previously published materials included; and any advice given or actions advocated are solely the responsibility of the author, who assumes all liability for said work and indemnifies the publisher against any claims stemming from publication of the work.

Printed in the United States of America
ISBN 978-1-64133-796-0 (hc)
ISBN 978-1-64133-794-6 (sc)
ISBN 978-1-64133-795-3 (ebk)

This book is printed on acid-free paper.

2025.01.14

BlueInk Media Solutions
1111B S Governors Ave
STE 7582 Dover,
DE 19904

www.blueinkmediasolutions.com

In loving memory of

Mr. Booker T. Hall Sr.

A great man and loving father

Dedicated to my beautiful family

James Sr.
James Jr. and
Danielle Liggens

Table of Contents

Chapter 1	Our Sister-Theola	1
Chapter 2	Decisions, Decisions	5
Chapter 3	The Conversation	15
Chapter 4	The Delsin's Surprise	22
Chapter 5	A Near Death Experience	29
Chapter 6	First Time Meeting Strangers	36
Chapter 7	Inquisitive Trucker	42
Chapter 8	A Chance to Stay in Touch	46
Chapter 9	Edward's True Love for James	50
Chapter 10	A New Challenge	54
Chapter 11	Sarah's Sister-Leona	59
Chapter 12	Ms. Sarah's Kindness	65
Chapter 13	Burt's Love for Sarah	72
Chapter 14	Getting Through a Hard Time	77
Chapter 15	The Good News	80
Chapter 16	A Growing Friendship with Sarah	82
Chapter 17	A Potential Job	89
Chapter 18	The Encounter with Strangers	92
Chapter 19	The Argument	98
Chapter 20	Henrietta's Restless Night	101
Chapter 21	James's First Public Bus Ride	105
Chapter 22	The Post Office Job	109
Chapter 23	Theola's Close Encounter	115
Chapter 24	Granny and the Ride Home	118
Chapter 25	The Baby	121
Chapter 26	The Surprise Homecoming	127
Chapter 27	The Moment of Truth from Rena	136

Chapter 28	Spreading the Word	140
Chapter 29	The Surprise Phone Call	145
Chapter 30	Words for Edward	151
Chapter 31	The Promotion	154
Chapter 32	James and Theola Move On	157
Chapter 33	Does Hard Work Pay Off?	159
Chapter 34	The Gathering of Minds	163
Chapter 35	The Diaper Change	166
Chapter 36	Going to Church	170
Chapter 37	The Same Symptoms	173
Chapter 38	Envy and Jealousy Arises	180
Chapter 39	Is James in Trouble?	183
Chapter 40	New Born Stress	184
Chapter 41	Don't Leave Me	187
Chapter 42	Being Nosey	191
Chapter 43	James's Submission	196
Chapter 44	Lee Roy	199
Chapter 45	Another Surprise on the Way	203
Chapter 46	The Conspiracy	213
Chapter 47	The Conspirators in Action	217
Chapter 48	The Backstabber	226
Chapter 49	Chaos in the Post Office	230
Chapter 50	Confronting a Friend	234
Chapter 51	Friendship	236
Chapter 52	Sandy Tells James	239
Chapter 53	Theola's Plan for the Children's Future	242
Chapter 54	Good Friends at the Right Time	251
Chapter 55	Another Plot Unfolds	253
Chapter 56	The Plot Thickens	255
Chapter 57	Breaking the Bad News to Theola	260
Chapter 58	A Good Lawyer	264
Chapter 59	The Surprise Visit	267

Chapter 60	Sandy's Conscious	272
Chapter 61	Where Will We Go?	274
Chapter 62	Sandy's Dilemma	277
Chapter 63	Perseverance	278
Chapter 64	A Joyful Moment	281
Chapter 65	An Unexpected Visitor	283
Chapter 66	Can You Count?	287
Chapter 67	Where Is James?	291
Chapter 68	The Payback	294
Chapter 69	The Boot	298
Chapter 70	Over Worked	302
Chapter 71	Surprise!	305
Chapter 72	Missing Person	309
Chapter 73	The Agony of Pain	310
Chapter 74	Hospital Stay	317
Chapter 75	Emergency/Help!	319
Chapter 76	Desperation	323
Chapter 77	Sisters to the Rescue	325
Chapter 78	Our Love for You Theola	329
Chapter 79	Doctor's Diagnosis	336
Chapter 80	James's Dilemma	337
Chapter 81	Remember Our Love	343
Chapter 82	Love of My Life, Forever	347

Chapter 1

Our Sister-Theola

*I*n a quiet little southern town, on a warm, humid night, in an air-conditioned house, Theola lay awake in the top bunk of her bedroom. Sweat dripped from her forehead while her cotton sack nightgown that was over her street clothes clung to her body from perspiration. Nervousness overwhelmed the pit of her stomach. She pretended to be asleep. Theola waited for hours until she felt everyone in the house had fallen into a deep slumber. Very cautiously, she sat up. By the glimmer of the kerosene lamp that sat atop their only bedroom dresser, Theola leaned gently over the side to see if her nine-year-old baby sister was still asleep. She then slowly moved to the edge of the bed to climb down the side ladder, praying not to disturb her other two younger sisters who lay across the room in another bunk bed, only a few feet away. As her bare feet gently touched the cool linoleum floor, she bent down slowly to reach under the bed of her baby sister. She used the glare of the kerosene lamp that barely lit the room to grab a brown bag filled with bread and peanut butter that she had hidden earlier in the day. She gently pulled the bag from under the bed. She watched her baby sister the entire time, trying not to disturb her sleep. Once Theola had fully retrieved the bag and shoes from under the bed, she sat on the floor to place her tennis shoes on her feet. Then she tiptoed ever so softly to leave the room without disturbing a soul. She turned to take one last glance at her three sisters. When she did, Theola saw the whites of a pair of eyes peering at her through the dimness of the room. Deborah was sitting on the side of her bed. Half startled to see her there, Theola covered her heart with her hand, but she didn't scream or drop her bag of food. Theola took a deep breath.

"Deborah, you scared me. What are you doing up?" Whispered Theola.

"Konee told me everything."

"What! I asked her not to tell. I know you're older than Konee. I would have told you, but you're too excitable. I felt you would have told Mom and Dad."

"I told her I would keep this secret for you."

"How did you get Konee to tell? She is very good at keeping secrets."

"You have been acting very strange. I noticed you sneaking around at night when you thought everybody else was asleep."

"I'm sorry, Deborah."

"Theola, what you're doing is wrong. You're our sister. We are a family. We can work these problems out. Don't run away. We all love you. Your brothers are going to miss you too. Mom and Dad will surely miss you. You're going to hurt them, Theola, deeply. Please don't do it." Tears started to flow.

"Don't cry Deborah. Don't make this any harder than what it is. James is meeting me. I'm running late."

"I don't like James!" The other sisters shuffled in their beds from the tone of Deborah's voice.

"Shhhhhhhh! Before you wake everybody else."

"Don't you want me to wake Konee?"

"No, we have said our goodbyes. She didn't want me to wake her." Deborah started sniffling. "Don't start crying, please."

"He's taking you away from us," Deborah spoke softly. "He was always sooo quiet when he came around. Daddy said the quiet ones are always sneaky."

"Don't do this Deborah. James isn't like that. I'll try to explain everything later." Deborah wiped the tears from her cheeks with the back of her hand. Theola felt regret. "Deborah, I love you all too. If I felt there was another way to do this, believe me with all my heart, I would."

Deborah stood from her bed. Her petite, slender body was outlined in the faintness of the light. Tears still trickled down her cheeks. Sadness gleamed on both their faces. Deborah stretched her skinny arms out. Theola eased her bag to the floor and gave Deborah a lasting hug.

"Deborah I must go now. Kiss my brothers and sisters for me. Tell them that I love them too." In her anxious moment to hurry and meet James, Theola turned to walk away.

Deborah bowed her head and quickly noticed, "Theola," she whispered. Theola turned and glanced at Deborah one last time. "You forgot your bag." Deborah picked up the bag from the floor and handed it to her.

"Deborah don't look so sad. Please stop crying. We will see each other again. It's not goodbye, it's see you later. I will be back, I promise. I love you all too much not to ever see you again. So wish me the best and I will keep in touch with you through James's parents."

"James's parents… ? How?"

"Look in Konee's drawer after I'm gone. You'll find their phone number."

"But what are Mom and Dad going to say?" Deborah sniffled. "What do I tell them when they ask?"

"Deborah you don't have to say anything. I left Mom and Dad a note explaining almost everything, so please don't speak a word to them. I love you. Got to run."

Deborah sat back down on her bottom bunk and watched Theola slowly creep out of the room into the darkness of the hallway. She laid back down in her bed with tears streaming from her eyes. The pit of her stomach was heavy with grief. She felt deep in her heart that she would never see her oldest sister again, no matter how Theola had promised.

Chapter 2

Decisions, Decisions

Theola knew she had to hurry to meet James before he felt she wasn't coming and he started to go back home. But first, she had to leave her house without her parents realizing she was gone. Theola walked gently down the stairs and through the living room, easing one foot down at a time, missing the specific spots on the floor that creaked. Being five feet nine inches tall and weighing one hundred and eighty pounds made this task a little difficult. After several nights of practicing, on this night, she succeeded in reaching the front door without waking her parents as she had once before. Theola slightly opened the door, only enough to squeeze through. She eased the door closed and turned the knob very carefully to lock the door back and not be heard. Slowly, she walked down the front steps of the porch. When she felt she was a safe distance from the house, Theola ran as fast as she could to meet James at the old school house, where they had met many times before. She darted through the backyards of houses, brushing pants, blouses, and sheets that hung from clotheslines out of her way. She dashed down dirt trails and dense wooded paths to reach the only boy she had known intimately since the eleventh grade. Minutes later, drenched in sweat, Theola approached the schoolhouse. By the streetlight that lit the road, she could see James pacing in front of the old school building. She waved her arm frantically so that he could see her coming. James stood with his arms folded, watching Theola race toward him.

"Theola Delsin, you bout as slow as molasses in the wintertime. It's fifteen minutes afta midnight! I was two shakes of a dog's tail from walkin' away. Ya said you'd be here by midnight."

Theola, out of breath, dropped the bag she was carrying and reached for James. She grabbed him by his shoulders. He held her close for a few moments, until she regained her composure. Soon she started to breathe a little easier. She pushed back from James and looked down upon him. He was only five feet seven inches tall with dark brown skin, naturally coarse, thick, bushy black hair, brown eyes and a stocky build.

"Why James Paul Taylor, you know I had to wait until everyone was asleep. If my parents had caught me, I would be in deep trouble right now," sighed Theola, still catching her breath. "Look at me. I'm still in my nightgown." Theola shredded the nightgown only to expose her white blouse and blue jeans. She placed her gown in her brown paper bag.

"Since I've been standin' here waitin' fo ya, I've been thankin'."

"And just what have you been thinking about James?"

"Perhaps what we're doin' is all wrong. Yo folks are church-goin' people. God lovin' people. Look at me. I dress plain, my folks dress plain, except for my sister Rena. Your whole family dress like you got money. Why ya wanna ruin all that?"

"It's not goin', lovin', and wanna James. It's going, loving and want to."

James continued as he paced the grounds. "I knowed they'd hate fo ya to leave and git married like dis. They have such high hopes fo ya. And I don't thank runnin' away with me was one of their plans fo yo future."

"James Paul Taylor I didn't run all the way out here to listen to excuses from you why I shouldn't leave home! Do you think I wanted to do this? I hated walking away from home. I love my family. Do you know what I have in this sack I'm carrying?"

James stopped pacing. "Well, I know ya gotta nightgown in there."

Theola opened the sack and threw the nightgown to the ground. She shoved the bag into James's face. "Look in there. I have a comb, a toothbrush, peanut butter and a loaf of bread. Does that appear like I know what I'm doing! I'm just as scared as you are!" She closed the bag and threw it on the ground.

"You don't have ta scream. You bout as loud as somebody shakin' a rock in a tin can. Calm down Theola. Ya gonna blow a gasket girl."

Theola realized her temperament. She relaxed and began again. "James," she spoke softly, "I know my parents love me. I know leaving them like this will hurt them. But they want me to stay here, in Rayville, Louisiana, go to college and become a school teacher."

"What's wrong wit dat?"

"Don't you want more out of life? There's a whole world out there we haven't seen. I haven't been outside Rayville. Have you?"

"Well ahhh…"

"I thought so. There are only two kinds of jobs in this town that black people like us can get that pays pretty good money and a half way decent job. That's a schoolteacher and cotton mill worker. Is that what you want to be?"

"And what's wrong wit dat? A schoolteacher ain't all dat bad."

"Ain't is not a word of the professional language."

"Well I like it. Stop tellin' me how ta talk Theola. Please. I don't much like it."

Theola didn't argue about the correction. "James there is no future here!"

"Ya gettin' excited again. Yo gonna pop a cork. Calm down."

Theola lowered her voice. "I want more James. There's a whole world out there that we haven't even begun to explore. I know there is more to life than Rayville. And I don't want to be a schoolteacher. I want to be a lawyer."

"A lawyer?" James was puzzled. He had a smirk on his face. "What kinda lawyer can you be? You're a woman. How many Negro women… hold on, I mean, how many half-negro, half-Indian women do ya see as lawyers? You thank yo tan skin, long black hair, brown eyes and good looks are gonna git ya into law school? Even if ya made it through law school, which I doubt will ever happin', what firm in this country would hire ya? This is the fifties woman, ya better thank."

"I am thinking James. This is not the life for me. I'm going to be a lawyer!"

"Yo gonna have a stroke if ya don't calm yoself."

Theola spoke softer. "If it's one thing my parents have taught me, it's to set a goal and go for it James. Believe that I can achieve it and with God's help, I can."

"And ya believe you can be a lawyer? Well ya gonna fo sure needs God's help." James started to laugh.

Theola picked up her bag and stuffed her nightgown in it. She started to walk away. James saw that Theola was serious. He picked up his container of water and followed her.

"Hold on there girl!" He ran to catch up with her. "Ya take stuff too seriously." When James reached her side, he grabbed her by the arm and stopped her from walking further. "Hold on now Theola."

Theola stared straight ahead, expressionless. Tears streamed down her smooth, light-skinned cheeks. James stood in front of her tearing eyes.

"Have ya thought about what we doin'? Where we goin'? How we gonna git there? How ya gonna start this career of yos? I can't support myself, not ta mention supportin' you and me."

Theola listened with frustration in her heart. She dropped her blank stare. "James do you love me? Do you love me? Yes or no. No maybes or perhaps. Do you love me?"

"Baby I love ya like I love ice cream on a hot summer's day. Do ya thank I'd be standin' here on one of the hottest days in May, in the middle of the night with a container of water in one hand and just the clothes on my back, tryin' ta run away from home to God knows where? If that ain't love baby, I don't know what else is."

"Well you mean the world to me James. When I met you, there was just something about you I liked right away."

"Ohhhhh, is that why ya played hard to git because ya liked me right away?"

"I saw you had a different girl every week holding your hand and cooing over you. You were quite the lady's man."

James flexed his biceps, "Baby I don't work out fo nothin'." James smiled. Theola started to walk away. James grabbed her arm quickly. "Did it ever occur to ya they might be chasin' me?"

"I didn't see you playing hard to get."

"What man would? I would never turn a lovely lady away in her hour of need." James paused, "Fo companionship and friendship, I mean."

"Of course." Theola smirked. "If I had just given in the first time you said *hi* at school, you would have thought I was an easy girl to get."

"So ya made me chase ya fo three months, just so I wouldn't thank you was easy? Come on Theola. Give me better credit than dat. Those 'get out of my face' words and hands on hips and shaking your head from side to side, said a lot. I may have been born at night, but it whan't last night. I could tell ya didn't like me. I almost give up on ya. But my mom told me that anythin' worth havin' is worth fightin' fo."

"Alright James, you're right I didn't like you when you were trying to talk to me. But you wore me down. You didn't quit. And now I love you and I am going to have your baby."

James dropped the plastic water container to the ground. With his eyes bucked and mouth open, he placed his right hand to his forehead and rubbed across it very hard. Suddenly his expression changed again. A huge frown came to his face. He squinted his eyes and tightened his lips. Before James exploded with anger he wanted to be sure he heard correctly.

"Got daw…" James paused and spoke softly. "Baby, ya almost made me curse ya and I know you don't like dat. Could ya say what ya just said one mo time? I don't thank I heard ya rite."

Theola placed her bag on the ground and reached for James's hand. He stepped back. "I'm pregnant with your child."

"Oh no, oh no! I only made love to ya once. One time Theola, dat's all. How? How can you be pregnant from just one time?"

"I am James."

James thought. He waited for laughter to come, but none did. "This ain't a joke? How ya just gonna blurt somethin' out like dat?" He paced the grounds. He paused and thought again. Then he stood before her. "Well, I'll be got damn! How could ya do this ta me? When were ya really gonna tell me? When we were halfway ta Tin Buck Too and couldn't git back home?"

"I had to do it this way James." Theola sounded frantic. "If I had stayed at home, my parents would have been ashamed of me. The neighbors would have talked about me. My hopes for college would have gone out the window. They already said they have eight children and they aren't raising any more babies. They would have made me get rid of the baby."

"Yo parents are God lovin' people. You live in a house that has bricks on it. Ya gotta preacher fo a daddy and a schoolteacher fo a momma. They have mo money dan most Negro folk do. They could take care of you and yo baby. They won't make ya git an abortion."

"No, I don't mean an abortion. I would have to put the baby up for adoption. I know I couldn't live with myself knowing I had a child in this world and didn't know where or who he was. Or even get to name the baby. I just couldn't do it James. This way, with you and me working together to raise the baby, I can have our child and go to college too."

"So you made this decision all on yo own ta have this baby. Did ya stop ta think how I might feel?"

"James please."

"So all this I love ya and wanna be with yo crap is only 'cause ya havin' my baby." James paced the grounds and shook his head again.

"How can you say something like that? I do love you James." Theola watched James's expressions of disappointment. James continued to pace. "Sweetheart, in the beginning, no, I didn't want to be with you, but like you said, you didn't quit, you wore me down and I fell in love with you."

"How do I know ya not just sayin' that cause ya havin' my baby? If you love me and trust me to love ya back, why didn't ya tell me ya were pregnant before ya got me out here in the dark and miles from home? Did ya thank I would leave ya if I knew? I thought we loved and respected each other, mo dan dat?"

"I don't know?" remorsefully spoke Theola.

"Did ya thank I wouldn't want the baby? Well, that just shows me how well ya trust me. What kinda relationship are we gonna have if ya feel ya have ta finagle me into doin' thangs?"

"I'm sorry James. You're right. I should have told you. I know it's a little late, but it's not too late for you to go back home before your parents miss you."

James pondered for a moment. He walked closer to Theola. He gazed into her beautiful brown eyes and gently touched her long, silky black hair.

"Is the baby mine?"

Theola reached as far back with her right hand as she could and struck James with a mighty blow across his cheek. His face turned to one side.

James reached down, picked up the container of water and handed it to Theola. "Here sweetheart, ya gonna need this water on yo journey ta wherever."

Theola snatched the water container and grabbed her bag from the ground. She immediately began walking down the long dark dust covered road. James watched her. Her pace increased each step she took. James turned in the other direction and took two steps toward home. He hesitated for an instant and realized that she was the only girl he had ever loved. For him to abandon her now, with his baby on the way, would not be the proper thing to do.

James reversed his direction. "Hold on there girl!"

She waited. When he caught up with her, he stared into her watery eyes, lovingly.

"What!"

"I know that the baby is mine, but that hurt you fo me to say that, didn't it? I just wanted you ta know how bad ya hurt me for not trustin' me." He kissed her on the chick. "I do love you Theola, but let's git one thang straight. No more hidin' thangs from each other. If there's a problem, we gonna work it out tagether. Understood?"

"Understood."

"If it's a boy, he's a junior."

Theola smiled. "Deal. But what if it's a girl?"

"Then she's a juniorette." James grinned.

She dropped the water container and her bag to the ground. She leaned slightly downward, only to give him a big kiss on the lips and a lasting hug.

"And one more thing." Firmly spoke James, stepping back from her embrace.

"Yes sweetheart."

"No mo correctin' me fo the way I talk. And I'm sorry I let ya meet my mom. Since you had been workin with her over the past few summers teachin' her thangs in the books, she been readin' and learnin' new words and tryin' to correct her talk and my talk. She even got my sister doin' it."

"Rena too?"

"Yeah, even Rena reads mo now and tries to correct my talk."

"That's great James," Theola smiled. "What about your dad?"

"If my Dad touches a book, it's to kill a roach. My Dad ain't haven it and me neither. I am who I am. The way I talk is who I am. Either ya take me fo what I is, or I can take my country talkin' butt back home."

"No James."

Theola was so happy that he agreed to be with her. James reached down to pick up the water container and the food. "Com'on then woman. I kan't let ya carry all this stuff. We gotta watch out fo the baby."

They both gleamed with happiness. He held out his arm. Theola's grabbed it tightly and squeezed. He gave her one last chance to change her mind.

"Theola I know you may not want to hear this. But once we start down that road, there ain't no turning back. If we abort the baby, ya can go back home, finish high school and our parents will never be the wiser."

"How would we pay for this?"

"My Mom would give me the money. I kan't tell her the truth though, but I could thank of somethin'. I could steal my Daddy's car. I know a friend that could set ya up with a friend doctor that could help and no one would ever know."

"I would know James. And just like I couldn't live with myself knowing I had a child somewhere in this world, I most certainly couldn't live with myself knowing that I took my child's life."

"Theola I am only thankin' of you and yo future."

"I know what you are trying to do. But I have made up my mind. My parents will get over it."

James nodded in submission of her desire. "Let's go."

The two began their long journey into the darkness of the night on a stretch of road, uncertain of their fate. James thought of his parents and his sister. He knew he wouldn't be missed, except for his mother. His life would now be what he'd make of it. Theola was leaving her beloved family and friends. She had contemplated her decision to leave for days. But now, how would James react to being a father. Would he really stay by her side? Would she be able to finish college and return home and still have her parent's love? She felt she had made the right decision and her determination to achieve her goal was enough for her to succeed. But deep in her heart, she was troubled and didn't know why.

CHAPTER 3

The Conversation

fter a couple of hours of walking in the smoldering humidity of the night, James was curious about Theola's condition. He brushed the sweat from his brow with his forefinger and thrust it to the ground.

"How many months are ya? Ya don't look pregnant."

"I'm just two months. That's why I needed to leave. I would have started to show pretty soon."

"Won't yo parents come lookin' fo ya?"

"With seven other children to raise, I doubt it very much. I told you I was going to leave them a note that I was running away with you. And I did. I left it in the living room on the coffee table."

"Good fo you. At least they will know what happened."

"What about you James?"

James smirked and sighed, "Yeah, my Dad and sister will be bustin' with joy when they find out."

"You mean they will be happy that you're gone?" Theola was perplexed by the comment.

"Are you kiddin'? Do dogs bark? My Dad will jump for joy, my sister will probably say, mo room fo her and her thangs, but my Mom will probably be a little sad. But kinda glad fo me too."

"Why would your Mom be glad?"

"Well, my Dad don't thank that I'm his child."

"What!" Theola smiled with disbelief.

"My Dad thanks my Mom was sleepin' around on him when I was born. So he kinda treats me with no respect. Anytime I did anythin' wrong, I got a beaten. No second chances. The older I got, the beatens went from switch to belt to extension cord. Anytime my sister did anythang wrong, I got a beaten."

"Why did he beat you for something she did?"

Theola reached for the container of water. Perspiration consumed her clothes. James stopped walking, took the top off the container and handed it to her. She took a sip and gave the container back. They continued their slow pace down the road.

"I'm the oldest he said and should know better. I should try ta keep her in line. But my Dad is partial ta my sister. My sister would do thangs on purpose to git me in trouble. She knew Dad would beat me fo whatever she did wrong."

"Where was your Mom?"

"She was there. But he'd threaten ta beat her too, if she tried ta stop him. My sister would watch our Dad beat me, especially if it was somethin' she did on purpose. It was always blackmail with her. If I didn't do what she'd said do, when she said to do it, she promised I'd get beat by Dad."

"Was she always right?"

"Do chickens have feathers? She'd be smilin' as Dad whooped the tar off my back with his belt. He ain't beat with the flat end. He'd beat me with the buckle. Dad would watch my sister. The mo she smiled, the harder he'd beat. And he would have this sayin' just befo he'd git ready ta make his first strike. He'd always say, 'This is fo old and new.' Wappp! 'This is gonna hurt me mo than it's gonna hurt you.' Wappp! And the whole time I was gittin' beat, I didn't see how it was hurtin' him when he was doin' the beatin and I was doin' the receiven. He wouldn't stop til he drew blood from my back. When my sister saw blood, she felt kinda sorry fo me. When she frowned, then he'd stop the beatin'."

"I'm so sorry James."

"Sorry!" James was angered by her words. "Don't be. That was how it was in my house."

"So what did your mother do while all this was happening?"

"She left the room long before he'd git started and began to pray for me, that he wouldn't kill me. Sometimes it hurt sooo bad, I woshed he'd kilt me. She knew that he believed that I wha'nt his son. He'd made dat perfectly clear ta her when I was knee hi to a dog."

"That's terrible James."

James continued. "So when the beatin' was all over, Mom would take me ta the kitchen. She'd put some lard and ma-cura comb on by back along with some of her special homemade sav. Then she'd nurse me back to health fo the next few days and nights until I healt up."

"How long did this go on?"

"Until I was fourteen." James thought for a moment and smiled. "Ya know Theola, my Mom is completely different from my Dad. She wouldn't whoop me like my Dad. She would never lay a hand on me. She'd always chastise me with words of wisdom from the Bible. Sometimes, her words hurt worse than Dad's beatens. I always felt lower than a snake in the grass after she explained ta me why I was wrong in goin' against her words. Even after I'd rocked her trust in me, she never laid a hand on me to hurt me, only ta love me."

Theola reached her arm around James's shoulder to show sympathy as they walked that lonely road. "I know what you mean James."

James shrugged his shoulder to remove her arm. He was still upset just from talking about it. "No you don't Theola! You da had ta gone through it. I don't need yo sympathy."

Feeling remorseful for James, Theola continued. "I'm sorry James. I just want to understand. Why did he stop beating you at fourteen? Did you finally stand up to your father?"

"There ain't no standin' up to my Dad. He woulda kilt me if I had."

"So what happened?"

"My mother realized one day what my sister was doin'. She had observed my sister and me out in the front yard. She overheard the conversation. She overheard Rena blackmailin' me. This took place before my Dad got home that day. My Mom didn't say a word to my sister. She just stood at the screen door and listened. My sister faced me. She didn't see Mom standin' at the door. When my sister was done layin' down the law ta me, my Mom moved away from the door and went to the kitchen. Rena turned from me and went into the house. I passed Rena in the kitchen helpin' Mom cook. I didn't hear any words about what was spoken in the front yard as I passed through the kitchen. I went ta the backyard ta feed the chickens. I guess Mom wanted ta see if Rena was gonna do what she said she would."

"Did she?"

"Can rooster's crow? Can alligators bite? My Mom and Rena were in the kitchen. At 4:00 o'clock, when Dad opened the screen door ta the house, my Mom saw my sister chase Dad down before he could git one foot in the door good and tell him somethin' I did ta her ta embarrass her at school. Without hesitation, he came into the house after me. Rena went back into the kitchen with Mom. Dad didn't say or ask me what happened. He got the extension cord from the dresser drawer in the livin' room. I was still in the backyard feedin' and playin' with the chickens we raised. He raced past Mom and Rena in the kitchen. He came barrelin' through the back screen door with dat extension cord in his hand. He wrapped me rite across my back. He caught me by surprise. I screamed so loud I knowed they heard me in Texas. Mom came runnin'. Before he could get off another blow, she had come racin' through the screen door, down the backyard steps and grabbed his arm that was holdin' that cord. At that point, I saw Mom like I'd never seed her befo."

"What do you mean?"

"Holden his arm, she stared Dad straight in his dark brown eyes and said, "If ya lay another hand on our son, I'm gonna ta leave ya." She said this with conviction and no remorse. He knew she meant what she said. He put his arm down, dropped the extension cord on the ground, went back into the house and never said another word. He looked at Rena standin' in the kitchen and passed her by with his head down. My Mom isn't a big woman and not very strong, but she stood her ground that afternoon. From dat day ta this, he never laid another hand on me, no matter what my sister said."

"Wow! Your mother did that?"

"I was surprised too. It takes a lot ta get her angry. But I guess that day she had seed enough. Especially when she knew he was wrong."

"I guess your Dad really loves your Mom." Theola wiped her forehead with her arm to stop the sweat from running into her eyes.

"No, not really. I don't thank he would have cared if she'd left and taken us with her. But as strange as it may seem, my Dad lives in the church, but he is not a religious man. So to let his wife and children leave him would have appeared disgraceful in the eyes of his church members as a good Dad and lovin' husband. He cared what the peoples would say."

"So what if you weren't around when Rena did something wrong?"

"Dad always forgave her. Ya see, my sister is very beautiful. Ya seen her."

"Yes. She is beautiful."

"She's light skinned and I'm dark skinned compared ta her. So Dad thanks that our skin color should have been the same. That's why he thanks I'm not his."

"That's absurd."

"That's what he told my Mom."

"I know your mother. I have talked to her on many occasions. We've read poetry. We have studied many books together, including the Bible. She is the most loving, kind-hearted, sweet and gentlest woman I have ever met. I know her heart. She lives by the word of God."

James raised the water container to offer Theola a sip. She accepted graciously. Theola swallowed a huge gulp and handed it back to James. James didn't take a sip. But he did unbutton his shirt. They continued on their journey.

"Does Rena believe that you aren't her brother?"

"Rena don't care if birds sing or cows give milk as long as it don't touch her lifestyle. It don't matter none ta her one way or the other 'bout nobody else. Rena is all Rena is worried about."

"Doesn't your Mom speak to Rena when she chastises her and give her words of wisdom like she does you?"

"Yeah, my Mom chastises Rena the same way she does me. The difference is, I listen most of the time. And ya're right Theola. My Mom trusts and believes in God with all her heart. She believes in doin' the rite thang at all times. That's how I know my Mom wouldn't da had an affair with another man. She lives what she teaches. Even though I thank Dad sleeps around on her sometimes."

"Why do you think your Dad is unfaithful?"

"On occasion, three or four nights out the week he don't come home till three or fo in the morning. The bars only stay open till one. There is only one all-night bar and dat's too rowdy fo him. He afraid some dem young duds in there will kill him and take his money."

"That's awful."

"My Mom done got used to it. It don't bother her no mo."

"What a terrible way to live together."

"Yeah, but I'm glad she didn't walk out on him and leave us behind. I knowed I wouldn't da made it without her love fo me."

"I don't want our relationship to be like that James."

"It won't. My Mom has taught me to love and respect a woman when she may not even respect herself."

"Oh really? And your point?"

"Like you. Just like a flower that is plucked from the stem that nurtures it. I'm plucking you from ya home, ya shelter, ya parents love and care. They fed ya, clothed ya and watched ya grow. Now that ya all grown up, I am about ta take ya away from all that. Now it's my responsibility ta feed ya, clothe ya and hold ya tightly, so dat ya are well taken care of. And this is what my mother taught me."

Instead of listening to the beauty of the lesson, Theola took the offensive. "So you think I'm not self-respecting?"

"No, no, no, not at all. I didn't say that. That's why ya are the only girl I have been with my eighteen years of livin'."

"That makes me happy James, because you are the only boy I have been with my seventeen years of existence."

James knew he had said more than enough and should end the conversation before anger intruded. "So where we goin' from here Theola?"

"I've always been partial to Chicago. It's been like a dream of mine. Let's say we head that way?"

They continued their pace down the road, holding hands and wiping perspiration from their faces. They felt secure in each other's presence, but they knew the road would be filled with unfamiliar paths.

Chapter 4

The Delsin's Surprise

*J*ust as the morning sun struck the windowpane of the Delsin home. Konee awoke only to look across the room and see Theola not in her bed. Immediately, Konee woke Deborah.

"Deborah, you saw Theola?" questioned Konee. The third oldest sister. She was just as petite and tall as Deborah, with dark brown eyes and coal-black short hair.

"Ahhhhhh, yes. And what are Mom and Dad going to say when we tell them Theola is gone?"

"We are not going to tell them. That's why Theola didn't want to tell you. We will let them find out on their own."

"But Konee, we knew what she was going to do. I tried to talk her out of leaving last night. I know I told her I wouldn't tell, but I feel we should."

At that moment, Keshna turned in her bed. "Shhhh, lower your voice. We don't want Keshna waking up asking questions."

"Konee, at nine years old, I think saying your sister has run away will be easy for her to understand."

"Let it be. Let's not combine insult to injury. Keshna will be devastated."

"But Mom and Dad need to know!"

"Are you crazy!" whispered Konee. "That's why we aren't going to say anything. We would be blamed for this because we knew and didn't tell them. Dad stands six feet tall and towers over all of us and Mom too. I can just see him now looking down at me and you with his deep voice and angry dark brown eyes. *Both of you are going to get your butts tanned. No one leaves this house without my permission.* Besides, Theola said she left a note for mother and father. "We will act just as shocked as everybody else. Okay?"

Deborah thought for a moment and realized the wrath of her father. "Okay. But I hate that James Paul Taylor for taking our sister away from us like that."

"He's not on my favorite list of people either. Now, let's pretend we are still asleep before Mom walks in here and finds us talking."

Konee and Deborah lay back down. They knew on Saturday mornings no one got up early but Mom to fix a good breakfast. They could smell bacon frying and the aroma of homemade pancakes filled the air. Not long after their conversation, they heard a voice call.

She knocked and cracked the door. "Wake up girls. Time for breakfast." She went into the next room to wake her sons. All three girls arose, yawning and stretching. Their mother came back into the room and stood by them. She smelled of bacon. Only three daughters were standing in the middle of the floor.

"Where's Theola?" spoke Konee aloud.

"Yes, where is your sister?" asked their mother.

"Perhaps she's already in the kitchen," said Deborah.

"No. I just came from the kitchen. She isn't down there."

"Maybe she is in the bathroom. She is always there first, so she can stay in there a long time," spoke Konee.

"No. I went by the bathroom when I went to wake the boys. The door is open."

Konee shrugged her shoulders. Keshna, being the littlest, said not a word. Deborah shook her head. The boys would race to the bathroom to brush their teeth and comb their hair so they could be the first at the breakfast table. Keshna thought she would beat her brothers that day and dashed away.

"Don't run Keshna!" her mom yelled.

Keshna knew the boys always had to let the girls go first in their house. Even if they were in there first, they had to come out. Their ages ranged from seventeen to nine, just a year apart. Theola was the oldest, Deborah was next, Konee, the four brothers, and then Keshna.

Their mom thought for a moment. "Maybe she's already in the other bathroom downstairs getting cleaned up? But I can't imagine why. But, I'll check." She went back downstairs to finish breakfast and look for Theola.

"Konee, what are we going to do?"

"Nothing Deborah! Now act like Theola is somewhere in the house."

"I really didn't think she would do it, knowing how strict Dad is on all of us."

"Where do you think Theola gets her stubbornness from? She's just like Dad. Once she makes up her mind to do something, count on it. Because it will get done."

The girls finished getting dressed and made their way to the kitchen table. The four brothers were already waiting for breakfast when the girls arrived. All were seated at the table, except Dad. Their mother served them. Suddenly, they heard a curse word from a distance. The children were in shock and disbelief at the words their father spoke. Their mother dashed from the kitchen toward the living room. Knowing their father never cursed, the children knew that whatever it was, it was serious.

"What is it dear?"

Dad stood at the kitchen door with rage in his eyes, holding a crumpled note by his side. Their mother reached for the note as she approached him.

He let her have it. He stood in the doorway facing the children, puzzled from the words he had read. Their mother began to recite the letter.

"Dear Mom and Dad,

Please don't hate me for what I have done. James and I love each other and want to be together. Once I have established myself and finished my college education like you have always wanted me too, I will contact you. Until then, give my brothers and sisters my love. I love all of you.

Your loving daughter,
Theola."

"Oh, my Lord! What has happened here John?"

"She's run off with that James Paul Taylor boy. I never did like that boy! I thought he wouldn't amount to nothing and now he's run off with our baby girl. If I ever catch that boy or get my hands on him…"

"Now John, don't say things like that. We just have to place our trust in the Lord and let Him take care of her now. But in our prayers, we should ask the Lord what we should do about this situation."

"Do!… Do!… This is your entire fault, Beatrice, for wanting me to be liberal with dating young men. Now, look at what has happened. And now you want to know what we are going to do!"

"Be careful dear. Remember your blood pressure."

He left Beatrice standing in the doorway and he sat down at the head of the kitchen table. Emotionally disturbed, he glared into space for a brief moment as he regained his composure. Everyone was silent, afraid to utter a word.

"Nothing Beatrice, we will do nothing at all. Our little girl is about to make her bed hard. So let her lie in it. She will learn what we have been trying to teach her about establishing her goal first and then establishing a relationship."

"But John…" Beatrice made her way to the other end of the table and sat before him. She was deeply heartbroken from the words he spoke.

John's eyes focused on Beatrice. "Let her grabble with the chickens! She will soon be a chicken. She will amount to nothing! My instincts told me that boy was bad news when I laid eyes on him. I tried to be lenient with her because of you, Beatrice and now where is she!" Anger overwhelmed him. He slammed his fist to the table. "I lost my oldest daughter!" John screamed at the children. "The rest of you girls can just forget dating!" He paused. "EVER!"

"What about the boys Daddy?" asked Deborah.

"The boys too!"

The children were all sitting dumbfounded at the table. Ronald smiled at his dad. John turned his attention to him. The smile soon disappeared.

"What were you smiling at boy? Are you glad your sister is gone?"

"Maybe the rest of us can have more time in the bathroom with one less sister."

"Son how old are you?"

"I'm eleven Dad."

"If you want to live to see twelve, I suggest you keep comments like that to yourself. You understand me!"

"Yes sir." Ronald took his eyes from his father to his plate.

The rest of the table went totally silent. Beatrice got up from the table and walked into the living room. Tears streamed down her cheeks. John followed. The words he had spoken stuck like a dagger through her heart. She stood in the middle of the floor, grieving. John grabbed her shoulders from behind and turned Beatrice to face him. With a loving and soft touch, he pulled her close to his chest and held her tight.

"Come dear, I'm just as torn up about this as you are, but we do have seven other children. We must try and continue to raise our children the way God wants us to."

Beatrice's watery eyes met with her husband's stern look upon her. "I know you are right John, but how can I, when I am missing one child."

"Then know this, my darling wife. I know I blamed you in there. But I was wrong. We both raised our children to know right from wrong. We have done our best to teach them the ways of the Lord. It's up to our children to choose what path they will take. Our oldest daughter has chosen a path that we wouldn't have selected for her. But honey, we have to live our lives knowing that we have done the right thing by all our children, and that's where our peace will come from." He kissed her on the forehead and glanced back into her eyes. "Now, let's go back into the kitchen and let our other children know we still love them too." Beatrice smiled. John took a handkerchief from his back pocket and wiped the tears away. "We also must let them know we are strong. Although we are saddened by Theola's departure, it will not bring us down as a family."

"That's why I married you John. You are so full of wisdom."

"Thank you dear. But they still aren't dating until they are out of our house."

Beatrice smiled. They both walked back into the kitchen and all were still seated at the breakfast table. The children were finishing their breakfast.

John stood at the head of the table. "Girls and boys, I want to tell you all something."

All the children, especially Deborah and Konee, gave their father their complete attention. Their mom sat down with tears slowly streaming down her cheeks.

"Your sister has run away with that boy named James Paul Taylor. She left a note saying she would contact us once she is established. But don't expect to hear from your sister for a long, long time. Your sister has defied our rules and taken it upon herself to become a woman before her time. I'm disappointed in her because I thought she would help the rest of you go in the right direction. Apparently, our teaching and guidelines were not good enough for your sister. From this day forth…" John glanced around the table into the eyes of his family and made his proclamation, "Theola is no longer welcome in this house."

All the children froze at that moment. A bewildered expression engulfed each child. In one single instant, all the children waited for some kind of retaliation from their mother to rebute what their father had spoken. Beatrice in total disbelief sat there for a moment and tried to compose her words without shouting.

"How could you John? What if she needs our help? We can't just turn our backs on her."

Deborah and Konee nodded their heads in agreement. All eyes were now on John.

"You mean the way she has turned her back on us. No Beatrice! Theola chose her own way of life. If this family is to move forward, we must put the past behind us. Theola is no longer welcome in this house and I don't want to hear another word about it! On this day and every day until the day I die, you girls and boys no longer have an older sister named Theola and we no longer have a daughter!"

Beatrice continued to cry even louder. Keshna followed her mother's lead. All the boys were saddened at the news, but not a tear fell. Konee and Deborah gave a grand performance, appearing stunned at Theola's actions. Tears fell like a waterfall from their faces and dad's unforgiving attitude and stern expression left no one to wonder how he felt.

CHAPTER 5

A Near Death Experience

While tears flowed heavily in the Delsin house, Theola and James had walked for several hours along the back roads and no one had stopped to aid them along the way. Fatigue was setting in, but they still maintained a slow steady pace. As the new morning sun beamed down on their faces, Theola contemplated how their future would be.

"When we get to Chicago, you'll find a job and I'll go back and finish my last year of high school. We'll find someone to take care of the baby that first year. The following year, I'll start college. I'll take classes at night while you work during the day. That way, we will have the baby covered both day and night by one of us."

"I see ya done thought this all out."

"We've been walking for hours. That's all I have been doing, thinking. I just don't want our baby raised by a stranger because no one else can love her like we will. Our child comes first. But I want to go back home someday, too. That's why I have to finish college," remorse gripped her words.

James nodded, trying to conserve his energy. They walked hand in hand, leaning on one another for strength in stifling humidity, eating peanut butter sandwiches for nourishment. They gulped their water. Soon, the water they had drank, now drenched their clothes with perspiration. Later that morning, they finally reached the main highway. The humidity and the intense heat from the rays of the sun made the journey more difficult. They watched cars and trucks whiz by, blowing hot air back into their faces as they strolled along the side of the road. Theola reached for the container of water from James's hand to wet her parched lips. She touched the spout to her mouth, but only a drop came out.

"James I'm sorry. I drank most of the water. It's all gone."

"I know baby. It's alrite. I wasn't thirsty anyway. I'd rather fo you and the baby ta have it."

"I guess we can get rid of this empty container." Theola motioned to toss it into the bushes.

"No! Let me have it, just in case we find a place to fill it." James continued to carry the water container and the remainder of the food. They sauntered for a couple more hours. The heat was beginning to take its toll upon their bodies.

"James, I'm getting extremely tired. I need to rest."

"Well we can't stop along this highway. It's not safe. Lean on me Theola."

She rested her arm on his shoulder as they walked. Hour after hour, her pace became slower and slower. James was almost dragging Theola with his arm around her waist. He realized she could no longer walk.

The sun was extremely hot without a cloud in the sky. By late afternoon, Theola was no longer walking, but being pulled by James.

"Let me try a thumb. Maybe we can hitch a ride ta Chicago, ok babe?"

The sun would soon ease to the west, but it seemed like an eternity to Theola and James.

Theola leaned her head on James's shoulder. "Right now, I really don't care what direction cars are headed. I just need to rest. James don't try thumbing with a black shirt on and blue jeans when it gets dark."

James ignored her comment.

He stopped trying to drag her. James peered in every direction. All he could see was swamp and trees. Not a barn, not a house, not even a shed in sight for miles around, just an old rusty wired fence with wooden poles to hold the wire in place that stretched for miles along this lonely highway. Perhaps the fence was there to keep things from wandering out of the swamp or from trucks and cars driving in.

Whatever the reason, James helped Theola to sit down as far away from the highway as she could. He rested her against one of the wooden poles. The blistering hot sun had scorched their faces. Their lips were chapped. Their tongues and throats were dry. Theola's eyes were almost closed. With no shade or shelter from the elements, James knew he had to find help soon. He took off his shirt to cover her face from mosquitoes and flies. Theola didn't move or say a word. He feared for her condition. He proceeded to stand close to the road and hold a thumb out for a ride.

A few minutes later, he turned to check on Theola. Her body had slumped against the wooden pole and she had fallen fast asleep from exhaustion and hunger. Feeling desperate, James focused his attention back on the road to quickly find help. Trucks and cars still passed them by for hours. James' thumbing had failed. He awakened Theola from time to time to make sure she was alright, but her pulse was slow. The heat had taken its toll. She continued to sleep. He went back to the highway and began to thumb once more. With no shirt on and nothing to shade his body from the remaining sunlight, James began to weave and wobble while standing.

Another hour passed. The darkness was upon them. The roads were not lit with light poles. James's dark skin and clothing did not give any reflection to headlights. James knew he could not fall asleep where he stood or he might become a victim of a hit and run or worse, road kill. Relentless, James stood thumbing. Hours and hours later, James looked to the sky. A beautiful dawn rose in the distance. He had stood all night with his thumb pointed in one direction. James could no longer ignore the signals of his body. He felt faint.

At that moment, a trucker was driving in their direction and saw James fall to his knees and then to the ground. From the brightness of his headlights, he also noticed another body, Theola, slumped against a fence. The trucker immediately stopped and got out. He raced to James and touched his wrist. James's pulse was slow. The trucker raced toward Theola. He could barely feel a pulse. He ran back to get a bottle of water from his truck. He kept a cooler for the stretches of land that had no store, gas station or town for miles. As the trucker jumped from his cab, James groaned. He gave James a sip of water first, dragged him to the front wheel of his cab and rested James against his big wheel tire. He went to Theola. He took the shirt from her face and wet it with the bottle of water. He placed the cooled shirt back upon her forehead and set her up against the fence. The trucker was afraid to move her. So he waited and waited throughout the morning, periodically checking their pulses and giving them little sips of water until the coolness of the shirt lowered Theola's body temperature and James regained consciousness.

"Ohhhhh, where am I?" James spoke, still groggy.

The trucker was standing in front of his truck, having a cigarette, when he heard James speak. He turned to see James trying to shake off the effects of dehydration.

"Relax boy. You and that gal over thar almost met yo maker."

James immediately jumped to his feet, realizing the situation he was in. But just as quickly as he jumped up, he fell back down, flat on his face. The trucker placed his cigarette in his mouth, walked over and pulled James back to the truck.

"Theola?" James glanced up at this stocky, redheaded white male with a straw cowboy looking hat on.

"Relax boy, I'm takin' care of her too." James glanced in the direction where he left her. She was still unconscious. "I just changed the shirt on her forehead. She done cooled down a lot since I first found yawl. I been givin' her sips of water, just as I gave you. She fine fo now, I thank. She should be comin round soon too."

"Well, can ya git her out of the sun?"

"She alrite boy. Just settle down. The sun ain't hot yet. It's just 'bout nine. I'll git her in a few minutes and brang her over by the truck."

James weaved and bobbed, trying to push his body up with his hands, leaning his back against the big wheel. The trucker realized James wasn't going to be still. He placed his cigarette in his mouth, leaned one hand on the front of his truck and handed James the other. James grabbed his hand with both of his to maintain his balance. Once standing, James staggered his way to Theola, almost falling. James touched his shirt that rested upon her head. It was still cool. He felt her pulse. It was faint, but steady.

"May we please get her into the shade by your truck?" James begged.

"Boy…" The trucker sighed and shook his head.

He threw his cigarette from his mouth into the highway and walked over to help James. Heavy though she was, their right hands went under her back and left hands under her legs.

"On the count of three, we lift." stated James. The trucker nodded. "One, two, three."

Each man grunted as they lifted her body with all their strength. They finally picked her up. Theola appeared lifeless. They walked gently and slowly to the front wheel of his truck. James almost stumbled and fell, but he maintained his balance. They laid her where James had been only moments ago. James felt better now that Theola was in a shaded area. James leaned against the semi-truck, exhausted from carrying Theola only a few feet. He gently took his shirt from her face and placed it behind her head, resting her against the wheel of the truck. She was still sleeping soundly. James soon checked the area for the bag that had what little food remained.

"You need to set yo-self back down boy, befo ya fall down."

James just leaned his back against the passenger side door of the truck and rested there. He spotted the food bag not far from where the trucker found him. James, a little rested, walked a few feet to retrieve the bag and the water container they had left on the ground. He placed the items beside Theola and he leaned back against the truck once again. Curious about their dilemma, the trucker gave James the third degree.

"What ya'lll doin' way out here? Its twenty miles to the nearest town?"

"It's a long story mister. We sure 'preciate yo help. Ya saved our lives."

"Well, let's get yo gal and put her in the cab where it's cool. I done wasted a lot of time dealing with ya'll. Fortunately, I done dropped off my load and I'm goin' home."

The trucker went to open the passenger door, while James leaned down to help Theola up from the ground. Startled by the gentle touch of his hand on her shoulder, Theola slowly awakened to find herself against an eighteen-wheeler. Dazed by her ordeal, Theola tried to stand and regain her composure. James held her by the arm. She was still groggy from her long sleep.

James assisted Theola in the cab. "Be careful baby. Watch yo step."

She slowly climbed into the trucker's cab and sat down. James put his shirt back on. It was wet, but it felt good. He soon joined Theola in the front seat.

The trucker was already in the driver's seat. James placed what remained of their food on the floor before Theola. Then he got in.

"Let's roll on." The trucker eased back onto the lonely highway. "Where ya'll headed?"

"We are headed to Chicago," said James.

"Ya'll runnin' away from home?"

"Somethin' like dat."

"You mean you got her knocked up and ya'll kan't face her daddy. Ain't that rite boy?"

Theola said not a word. Still woozy from dehydration and long sleep, she felt their situation wasn't any of his business, however grateful they were for the ride and saving their lives.

"Rite mister."

"I tell ya'll what. I kinda sympathize with ya'll situation. I'm headed as far as Oklahoma City, but I know some of my trucker buddies go towards Chicago. I can see if I can get ya'll the rest of the way with one of them. Alrite?"

Theola and James smiled at each other. "Dat be fine sir."

"How long ya'll been walking that road?"

"Almost a day and a half and no one stopped ta help us sir."

"Well, it's lucky I came along. Ya know blackies on the road like that can only mean one thang?"

Too weary to challenge his statement, Theola rested on James' shoulder with her eyes closed.

"And what's dat mister?"

"Yawl in trouble with the law and done stole something, but since ya with this here gal, I figure ya got her knocked up?"

James couldn't take any more comments from the trucker. "If you don't mind, my gal and I gonna to take a nap. We a little tired."

The trucker nodded. Theola and James leaned on each other and enjoyed the ride, for it was at least six hours to Oklahoma.

Chapter 6

First Time Meeting Strangers

Theola and James could feel the rig slowing down. The hours seemed like minutes as the trucker woke them pulling into the truck stop in Oklahoma City.

"We's here. Good afternoon, ta ya'll. Yawl did some sleepin'."

Theola and James awoke, yawning, only to see at least twenty other eighteen-wheelers stationed at this truck stop. The trucker jumped out of the cab.

"Ya'll wait out here. I'll get some food and bring it out ta ya. Do ya'll have some money?"

"No mister. You don't have ta buy us no food. We gotta little peanut butter and bread, but no water."

"Now son, yo little lady bout ta have a baby. Ya kan't be feedin' it jest bread and water. Yawl waits here, niggas ain't allowed inside. I'll bring yawl somethin' good ta eat fo the baby."

James nodded and sat quietly in the truck cab. He noticed Theola out of the corner of his eye, staring at him. James knew she hated to be called out of her name. So he pretended not to notice her.

"James doesn't it bother you the way he calls us niggas and boy. Like we're nothing and you're some kind of child?"

Not really wanting to address the issue with her, he knew he couldn't just ignore her. "Do bunny rabbits hop? Do rattlesnakes rattle? Yeah, show it does." James was a little irritated. "But what am I gonna do. Insult the man while he tryin' ta extend charity ta us. I got a pregnant gal that needs a ride, some food and a place ta lay her head. We ain't got a pot ta piss in and a back door to throw it out of. What is my askin that white man ta stop callin' me boy gonna gain us, in gettin' us, where we wanna go?"

"How about a little respect? There is nothing wrong with having a little dignity. You need to stand up for yourself James Paul Taylor and show some pride in being a man."

"I can tell you feelin' better now."

Theola sighed. "What's wrong with wanting to be treated like an equal human being?"

"Nothin'! But I don't got two dimes to rub together Theola. You know they still lynch people in the south."

"Well that's why we are heading north."

"Well news flash. We ain't in Chicago yet and they ain't no different. They shoot Negroes in Chicago and make them dig their own graves befo they kill 'em and ya don't ever hear about it. They never find the body cause they make 'em dig mo than six feet. The south is just a little messy. They leave the body hangin' from a tree limb, sometimes butt naked."

"Oh James, do you have to be so vivid about it."

"You done led a sheltered life gal. We are Negroes in a white man's world. Hatred will always be there, whether we are in the south, north, east or west, cause the white man is everywhere."

"It's got to be different James. It just has to be different."

James smiled sarcastically. "Ya keep on believin gal. Maybe someday it will be different."

"James my mother and father taught me if you believe in God, then all things are possible."

"Theola my mother said the same thang ta me too. But she also said that ya can git a lot further with a grain of sugar than a spoonful of vinegar."

"And what's that supposed to mean?"

"It means ya can git a lot further with a little kindness, than a lot of bitterness."

"So you just let people run over you and abuse you verbally."

"Berbal what?"

"You just let them talk bad about you?"

"Nooo Theola. All dat means is, be kind no matter what's goin' on and thangs just might work out fo the better. My Dad said to look at life for what it is. Know who ya are and where ya stand. And right now, I'm a Negro man with a pregnant gal and no job." James stared at her to get some reaction to his comment. Theola gave none. "So we need to be as humble as starved kittens tryin' ta git a bowl of milk. We need ta purr and cuddle up ta a total stranger."

"James we have to believe that God will always make a way where there is no way."

"Yeah," sighed James.

"Look at this trucker and how he is helping us. He didn't have to do that."

"So why do ya want me ta make him mad if ya believe God done led him ta us?"

"I'm sure God wouldn't mind him calling you by your name. If letting him know you'd like to be called by your name is offending him…"

"Let it be Theola," James interrupted, "Your temper is goin' ta get us in a whole lot of trouble someday."

"Just because I don't like to be called out of my name, I'm wrong?"

James sighed and shook his head. He knew if he kept going, Theola would too. He said nothing further. At that moment, he saw the trucker come outside with a tray covered with a big white cloth. A man followed behind him. James opened the cab door. The trucker handed James the tray of food. James handed the tray to Theola. She didn't hesitate. Theola dug in and started eating without using a fork or knife. James jumped down from the cab to speak with the two truckers. James showed his humbleness by bowing his head and not looking either trucker in the eye.

"This here is a friend of mine boy. His name is Skip. He is headed to Illinois. I told him your situation. He said he'd be glad to help."

James raised his head to acknowledge the other trucker. He stood about six feet-four inches, with blonde hair and blue eyes. He wore a cap with the words Dallas Cowboys printed on the front, a red and white plaid shirt and worn-out blue jeans. James extended his hand. Skip shook it.

"I understand what ya goin through boy. Elrod explained everythang ta me. You ain't got no money and no place ta stay and ya don't know nobody. Well I can relate to that too boy." said Skip.

James bowed his head again. "Yes sir. You are rite."

"When yo gal finishes her meal, yawl come on over to my rig." Skip pointed to his truck. "It's the solid silver truck with black lettering and Chicago license on the front."

James raised his head to notice the truck. "We's be rite thar sir."

Theola continued to watch, eat, and listen. James climbed back into the cab and closed the door. He noticed the plate. "Can I have some?"

The two truckers stood outside the cab and talked. James was a little concerned with their kindness.

"Theola, don't you thank this is kinda strange that these white men are helpin' us like this?" James tried to take a chicken leg from the plate, but Theola guarded it with both hands.

"James I think you worry too much. God moves in unique ways. These men are showing kindness perhaps because they have been in similar situations themselves from what I heard."

"Can ya move yo hand so I can get some food too?" Theola moved her hand. "Well, I'm sho nuff glad ya feel so sure about their behavior. But I'm gonna continue ta stay on my p's and q's."

Theola spoke with a mouth full of biscuits and gravy. "If it makes you feel better James, by all means, do so."

Theola was almost done. But she had to know one thing. "James why did you bow your head and look away when you were talking to those men?"

"My daddy says never ta look a white man in the eye or he thank you an up-piddy Negro."

"Well my Daddy taught me I am just as important as any other person who walks this earth. Don't lose your self-respect James. We are all human beings."

James ignored the comment as he noticed Elrod was on his way around the front of his truck to get in and Skip had started to walk toward his rig. Elrod put the key in the ignition.

"Hey boy. I don't even know yo name."

James and Theola had their heads bowed in the plate eating chicken legs and biscuits.

James did not raise his head from the plate. "My name is James and dis is Theola."

James, Elrod and Theola noticed Skip had started his rig and had placed the air conditioning on as the windows were rolled up on the truck. Theola continued to eat.

"Well, James and Theola, this here is where we part. It's been nice ridin' with yawl, even though ya did sleep most of the way. Good luck with yo new baby and all."

Theola had just finished sopping up the gravy with a little piece of biscuit. James licked his fingers from the last small chicken leg he managed to grab in between Theola's eating binges.

"I didn't catch your name mister ....." said Theola, wiping her hand with the cloth napkin that came with the dinner.

"You can call me Elrod." He smiled.

Theola returned the expression, staring him in the eyes. James started to climb out of the truck. "Thank you sooo very much Mr. Elrod. Your kindness has made our day a little easier to deal with."

Theola passed James the empty plate and dirty napkin just as his feet touched the ground. James placed both items on a nearby trashcan. He noticed Theola still in Elrod's truck.

"Theola I thank Mr. Skip is waitin' fo us."

Theola eased her way to the ground. James slammed the door of the cab on Elrod's truck. They both strolled over to Skip's truck and climbed into the cab. They watched Elrod pull off and blow his horn.

Skip responded by doing the same.

"Ya'll ready ta get up outta here?" asked Skip.

"Yes sir," spoke Theola.

"Thank ya very much Mr. Skip," said James, peering out the windshield. Theola just shook her head at James's reaction of not making eye contact with white men when talking to them.

"You welcome boy."

Skip cranked up the big rig and let her roar. Theola cringed at the word *boy*, but she remained silent, trying to be mindful of what James had said. He pulled out onto the main highway and again, Theola and James were on the road.

CHAPTER 7

Inquisitive Trucker

James wasn't quite ready to go sleep. He needed to know that he wasn't headed for some dark lonely road and a bullet in his head. Theola tried to exercise her attitude on being kind.

"Mr. Skip we really appreciate all that your friend, Mr. Elrod and you are doing for us. Without your hospitality, we aren't quite sure where we would be right now," said Theola.

Skip was amazed at the clarity of her speech, being Negroes and from the South.

"Elrod told me you two were from Louisiana. You, young lady don't talk like most Southerners do. Why is that?"

"I come from a background of teachers and educators. My mother didn't like the southern drawl. Whenever she felt we were slipping in that direction, she would quickly correct our language."

"How about you boy?"

Again Theola cringed at that word. James noticed her reaction and hoped that Skip didn't. Skip had his eyes on the road and noticed nothing.

"My woman tries to correct me all the time. Not only does she not like the drawl, but she don't like the southern names either. But I don't sees nothang wrong with the way I talks."

"You mean names like Janny May and Billy Bob you don't like?"

"That's right," spoke Theola.

"I heard ya with a southern drawl when you and Mr. Elrod was standin' back there talkin' at his cab. Since we've been talkin' with ya, I don't hear it no more."

"You see James, well, I'm from Chicago. I pick up produce from Louisiana and drive it to Chicago on a weekly basis. Trucking is my life. Elrod is a good friend. We see each other every week at this truck stop. And I would say that eighty percent of the truckers at that stop have a southern drawl. So I only use it when I am around those guys. I sort of fit in with the group when we are sitting around drinking beer and talking dirty." Skip glanced over at the both of them. "You know what I mean. But I can drop the accent when I am in the company of others who speak without the drawl."

"I see. Oh that's good, you can change your accent to suit the social style you are involved with at that particular time."

Skip kept his eyes on the road. "I can tell your mother taught you very well."

"Yes, yes she did." Theola reminisced for a moment of being back home.

They were silent for a few moments, trying to think of something to say to discover the reason for his generosity. James nudged Theola to continue to prob. Not more than five minutes passed before Theola broke the silence.

"Do you like trucking Mr. Skip?"

"Trucking is my life young lady."

"It must be hard on you to maintain a family and be on the road a lot?"

"It doesn't leave me much time for a family. I love trucking. It's all I have ever known. My daddy was a trucker and his father before him. But that's why I can identify with what you are going through."

"How is that Mr. Skip?" asked Theola softly.

"Call me Skip. You see, I barely knew my daddy because he was on the road a lot and the same as his daddy before him. I missed not being around my father. So I promised myself that unless I was able to spend the time with my child that he deserves, then I wasn't going to have a child. But, a couple of years ago, I met this girl at a Chicago bar one night. I told her I was a trucker and eighty percent of my life is spent on the road. At first, it didn't matter. She said she would see me when she could."

"Sounds like she understood," said James.

"She did for the first year. It was ok. We were so compatible in the things we liked and did together. But the more we became involved, the more she wanted to see me. And I told her that wasn't possible, at least not right then. Well, six months later, she became pregnant."

"Then what?" asked Theola.

"I told her I loved her and if she wanted to get rid of the baby, I would pay for everything. She wouldn't hear of it. The baby was a part of me and her. She wasn't going to give up something we had created in our act of love and passion."

"Wat she do?" James was curious.

"I told her I wasn't ready to be tied down with a wife and a baby. If she wanted to keep it, I would help her pay for his upbringing, but I wasn't ready to be a father. She slapped my face and walked out of my life that day. I haven't seen or heard from her since. That was nine months ago. And now, not a day has passed that I don't wonder where she is or if she had a boy or girl, how they are doing, if they need my help or what. I did love her very much." Skip paused and sighed with an almost tearful tone of voice. "I guess that's something I'm going to have to live with for the rest of my life."

Theola's heart went out to this man she just met. "Maybe not Mr. Skip. Maybe one day she will give you that second chance that you so desperately desire. Then you'll have that opportunity to love your baby boy or girl."

"Perhaps?" Skip regained his composure. "I really hope you are right. "That's why I have respect for what James is doing for you. He could have run like I did, but he's not. He's facing his responsibilities of becoming a father to his child. Something I should have given a little more thought to before I told her I didn't want a wife or a child."

"I will pray for you Mr. Skip," said Theola.

Theola and James were silent after that comment. They realized Skip's motive for helping them was personal. They had a long journey ahead and decided to get some rest. They leaned on each other once more as the night began to fall.

Chapter 8

A Chance to Stay in Touch

That same evening the Delsin Family was preparing for bed. Still stunned from the words their father spoke about Theola, Konee and Deborah were in their bedroom discussing Theola.

"Deborah you heard what daddy said. Are we going to let Theola go out of our lives like that? She has always been a beautiful big sister to me. I can talk to her and tell her things that no way I would ever tell mom or dad or even you," said Konee.

"Me?"

"Yeah you, big mouth," smiled Konee.

"I guess I do talk a little bit more than everybody else. But I feel the same way you do about Theola. Before she left, she gave me the Taylor's phone number. She said she would keep in touch with them and to call them to find out how she is doing. But I don't want anything to do with James or his parents."

"Now Deborah, if we don't want to lose contact with Theola, we have to call them or we may never see her again."

"I know you are right Konee. Let's call James's mom and let her know we would like to be informed of the whereabouts of our sister and just how she is doing from time to time."

"It's late though. Do you think they would mind us calling after seven?"

"It's not that late. I'll get the phone number. Let's call now."

Deborah went to their dresser drawer. "Theola told me where she kept the number. I placed it in a safe place so mother wouldn't find it."

"Where?"

Deborah kept the phone number taped to the outside bottom of her drawer. She pulled the tape gently from the drawer so as not to rip the paper and destroy the phone number.

"I've got it." Deborah held it in her hand.

"Let's call," said Konee.

At that moment Keshna walked in the room. They both stared at her in unison. Keshna observed the surprised look upon their faces.

"What are you two up to?"

"Should we let her in on it?" asked Deborah.

"She keeps secrets better than you do," stated Konee.

Deborah gave Konee a sarcastic smile.

"Alright, Keshna we are going to call James's parents and let them know that we would like to be informed of how Theola and James are doing. Are you in with us?" spoke Deborah.

"Yes! I do miss her so very much. I would love to know how Theola is doing. When are you going to call?"

"Right now," stated Konee. "Alright, you go downstairs and see where mother and father are Deborah. If they are settled somewhere in the living room or kitchen, I'll go into their bedroom and use their phone. Where are our brothers?"

"They are in the kitchen eating dessert. They had just sat down when I was getting up. They should be in the kitchen for a little while," spoke Keshna.

"Ok Keshna, you stand at the top of the stairs and keep an eye on Deborah. She will give you a signal if anyone is coming and you will whistle to me to come out of the room, ok?"

"Got it."

"Alright, let's move into positions before our brothers make their way upstairs," stated Konee.

Deborah eased her way down the steps. She peeked into the kitchen. The boys were still there. She went into the living room. There she saw her mother knitting a quilt, instead of grading papers. Dad was reading the Bible. Deborah gave Keshna a thumbs up. Keshna gave the thumbs up to Konee. Konee entered the bedroom. She immediately started dialing. Each turn of a number on their rotary phone seemed like an eternity. She knew that if she was caught in her parent's bedroom, it could mean the whipping of her life. Finally, the last number was dialed. The phone rang. It was a woman's voice.

"Hello," answered a soft, pleasant tone.

"Hello Mrs. Taylor?"

"Yes."

"You don't know me. But my name is Konee Delsin. I am one of Theola's sisters. I believe my sister and your son have run away together."

"Yes, I know. He told me he might be leaving me soon and not to alert his father or sister of his departure."

"Mrs. Taylor, Theola said she would call you from time to time to let you know how she and James are getting along. We would also like to know how they are doing as well. We love our sister very much and we want to stay in touch with her."

"Why can't Theola call you directly?"

"Our father has forbidden us to ever speak to her or mention her name."

"Who dat on the phone?" shouted Edward from the kitchen to the living room. He was munching on fried pork chops, collard greens and mashed potatoes. "We eatin' dinner. Tell whoever dat is, dat seven-thirty is a little late ta be callin' on the phone."

"I'll just be another minute dear."

"I heard someone in the background calling you. Do you have to go?" asked Konee.

"No honey, it's alright. I'm sorry your father feels that way. Our children are our lives. And…"

"Yes ma'am." Konee interrupted her. "I've got to go now. If my parents knew I was talking with you, my rear end would need ointment for a week. Please, just tell me. Will you keep us informed about our sister?"

"Of course my child, here is what we will do. You call me every two weeks when you can and I will let you know if I have heard from them and how they are doing."

"That's wonderful Mrs. Taylor. Thank you so very much. Bye now." Konee hung up the phone gently. She noticed Keshna still holding her post.

Konee whispered. "Keshna I'm done."

Keshna called softly to Deborah. "Pisssst! Konee is done."

They all retreated to their bedroom.

"What did she say?" asked Deborah.

"She was very kind. No problem. She said we can call when we get a chance."

"Just about Theola, right?"

"I couldn't say that to her Deborah. It would have sounded like I didn't care about James."

"We don't!" added Keshna.

Konee ignored their comments. Deborah and Keshna were delighted at the news. They all embraced and rejoiced in silence over the kindness of Mrs. Taylor's attitude.

CHAPTER 9

Edward's True Love for James

Meanwhile, on the other side of town, in the Taylor household, at the dinner table, Henrietta caught Edward's wrath for not hanging up on someone who had called after seven at night.

"Why ain't ya tell dem you were having dinner? People don't need to be calling anybody's house after seven. It's almost time fo bed in another hour or so."

"Edward sometimes there are important things to say at any hour. You just have to be willing to listen."

"I ain't got time ta listen ta nobody, especially when I's sittin' at the dinner table. I don't listen ta you half the time and you stare me in the face. Next time, ya just call me. I will take care of it."

Henrietta mumbled under her breath. "Un-huh."

"Hmmmm, the nerve of some people. No respect fo the hour of the day." Edward continued to mutter to himself.

Henrietta stirred her food and ate very little. Edward and Rena noticed the sadness on her face.

"What's wrong Mother?"

"Yeah, Henrietta ya look like one of dem bastard hounds with the long ears. They looks like they bouts to cry any minute. Did dat phone call mess ya up some kinda way?"

"Edward dear, aren't you the least bit worried about our son? He's been gone all day. You haven't said a word, nor have you Rena."

"Hell Henrietta! I ain't cared for the boy since the day he was born. You knows that." Edward passed the mashed potatoes to Rena.

"I know, but he is still your son no matter what you say. Aren't you worried that he is not at our dinner table? Don't you want to know how he is doing or where he is?"

"Henrietta I could care less what dat boy has done. He probably, like I told ya earlier, ran off with that gull he'd been seein' fo the past two years." Edward took another bite of string beans.

"I know they have Dad. James had been talking about it to me. He said he wasn't going to do it," spoke Rena, cutting into her fried pork chop.

Henrietta was shocked that Rena knew, but she did not display any emotion. Rena must have found out through her grapevine at school and confronted James with the accusation. That would have been the only way she would have found out anything from James.

Henrietta continued the conversation like she didn't know as she sipped on her glass of iced tea. "Rena you're his sister. How come you didn't say anything about what your brother was thinking about doing?"

Rena placed her knife and fork down on her plate to address her Mother. "Mother, my brother's eighteen years old. I didn't think he had the guts to run away with some girl. Besides, he's old enough to take care of himself. And I need to concern myself with Rena and her future. I'm heading off to college someday. James is the least of my worries. And you know what else? I'm going to find myself a man while I'm in school and I'm not going to have to finish college. You know why?" Neither parent uttered a sound. "Because he's going to take care of me."

"Rena you should not think like that. Good men are hard to find. Your education should come first. Don't go down to Baton Rouge thinking some man is going to sweep you off your feet and you never have to work a day of your life."

"Oh Mom, look at you and Dad." Rena swallowed some iced tea.

"Yo Ma right Rena." Edward pointed his fork at her while he talked, his mouth full of food. "Ya git yo education first. If a man happens ta come along while ya gittin' yo studies done, ya keep him at a distance til ya finish college. Ya understand me?"

"Yes sir! Dad. I do." Rena had a smirk on her face and a slight tone of sarcasms in her voice.

"Don't take that tone with me honey. I brought ya here. I can take ya out!"

"Please Daddy. You have said that line a thousand times. But don't worry, I will be out of your life soon. My college days are approaching fast. Then you can just concern yourself with James Paul Taylor, your son." Rena stared at her father with conviction.

"Yo Mama son, not mine. As fo yo so call brother, James Paul…" Rena ignored her father and stared at her plate. "If ya make yo bed hard, ya gotta lie in it. And if he is out there with that gull," Edward turned his attention to Henrietta, "Den, he deserves whatever happens ta him and that gull too." Henrietta didn't say a word. "I told him ta stay here and start ta work at dat cotton gin. Now he dun run off." Edward smiled. "He ain't got no skills. What kinda job is he gonna find? He ain't got the sense of a dear that like to see itself in headlights."

"That's enough Edward. No more of your nonsense. We have to pray for them."

"I ain't gotta do nothin' but eat and go ta the bathroom. You pray fo 'em if ya wanna. They deserve what they gits."

Henrietta bowed her head in silent prayer for them. Edward continued to munch on his dinner. Rena just watched her Mother pray silently as tears streamed down her cheeks and no more words were spoken.

CHAPTER 10

A New Challenge

Miles away, James and Theola were nearing the state of her dreams. They awoke only to see a sign that stated, Welcome to Illinois.

"Hey...you two really took a nice long nap," said Skip.

"Yeah. We were kinda tired from the long walk and long drive with Mr. Elrod," stated James.

"Do you have a place to stay? I mean, where do you want me to drop you off?"

"Mr. Skip, you can drop us off anywhere. We don't know nobody in Illinois and we ain't got no place ta stay."

"You got a little baby coming. You got any money for a hotel, motel or an apartment? And please, call me Skip."

"No money either Mr. Skip," stated James. "I mean Skip."

"Well, you guys just happen to be in luck. I know a wonderful lady who runs a motel right outside of Chicago. She makes home-cooked meals, you get clean sheets on comfortable beds and she is really hospitable. I stay there when I'm just passing through. She's a friend of mine. I'll ask her to give you free room and board until you find a job and can pay her rent. Now, don't shirk her James. You seriously be hunting for a job to pay her back. I'll be coming through every now and then. If she tells me you're not trying to pull your weight, I'll have your hide."

"Don't you worry none Mr. Skip. I'll bust my britches ta git work. James Paul Taylor is a man of his word."

"Skip we promise not to take advantage of your friend's hospitality or dwelling. We will repay her anything we borrow or use. You have our word." Theola spoke with confidence. "We'll both work to pay her back."

"All right. That motel is just ten miles up this road. Her name is Sarah. She is a good person. She'll take good care of you if I say so."

Skip noticed the sincerity that reamed from their faces. He believed them. "We are almost there."

Several minutes later, he turned the corner down a long, unlit, deserted road. Theola and James were beginning to wonder if there was a motel. But far in the distance, you could see a little red blinking sign saying *'Rest Anytime Motel'* as it was early morning. That motel light was the only sign that could be seen for a good mile.

"Here we are you two. Let me go in first and tell her I have company this time around."

Theola and James nodded and waited patiently. They watched Skip climb out of the cab and enter the motel.

"Theola this motel is fur away from town. We are out in the boonies somewhere. When I find work, just how am I pose ta git there?"

"James you worry too much. We don't even have a room yet. Let's just take things one step at a time."

"That's easy fo ya ta say."

"We are in this together James. All the way. I love you. Let's just keep the faith."

"You keep the faith. I'll keep the reality."

Minutes later, Skip came from the motel. He stopped at the door and motioned with his hand for them to come in. Theola and James dismounted the cab. Skip held the door open and let them in. Sarah stood behind the desk register.

"Welcome. I'm Sarah." A soft voice and a beautiful smile stated as they both walked through the door. They both observed a pretty medium-height brunette with an hourglass figure. She pushed the register book toward James. James appeared puzzled as to what to do.

Sarah picked up on his hesitancy. "Sign your name and your friend's name in the book honey."

"Well, I'll be a monkey's uncle. Just sign rite here?" James pointed to a line in the book. He signed both their names as Theola noticed the surroundings. The motel appeared quaint. It was a huge solid brown oak desk Sarah stood behind. The lobby was filled with colorful flowered curtains, an enormous dark brown cloth sofa seat and a small wooden coffee table in front of the sofa. Nothing matched. A couple of leather lounge chairs were placed in the corners of the room. "Done ma'am." smiled James.

Sarah turned the book around to where their names faced her right side up. "Okay James Paul Taylor and Theola Delsin. I just so happen to have a lovely room available three doors down from the lobby. I do serve breakfast if there is anybody in the dining area at six o'clock, for anybody that wants to eat. Six to ten is breakfast. Room and board is thirty-five dollars a week. That does include your breakfast. You have to pay extra if you eat dinner here in the evening. There is a small kitchenette in the room, but I don't allow cooking after eight. If you have any questions about anything, just ask me or my sister. She helps me run the place. When you see her, she looks just like me. Her name is Leona." Sarah paused. She glanced at James and Theola. Neither one seemed confident in what they were doing. "Do you have any questions?"

"No ma'am. If we could just freshen up a bit and get some rest, we would appreciate it," said Theola.

"No problem. There are towels in the bathroom, in your room."

"Thank ya ma'am," said James.

"Call me Sarah."

"Yes ma'am," stated Theola.

"James for any food you eat at dinner and your room and board, I will let you run a tab until you are able to pay."

"A tab?"

"A bill," said Sarah.

"Well knock me in the head with a hammer. Yes ma'am, a tab."

"Is this your first time at a motel?" asked Sarah.

"Yes ma'am. This is our first time anywhere," said Theola.

Sarah and Skip sneered. James grabbed Theola's arm and headed toward the door. Skip made it to the door first and opened it for them.

"Oh James." Sarah called.

James turned. "Yes ma'am."

"You'll need this key to get the door open." Sarah was still smiling. Skip was too.

James, a bit embarrassed, walked back to the desk to retrieve the key. "Thank ya ma'am."

"James it's room five as you walk out that door to your left."

"Yes ma'am."

James and Theola walked toward their room, weary of the day's travel. Skip and Sarah were still enjoying the calamity of their actions.

"Sarah you see that they are young and confused and do not have a clue about things around them. If you can help them …."

Sarah interrupted, "You know I will Skip, but why such an interest?"

"It's a long story. Hey, when do you get off today?"

"I'm the boss. I'm off when I say I'm off. Here, take the key," Sarah reached into her apron pocket and threw Skip the key to her room. "Go shower. I'll be there soon."

Skip walked closer to her, leaned over the counter and kissed her on the cheek. With great pleasure, he headed for his usual room to rest for the day. Sarah soon followed.

CHAPTER 11

Sarah's Sister-Leona

Theola and James were so tired they just fell across the bed and slept a few more hours that morning. It was the weekend. This Saturday morning, when they awoke from a restful sleep, the day seemed strange for both of them not being in the comfort of their own homes. However uncomfortable they felt, they were starved and decided to take advantage of the breakfast offered by Sarah. When Theola and James entered the lobby, they saw Leona behind the desk.

"Good mornin' ma'am." James smiled.

"Good morning James and Theola," said Leona, without any impression.

"You know our names," replied Theola.

"My sister told me she had two Negro people staying in room five. See, we don't get many of your kind at this motel. It's kind of off the regular path for most folk like yourselves, if you know what I mean."

"No' I don't know what you mean. Why don't you explain it to me!" James grabbed Theola gently by the arm.

Leona stared at Theola a little strange. Shocked from her tone of voice.

"A little fire in you, ahhh, for a Nigra?"

Theola moved in Leona's direction, but James tugged her arm forcefully. Theola's expression left no one in doubt about the anger she felt behind the words that were spoken.

"Where the kitchen at? Ms. Sarah said breakfast was included in the room and we would like ta git somethin ta eat ma'am."

The estranged look at Theola left Leona's face with the softness of James's voice. Leona addressed James. "You can find my sister in the kitchen, past the lobby."

"Thank ya ma'am." James pulled Theola by the arm. Theola's eyes were squinted and lips were tightly pressed together. She stared at Leona all the way to the kitchen.

When they were clearly far enough away that Leona could not hear them speak, James reminded Theola of their situation. "Theola what are ya tryin' ta do?"

"Did you hear what she said?"

"I heard her Theola. And ya know what? We are at the mercy of her sister. If ya piss her sister off, where do ya thank we gonna be? We ain't got no roof over our heads, no food ta eat and not a dime in our pockets. Naw! Stop being so quick ta jump somebody when they call ya Negro. At least fo now, please!"

Theola shook her head in disgust. She hugged James as she knew he was right. "You will be the calm in the mix of my storm. But I hate to be called something else besides my name."

He put his arm around her waist and they went into the dining area. Sarah was shifting pots and pans and rearranging dishes. She heard the half-size kitchen doors swing open with a constant squeaky sound.

"Come on in and have a seat. You know I got to get them doors greased. They do get on my nerves sometimes."

James and Theola stood by the swinging doors. They noticed six clean tables with flowered tablecloths and four hardwood chairs per table. There was a little vase with a small artificial flower that looked like a rose. It was set in the center of each table in a tiny beige vase. Four place settings on each table, complete with napkin, fork, spoon and knife.

"Thank you Miss Sarah," stated Theola.

"Come on in now and sit down." They slowly moved toward one of the tables. James pulled Theola's chair out for her. Then he sat down. "Heyyyy, you two are up early."

"Yes ma'am, six o'clock in the morning is a bit early, but we's rested and sure is hungry."

"Well just name your appetite."

James and Theola didn't say a word. They just glared at each other for a minute.

Sarah noticed their hesitancy. "Since you have a hard time making up your mind, I'll whip you two up my special pancakes, eggs and sausage. How does that sound? Chased with some cold milk and orange juice."

"Dat's just fine ma'am."

"Call me Sarah, please."

At this point, Theola didn't care. The baby was hungry and so was she. James and Theola made little conversation and waited patiently. Moments later, Sarah returned with the fixings.

"Eat up!" Sarah brought hot breakfast plates of eggs, pancakes and sausage. She placed the food before them.

"Ma'am we just want to thank ya fo yo hospitality."

"Don't thank me yet young man. Wait until you get my bill." Sarah smiled.

"Yes ma'am, but a lot of people wouldn't da gave us this much with no money and all."

"Think nothing of it, really."

"Yes ma'am, we really do appreciate it Sarah." James smiled as Theola was following his lead on showing kindness.

"You know James and Theola, since today is Saturday, after breakfast, I can take you two around some places in the city that I know are open. You can see where you might want to apply for some jobs."

"Dat would be wonderful Ms. Sarah."

Sarah went back to the kitchen to prepare batter for more pancakes. James and Theola ate quietly for a few minutes until Leona came into the kitchen. Leona stared at them sitting at the dining room table. She walked up to Sarah standing behind the grill and whispered to her.

"I don't think they passed a law where we serve Negroes in a restaurant? What if some white people walked in here and saw you cooking for them?"

"First of all, this isn't a restaurant. This is my motel and my kitchen. Second, if they don't like what they see, they can leave after they pay for their room, of course."

"Sarah when did you start doing favors for niggers?"

"Since I met a man called Skip."

"Well why am I not shocked Sarah. I never did like that man anyway. He passes through here with his big red truck, satisfies himself with you and moves on. Never a mention of marriage. This time though, he drops a couple of niggers in your lap for you to babysit and you do it. If Mom and Dad knew, they would…"

"Drop it Leona. If you got a problem with them, then you can leave too."

Leona was stunned. She took a step back. "You taken niggers side over your own blood. You did lose your mind!"

"Keep your voice down."

James and Theola heard the shouting.

"If you still want my help at this motel, you'll get rid of them niggers!" Leona pointed in their direction and paused for an answer. Sarah didn't move or say a word. "Now!" screamed Leona. "And then apologize to me."

The tone of voice had James and Theola's heads turned to the kitchen area. Upset over her words, Sarah didn't want to talk about it.

"Just go Leona. Go home." Sarah spoke softly.

"Mom and Dad did not raise us to be nigger lovers."

"They raised us to love all people. You chose to hate. Not me."

"You love that no good trucker that much, to put niggers over me. Don't you?"

"Just go please." Tears formed in Sarah's eyes from the harsh words she spoke about Skip. Leona turned her nose up at Sarah and walked toward the door. But just as Leona placed her hands on the swinging doors, she had to say one last word.

"You're a fool. Skip is not good for you. He only uses you for what he can get for his own personal gain. What them niggers going to do for him or you, I'll never know. You fool!" Leona pushed the doors with such force that they swung several times back and forth, making a tremendous squeaking noise before coming to a complete stop.

"I love you too, bye." Holding back her anger, Sarah felt deep in her heart that she was extending an act of kindness to those in need regardless of how her sister felt.

Theola and James noticed the emotional stress upon their faces, the loud tone of voice and the way Leona stormed out of the kitchen. They knew they were the topic of that conversation and they felt they were in trouble. James noticed Sarah walking toward the table.

"Here she comes Theola. Whatever she says, let's just thank her, get our stuff and move on."

"Ok James."

When Sarah reached their table, they waited for her to ask them to leave. "Would you two care for seconds?"

To their surprise, she spoke words of kindness. "No thank ya ma'am."

"No thank you Ms. Sarah." Sarah started to walk back toward the kitchen. "Wait Ms. Sarah. We overheard some of the conversation. We do not want to create hate and discontent between siblings."

"Ohhh... that." While James was concentrating on what Ms. Sarah was saying, Theola reached into James's plate. "My sister and I argue at least once a day about something. Don't pay her any attention. She is the spoiled brat in my family. I just ignore her." Sarah smiled to reassure them of her friendship. "You sure I can't get you anything else?"

"Yes ma'am. Thanks Ms. Sarah fo the breakfast." James started to finish his food, but eggs and pancakes were missing. He glanced over at Theola. She was done eating. James and Sarah watched her gulp down her orange juice and milk.

"Well, when you two finish, if no other customers come in for breakfast by eight o'clock, come back at eight-thirty. I'll call a friend in a few minutes to see if he can watch the motel for me while we are gone."

"Great Ms. Sarah!" Sarah departed to clean up. "Are ya finished, babe? Or do ya see somethin' else on my plate ya would like ta chomp down on?" Theola shook her head. "Then let's go."

"Yes James." Theola dried her lips with the cloth napkin and rubbed her tummy. "Boy James, that was good."

James cheerfully commented. "Make sure most of that is for the baby. I don't want no fat woman."

"What you see is what you get. Take it or leave it." Theola followed James to the room.

Sarah watched while they left. She took the dishtowel in her hand and wiped the table clean of crumbs. Sarah cleared the dirty dishes, called a friend, and prepared to take James and Theola to town.

Chapter 12

Ms. Sarah's Kindness

n their way back to their room, James thought about the words and actions that had occurred between Sarah and her sister.

"They were arguing about us Theola?"

"Don't worry James. If she was going to toss us out, she wouldn't have offered to show us around Chicago."

"I guess ya right."

"Sure I am."

When they entered their room, James paused in his footsteps. He was staring at the clothes he had on.

"What is it James?"

"Damn! Theola. Freshen up into what? This all we got is the clothes on our backs."

"Please try not to curse. You know I hate cursing."

"Sorry baby, but what we gonna do fo clothes."

"I know. We'll wash our clothes in the bathtub at night."

"I guess we don't have much of a choice, being broke and all, do we? Runnin' away without a dime in our pockets! How stupid was I?" James stated sarcastically.

"Don't get testy with me James Paul. If I had even looked like I wanted to pack some clothes, my Mom would have had female intuition and realized I was up to something."

James sighed, "Me too. My Mom is the same way. Nothin gits passed her. She doesn't even have ta look ya in the eye and she can tell when somethin' is troubling ya."

"That's why I had to be extra careful how I acted around my mother and what I said."

"All right. I git yo point. Let's get ready fo our little trip. You can use the bathroom first, I'll wait."

James sat on the edge of the bed. Theola noticed the worried expression upon his face. She sat beside him.

"James I know things seem bleak right now. But I'm still keeping my faith in Jesus to see us through this." Theola placed her arm around his neck. A whiff of bad order hit him in the face. James reached around his neck and grabbed her hand and pulled her arm down.

"Whooooo, okay woman, go git washed up. We'll take our punches as they happen."

Theola jumped up from the bed, she laughed at James and then kissed him softly on the lips. "I love you."

"Yeah, yeah. I love ya too. Now go git cleaned up woman."

Theola dashed off. Moments later, she came out and James went in. Minutes later, he returned.

"Are we ready for an adventure Theola?"

"We have about a half-hour wait James."

"Let's wait in the lobby. This way it'll look like we're eager to find a job."

"Okay."

Theola and James made their way to the lobby entrance. When they entered, there was a strange white man at the front desk. He stood medium height, medium build, dark hair and about as tall as James. He was shocked at the presence of these two individuals in the lobby.

"Who are you people?" asked the man.

Theola was incensed by the question.

"We're waiting for Ms. Sarah," James quickly spoke before Theola could say something derogative.

"Well, you can just wait outside. I'll get her," said the man. James and Theola didn't move. The man was astonished at them not responding to his command. "I said you can wait outside," he repeated louder.

"She is expecting us in here!" Theola shouted.

"Wait here." The man said calmly and dashed off to get Sarah.

"James I've had just about enough of these insolent fools. Wait here, you people, nigra, what next?"

"How about coons, blackies, monkeys, spooks, coloreds, dogs and probably some I ain't know. Have ya heard all those befo?"

Theola shook her head. "I thought the north would be different."

"I told you hatred is the same no matter where ya go. The punishment might be a little different, but the end result is the same. Defiant Negroes die. However, I thank ya a little on the edge. Cool down. What he said was not any different than what I woulda said if I was standin' in his shoes."

"But look at Ms. Sarah."

"Ya got some good and some bad Theola and the sooner ya realize that, the better off ya gonna be. Nothin gonna change yo skin color, ever. Wake up. But remember ya can go a lot further with a spoon full of sugar than you can with a cup of vinegar. So be nice no matter what."

"I'll try James. I'll try."

Just then, Sarah came from the kitchen wiping her hands with a clean plaid cloth. The man followed. She paused and turned to the man behind her.

"Burt, this is James and Theola. The couple I told you I was going to show around town."

Burt waved to them. He whispered to Sarah. "You didn't tell me they were Negroes."

"I didn't think it would have mattered to you Burt. I never heard you say an unkind word about any race."

"Ohhhh… You're right, but you could have warned me." Burt faced Theola and James. "I didn't realize you were friends of Sarah's. Any friends of hers can be friends of mine."

They just nodded their heads. Burt turned to Sarah with raised eyebrows and a fake smile.

Sarah ignored Burt and approached James and Theola. "Well I fed the last couple of fellows a little while ago. So let's go through the kitchen. The garage is closer if we go out that way and I can put this dish cloth away." Theola and James followed Sarah. Burt watched them leave.

"James I realize you don't have any transportation and I have two cars. You are welcome to take either one to work when you find employment. The closest town is twenty miles and there is only bus transportation to town. The problem is the bus station is eight miles from the motel."

"Yes ma'am."

They reached the garage.

"Wow! A 1949 Hudson Super Six Club Coupe."

James walked around the car admiring its beauty. He gently touched the exterior of the car with his fingertips. "Black on black with white-wall tires." James glanced to the left of the garage. "Plus a 1950 Ford pick-up, very nice."

Theola was unimpressed.

"Hop in the Hudson. We'll see what we can find."

James opened the passenger side for Theola. He got in the back admiring the leather interior. Sarah opened the garage door and walked to the driver's side. She started the engine. It purred like a kitten. James adored the sound and the feel of the car. When she hit the main highway, James was a little nervous about a white woman having two black people in the car, even though Theola was the same gender.

"You know Theola, I was thinking," said Sarah.

"Yes ma'am."

"Since my sister quit on me and you are about to have a baby and all, why don't you help me out at the motel? That way you don't have to leave the comfort of your room until about eight-thirty in the morning, have some breakfast and start to help me by nine o'clock."

Sarah kept her eyes straight on the road, both hands on the steering wheel and drove with her gas foot to the floor. But James and Theola gave the appearance that her driving was fine. Theola glared straight ahead and said nothing. James observed the scenery from the back window, trying to ignore trees and landscape, that appeared to be a blur from the side window as Sarah drove from the country to the city.

James thought Theola would acknowledge her comment, but she did not. "That would be wonderful if Theola could work for you." James stared at the back of Theola's head, wondering why she didn't respond.

Theola thought that Ms. Sarah may want her to work for her forever. "That would be fine Ms. Sarah, except I do plan on going back to school to finish my high school education."

"I don't want to interfere with your education at all Theola. When school starts, we can shift your hours to the evening. You can sit at the front desk and sign customers in the book. You don't have to do anything strenuous the closer it gets to the time for the baby to come."

"Okay," said Theola solemnly, relieved of the fact that Ms. Sarah knew she was only going to work for her until the baby was born.

"I'll pay you twenty-five cents an hour for an eight-hour day."

"Yes ma'am. I am most thankful." Theola thought the hourly rate was a little low, but she remembered what James said about kindness.

James leaned forward a little to try and see the expression on Theola's face. There was none. So he had a feeling that Theola was not happy. Sarah continued to drive faster than the posted seventy-five-mile-an-hour speed limit. All was quiet for about five minutes. They were now approaching Chicago. Sarah drove around stores and auto shops. She let James get out and do the talking. Hours later, still no success. Theola was growing weary and hungry. Sarah noticed Theola's tired exterior. James was on his way back to the car from a stop they had made at a gas station. He got in the back seat.

"Any luck?" asked Sarah as she drove off.

"No ma'am, none. He said he don't need no mo people rite now pumpin' gas."

"It's getting late James. The workday is almost over. Plus, I believe Theola is a little tired and I'm hungry too. We'll head back to the motel and call it a day."

"Yes ma'am."

Theola felt honored that Ms. Sarah had taken the time to help them this entire day. "I'm not tired Ms. Sarah. I can go on."

"I know, but I'm hungry now. But Monday, if I can find somebody to cover for me, we'll try again."

"I'll cover for you," said Theola.

"Oh no! I'm not riding in this car alone with Ms. Sarah. Back in Louisiana, they would lynch me for sure."

"James we don't lynch people in Chicago."

"No ma'am. Yawl mo sophisticated here. Ya just shoot Negroes. I'm sorry. I want work, but not if I have ta ride alone with ya ta find a job. Nothin' against you Ms. Sarah."

"Let's go back to the motel and get something to eat and think about it."

"Yes ma'am," said James.

Theola was in total agreement about James finding a job on Monday. She was hungry and tired too, but she did not say another word.

Sarah got back on the highway and headed home as quickly as she left. No more words were spoken. They glanced at each other. James shook his head. He knew if her driving didn't kill him, the Klan would.

CHAPTER 13

Burt's Love for Sarah

Minutes later, Sarah, Theola and James arrived back at the motel. When they entered the lobby, Burt was still at the front desk. Theola and James headed straight for their room to rest.

"Come back in about an hour you two. I'll have some sandwiches and drink ready."

They both nodded and walked out the front door. Sarah pulled her purse off her shoulder and placed it on the front desk where Burt stood.

"Hey Burt, were things pretty quiet?"

"Yeah. No one dropped by." Burt noticed Sarah's worn facial expression. "What's the matter Sarah? Is there something I can help you with?"

"Not unless you can hire a Negro boy at your company."

"Does it mean that much to you for him to get a job?"

"That boy got that girl pregnant. They ran away from their homes with no money and no food. I'm trying to help them out as much as I can, but they have to make their own way."

"I knew you had a kind heart Sarah. I wouldn't have given up my Saturday for anyone else but you. You have always been a good listener for me when I needed one. Tell you what I'm going to do. I have some friends at the post office. I'll speak to them on Monday. By Tuesday, he'll be working."

"You mean it Burt?" Sarah beamed with joy. Burt walked around the front desk to get closer to Sarah.

"Only for you, only for you." Burt smiled and reached out his arms. Sarah mimicked Burt and they embraced.

"Say Sarah, how about you and me painting the town tonight?"

Sarah pushed back from Burt. "That was just a thank you hug Burt."

"I know that. I just want to spend some time with you."

"I wish I could Burt, but Skip is supposed to be coming through about nine. I told him I would be waiting."

"Sarah, Sarah, Sarah. When are you going to give that man up and give me a chance? He means you no good the way he treats you. No commitment, just in and out of your life. I don't know what you see in him."

"Drop it Burt. I know what I'm doing."

"Do you Sarah Styles? Do you really know what you are doing? You don't know Skip."

"And you do, I suppose?"

"Ok Sarah…I'm going to tell you a little story. I was hoping you would eventually see him for what he truly is." Burt gently grabs her by the arm and sets on the lobby couch. He looks into her eyes. "You don't know how Skip got his name, do you?"

"He said the guys just gave it to him."

"That's right. He got that name by skipping out on so many girls he dated before they could ask for a commitment from him."

"Just how do you know all this Burt?"

"Because six months ago I stayed at this motel for five straight days waiting for him to arrive, just so I could bust his head open."

"Why?" Sarah was confused and stunned from the remark.

"Your darling Skip was dating my baby sister. He stuck with her longer than he did most of his women. He thought everything was going fine until my sister told him one day when he was passing through, that she was pregnant with his child."

Sarah got quiet and stood from the couch. She turned her back to Burt. No expression appeared on her face for a small period of time. Then she stared at him. Burt pulled her arm for her to sit back on the couch. Sarah responded, she sat back down more inquisitive than before.

"And then what happened?"

"He asked if she was sure she was pregnant. She told him yes. Then he said he'd help her get rid of it."

"What! Not Skip?"

"Yes, your precious Skip. She told him she'd run off and have the baby alone before she would destroy a life that God created. He told her that she knew he was a truck driver and he couldn't be committed to a wife and family. She'd have to make it the best way she could. And he walked out. She hasn't seen him since. That's been about a year ago."

"How did you find out that Skip was here?"

"My sister told me he stays here if he's too tired to make it to her place. She described him to me. And so I waited. While anticipating his arrival, I thought to myself, he hasn't done anything any other man hasn't done to a woman. So why should I bust him up for something I've done myself."

"How noble of you Burt?" sarcastically stated Sarah.

"While waiting for him, I noticed you. I love your aggressiveness in ruling your motel with an iron hand, yet the feminine side greets each customer with a smile. That's why I always come back here in the evenings to have dinner. I was hoping to get a chance to be more than just an acquaintance."

"Really Burt?"

"This place is miles from town. I travel forty minutes past an old-fashioned Mom and Pop diner with good food just to see you. You are a beautiful woman. I think you are a heck of a lady and well worth the drive.

That's why I introduced myself to you on the third night I was here. Our conversations have been great. I think we have a lot in common. So I said to myself, forget my sister. She knew how he felt. She allowed what happened to happen." He stared deeply into Sarah's eyes. "Now, how about that date."

"What? You're full of it Burt. If all this is true, what did your sister have?"

"She had a boy. And you know what she named him?"

"Let me guess, Skip?"

"No. She named him Stephen "Stay" Hudson."

"What kind of middle name is *Stay*?"

"So he wouldn't run from a commitment to a woman when he got older."

"Right…" Sarah laughed. "I knew from your actions and occasional stares that you wanted to get next to me, but what a fairy tale story. You expect me to believe that?"

"Ok. The middle name isn't true." Burt smiled. "I didn't make all of it up. You don't have to believe me. Just ask Skip next time you see him."

Sarah was still in disbelief at Burt's story. "Thanks for the tip Burt. I consider you a very dear friend, but if I say I'm going to continue seeing him, you won't go back on your word about James because of this, will you?"

"Noooo…Sarah. I won't. We have a Negro male working with our company. I wish I had ten more like him. He works harder than the other five white guys I have. But no, Sarah. I still care for you. I can wait. One day he will walk away from you too."

"Oh Burt…please."

Burt got up from the couch. He kissed Sarah on the cheek. "I'm going now. I'll call you Monday." Sarah stood from the couch. "Oh Sarah, he better be a good worker. I'm sticking my neck out if he doesn't perform."

"Don't worry Burt. Everything will be fine."

Burt gave a slight grin. "I care a lot for you Sarah. Just say the word and I'm yours." Sarah smiled and didn't comment as Burt walked out the lobby door.

Sarah went to change and fix sandwiches in the kitchen. She thought about what Burt said. Perhaps some of it was true. But her heart still belonged to Skip.

Chapter 14

Getting Through a Hard Time

As they sat on the bed in their motel room, Theola and James pondered their situation of joblessness. How could they borrow before they knew how they were going to pay back what they owed?

"Theola I'm sorry. This is not how I wanted our lives ta start. I had thought about me workin' at the cotton gin, you a housewife and ten kids runnin' around in the yard. I come home, ya have my bath water run, dinner ready, I kiss the kids, grab a beer from the frig and plop on the couch ta watch the tube fo the rest of the evenin'."

"What! Are you nuts? What kinda life is that? I'm pregnant all the time and you want to watch television all evening, every day!"

"Theola don't get so angry. Ya gonna pop a gasket. Dat was before I knew what yo dream was. Now, I won't do nothin' ta try and stop ya goal. I love ya. Although I thank yo dream is a little too high ta reach. I'm yo man and I will try ta back ya all the way."

"I'm sorry James. I'm not use to sarcasm. My mother would always try to joke with my father and he would tell her that life is not a joking matter. Please forgive me, but jokes came few and far between in my house."

James was serious, but he was glad she thought it was a joke. So he played along.

"Don't give it a second thought. But sometimes ya have ta find a little laughter in life. Otherwise, you'll get gray hair at an early age." James glanced at Theola's head. "Like that one in the top of yo head."

"Where?" Theola leaped to her feet to go to the mirror.

James just started laughing. She realized it was another joke. She stopped in her tracks and leaped on him, bringing him to the floor. They laughed and rolled around for a moment.

James stopped. Theola's smile captivated his attention with warmth and understanding.

"Dat's better. Just know in yo heart I'm yo man."

Theola's smile went away. She stood before him. "I'm concerned for our future."

"So am I." James got up from the floor. "But I have to tell ya Theola, when I got out the car today ta talk ta dem white men bout a job, they probably heard my knees knockin'. And as I stood befo dem, my voice trembled. They probably looked at me and laughed inside the whole while I was standin' there."

"James don't cut yourself short. We are new at working, finding jobs and asking the right questions about anything. We are just going to have to learn as we go and hope and pray the pain of experience isn't too harsh on our lives."

"What are you? A phila, philapher?"

"Philosopher."

"Yeah, one of dem."

"No James, but I do read a lot. That's how I know there is a better life for us out there, be we Negro, Indian or whatever. We can make it if we try."

"Well girl…at this crossroad in our lives, we ain't got no other choice but ta try. I ain't never held down any kind of job befo, other than workin' in the cotton fields back home."

"All you have to do is what you are told and do it well. But to get ahead of the rest of your peers, my daddy always told me not to just look at what has been given me, but look at better ways to do things."

"Come on Theola, a white man takin' suggestions from a Negro?"

"Just try it. First learn the system. See how things operate. Then when you know what you are talking about, approach your supervisor."

"Yeah…right." James displayed even less confidence than a minute ago. He turned his back to her. Feeling his rejection, she changed the subject.

"It's about time to meet Ms. Sarah for those sandwiches. We're starved." Theola gently rubbed her stomach.

"Ok babe. Let's go."

They ended their conversation and headed to the lobby.

CHAPTER 15

The Good News

Minutes later, Theola and James were in the kitchen. Sarah had made some lemonade. The sandwiches were already prepared. Sarah invited them to be seated at the table.

"There wasn't anybody in the lobby when you two passed through, was there?"

"No Ms. Sarah," said James.

"Have a seat you two. I got some good news."

Sarah placed the sandwiches on the table and went to get the lemonade from the counter.

"What news is that Sarah?" asked Theola.

Sarah sat down at the table. "I got James a job working at the post office in the city." James and Theola appeared astounded at the news. "He can probably start on Tuesday because Burt will work his magic on Monday."

"How Ms. Sarah?" questioned James.

Sarah poured herself some lemonade. "My friend Burt knows some of his friends who might be willing to help. He said he would see what he could do. But with Burt, if he says it's so, it will be so." Sarah leaned back in her chair and placed her hands on her hips. She observed their faces. They were shocked. "Well ...."

"Grrrreat! We don't know how ta thank ya enough." James was elated. Theola, with her mouth full of food, smiled and nodded at Ms. Sarah.

"You can start by doing an excellent job because Mr. Burt is depending on you not to make mistakes and tarnish his name."

"Oh yes, ma'am. You don't have ta worry bout dat. I will be the best employee the post office ever seen. I won't let you or Mr. Burt down ma'am. Dat's a promise." James reached for a sandwich.

"Alright James. That's what I want to hear. I'm counting on you."

"Yes ma'am."

Theola glanced at James chewing vigorously and smiled.

"Theola you can start to work for me on Monday at nine. The two of you enjoy the rest of this weekend. Monday morning will start a new life for the both of you."

James and Theola ate heartily and rested for the remainder of the weekend.

CHAPTER 16

A Growing Friendship with Sarah

Monday morning came early for Theola, but she was on time for her first job. She didn't know what to expect, but take her own advice that she gave James and do the best job possible.

"Good morning Ms. Sarah," Theola spoke as she walked into the lobby.

"Sarah, please." She was checking the logbooks and placing dollars in the cash register.

"Come on in Theola. You are right on time. I realize your condition is delicate, so the things I'll have you do will be really easy. I told you I would pay you ten cents an hour, wasn't it?"

"No ma'am. You said twenty-five cents an hour." Theola gave her a bewildered stare that seemed to insinuate she was a cheap skate.

Sarah shook her head. "I'm sorry Theola you're right. I've had so many things on my mind here lately, that I'm just getting forgetful. Ok, twenty-five cents an hour."

"Yes ma'am."

"Theola may I ask you a personal question before we get started? Have a seat on the couch."

"Yes ma'am." Theola sat quietly and waited for her question. Sarah sat beside her.

"Are you happy about this baby?"

"Ohhhh yes ma'am. I do love James very much. James and I met in high school. We went to the same church. That was about two years ago. We have seen each other ever since. But I didn't plan on getting pregnant. We thought we'd try sex once before we got married, thinking nothing would happen on the very first time." Theola bowed her head slightly from embarrassment. Theola rubbed her stomach and placed both hands around her belly. "You see that I was wrong."

"Well don't feel bad honey. We all make mistakes."

"I just wish my parents had talked to me about sex and been truthful. My Mom told me I would get pregnant if I kissed a boy."

"Parents do what they think is best for you. Sometimes it's not always right. She was hoping that would frighten you away from a physical relationship. When is the baby due?"

"Around Thanksgiving."

"What a beautiful blessing you'll have."

"Yes ma'am. I'm looking forward to it. Enough about me, what are the chores you would like for me to do this day?"

"I'm going to teach you how to use the cash register and run the logbook for people signing in. Until someone comes in, you can dust the furniture in the lobby. What's James going to do all day with you in here?"

"He said he was going to relax."

"If he wants, he can borrow my car and go into the city to get familiar with roads and places in Chicago and find his way to the post office."

"That's very nice of you Sarah, but I'm sure James would be very nervous about taking your car into the city without you. Some may think he stole it."

"If that is so, then I will take him to the bus stop. He can catch the bus to the city."

"James has never ridden a bus before. That will be a new experience for him."

"Then he will soon get used to it."

"Yes ma'am."

"About the baby…"

Theola stood from the couch. She didn't want to talk anymore about her situation. She thought Sarah was trying to make her feel stupid about not knowing you can get pregnant on the first try. She went to the front desk and started to fiddle with the cash register. Sarah noticed her discomfort about their conversation and followed her lead.

"Let me show you how to do that. After you tell them the price of the room, this is the register book. Once you place their names in the book, you look at the key rack and see which rooms are available. Then you put that key number beside their name in the book."

"Yes ma'am."

Sarah, thinking about the baby, wanted to assist Theola financially. Sarah quizzed Theola again. "By the way, when is your baby due again?"

"In November Ms. Sarah."

"Call me Sarah, please."

"I thought while I was working, I would call you Ms. Sarah."

"Your choice." Sarah thought for a moment. "You know November is just six months from now. Are those all the clothes you have on your back?"

"Yes ma'am. Why do you ask?" Theola appeared sad. Her goal in life was never to be dependent on anybody for anything, not even the man she married. And yet, here she stood at the mercy of a woman she had only known for a few hours.

Sarah suddenly appeared emotionally stressed, almost tearful, before she spoke. Theola didn't know what to think after seeing her expression. So she tried to guess. "As soon as I make enough money Sarah, I can buy myself another dress. Please don't cry for me. I won't embarrass you by wearing the same clothes all the time."

Theola wanted to come around the desk and place her hands on Sarah's shoulders to give her comfort. Sarah's head was bowed. She held her face in her hands. But Theola did not comfort her. Unsure of why the tears were falling, she stayed behind the desk.

"Ohhhh Theola, that's not why I'm crying."

"Then why?"

"I want what you are about to have. Look at me. I'm close to my mid-30s. I just have a body that every man wants and no man wants to commit to. I've never been married. And I ask myself, why?"

"Look at where you are. Trucker's come and go every day. They are the only men you see. Finding the right man takes time and truckers usually don't have time to give."

"Neither do I anymore. Time is slowly running out on me. I want a family. I want a husband who loves me for me and not just my body. I want to raise five or six kids. I want a small ranch with a little white picket fence where we can have cows, dogs, chickens and a couple of horses. Raise our kids in a loving environment as husband and wife. Is that too much to ask for?"

"No Sarah. I think that is just about what every woman wants at some point in her life. But my Daddy used to say that love is hard to find, but if you stand still long enough, don't look for it...love will find you. That's the way it was for James and I. When I first saw him, I thought I didn't want a boy who was shorter than me and I didn't like the way he dressed. He wasn't my type and he talked funny. I ignored him for months. Then, one day at church, we started talking. We found we liked some of the same kinds of foods. We went to the same school. I just never noticed him, but he always had his eyes on me. We like a lot of the same subjects in school and on and on. Until his personality finally won me over. He was the perfect gentleman at all times. He never tried to take advantage of me at any time in our relationship. And he spends most of his time trying to make me laugh. He says I'm too serious. I wasn't looking for him, but he found me and I love him very much."

"Did he ever ask?"

"Ohhhh, he asked lots of times. I just said no lots of times. As usual, he was persistent in asking until I finally said yes to having sex, thinking nothing would happen the first time."

"I'm sorry Theola."

"Ohhhh, don't be sorry. I couldn't be happier about the baby. It's just that I had my life planned without a baby and without a man. They were to come after my college degree. Unfortunately, I made a mistake. Now I have to plan for our future. James and I don't even know what our future has in store for us, but now we have to take it one day at a time with our child on the way. You see, I want to go back to school. I want to make a difference in my life and in the lives of others."

"I understand Theola and I want to help. I don't want to stand in the way of your desires. If you want to work extra to help pay for your schooling, you can do that."

"I'm hoping James will be able to come through on the financial end of things and help with the baby. I would like to concentrate totally on college instead of a job, school and a child."

"I don't know Theola. That's a pretty tall request for a young man. But I am behind you and James in whatever you decide to do. I will help wherever I can."

"Right now our concern is for the baby."

"Well I can loan you some money to buy clothes and things for the baby. I'll take you shopping this coming weekend if you want?"

"Why Sarah, you don't have to do that. We don't have any way of repaying you right now."

"I know Theola. Forget about a loan. We'll call it a gift. Just call it my gift to the baby. This will not come out of your salary from me."

"Sarah I don't know how to thank you enough."

"And while we are at it, we'll get you a couple of maturity dresses."

"I don't know what to say."

"Just say ok. We'll do it this weekend."

"Ok."

"Don't give it a second thought. I want to do it."

Theola didn't know what else to say.

Sarah smiled and patted her on the hand. "Enough talk. Let's get back to the chores at hand. Now let me show you how the cash register works."

Sarah for the rest of the day taught Theola the duties she would be responsible for each day. Theola dusted, managed the hotel books and waited on customers. Just as Theola was getting ready to leave at the five o'clock hour, the phone rang.

"Hello," answered Sarah.

Theola waved to let Sarah know she was leaving for the day. Sarah motioned her hand backward for Theola not to leave just yet. Sarah whispered, holding her hand over the receiver, "It's Burt."

Theola waited to hear what the conversation was about.

"Tell me the news Burt. Did you get James the job?" Moments of silence filled the room.

"Well?" Theola asked.

Sarah placed a forefinger to her lips for Theola not to speak. "Thanks Burt. I owe you one." She hung up the phone.

"Well Sarah?"

Sarah held out her arms, gleaming with excitement. "James got the job! He starts tomorrow."

They both hugged each other and jumped for joy.

"Sarah thank you so much. You're great."

"Why thank you Theola. I'd like to think so myself. You go ahead. Tell James the good news. Tell him Mr. Burt said he needs to be at work by seven on Tuesday and I'll see you tomorrow."

"Yes ma'am!" Theola started to rush out the door, thrilled to tell James the news. Just as Theola's hand touched the doorknob, she turned back to Sarah. "How is James going to get to work?"

"In the morning you both come to the lobby at six. I'll take James to the bus stop. The bus stops at several key buildings in the city and the post office is one of them. So all he'll have to do is catch the bus every morning. And the bus stop is just eight miles from here. Ok?"

"Yes ma'am." Theola walked out.

Sarah felt pretty good about what she had accomplished for this young couple.

CHAPTER 17

A Potential Job

Moments later, Theola found James curled in bed, snoozing with the television on. She gently tiptoed over to the bed and observed his face. From his coarse black hair to his dynamic chin, he appeared to sleep without worrying about the world for the moment. Theola then sat gently on the bed, trying not to wake him just yet. She stroked his forehead softly. She leaned over to touch her lips to his. James did not wake up from the gentleness of her kiss. She kissed him multiple times, softly, until James began to smile. His eyes opened. He reached up, pulled Theola onto the bed and he kissed her passionately.

"I love ya baby," said James.

"I love you too." Theola beamed. I've got some good news for you." James released her. Theola rolled out of the bed and stood beside it, grinning from ear to ear. "Guess what?"

"What baby?"

"Mr. Burt got you the job. He called a little while ago and confirmed it." James leaped from the bed. "That's wonderful. When do I start?"

"Tomorrow, just like Sarah said. Mr. Burt is a man of his word."

"Sarah? Ya call her Sarah now?"

"She insisted."

James just shook his head. "Ok. Oh man!" exclaimed James.

"What James? What's wrong?"

"I have the same clothes I had on for two nights. I'll be wearin' the same clothes every day until I can afford ta buy new ones. I knows ya git tired of washin' my clothing out every night in the bathtub."

"Oh James, those are small things. Besides, Sarah is taking me shopping this weekend to get some clothes for me and the baby. I think I can manage a couple pair of underwear and some pants for you."

"What? Why she doin' dat? Dat's just mo money we gotta have ta pay her befo we leave. No Theola. I don't wanna be dat much in debt, dat we kan't work our way out."

"James will you just listen for a minute? This is not costing us anything. She is doing it out of the kindness of her heart."

"In a pig's eye. Now tell me chickens don't lay eggs. We will either owe her money or a favor. Ya watch and see."

"She's not like that James."

"Mark my words Theola."

"We talked for a little while, I learned a little bit about her and she did the same with me. We understand each other. So what I'll do is ask her if she could buy you a couple pair of pants and shirts to see you through to your first pay check."

"No! Theola don't. I'll wash what I have out every other day. It will be fine, alright?"

"Ok James. You're just making it hard on yourself. Let her help until we can do for ourselves."

"No!"

"Alright, be that way, be stubborn!" Theola dropped the subject. "Oh, she said she will take you to the bus stop. We should meet her at six in the morning."

"We?"

"I start work tomorrow too. I'm watching the lobby, remember?"

"Ms. Sarah takin' me alone, just me?"

"Of course."

"No way Theola. I'm nervous when the three of us are in the car."

"James how are you going to get to work?"

"Walk."

"Stop being stupid. Walk eight miles every day? Why don't you duck down in the car, do whatever, but we need this job. You can't be late to work!"

"Ya ain't seen a black man lynched befo, have ya?"

"Will you stop with the lynching?"

"You want ta see me lynched, don't ya?"

"No James. I try to avoid such horrifying events. But do you think Sarah wants you harmed?"

"No."

"Then go, just tomorrow and see how things work out. If it doesn't work, then we will try something else."

"Alright Theola. But if they come to lynch me tomorrow night, then ya no why. My death will be on yo hands."

"Yeah, yeah, yeah." Tired of his whining, Theola sat on the edge of the bed. "Do you mind James if I take a nap? Sarah didn't work me very hard, but for some reason, I'm very sleepy. Wake me when it is dinner time, please."

Theola threw the covers back from the bed. She leaned back and placed her head on the pillows. James took her shoes off and placed her legs on the bed. She pulled the covers to her waist and she fell fast asleep. James watched her as she had watched him earlier. Moments later, he placed the covers up to her shoulders and sat in the cushioned recliner across from the bed. As he sat there, he thought he had the most beautiful, intelligent young woman in the world, but dumb as a doorknob to the racism of society.

Chapter 18

The Encounter with Strangers

James sat in the recliner for a couple of hours like a guardian angel until suppertime came. He gently walked over to the bed and kissed her on the forehead.

"Wake up sweetheart. Let's go get something to eat." Groggy and still tired, Theola awoke. She was hungry and ready to eat. Slowly, she sat up. Then suddenly, she raced toward the bathroom.

James watched her, "You alright Theola?"

"Yes James." Theola stood at the bathroom door. "I just felt like I wanted to throw up. Let's hurry and get something to eat. I seem to get a little nauseous when I haven't had something to eat in a while."

"Alright."

Theola washed her face with cool water and combed her hair. James stood at the bathroom door waiting. "Feeling a little better?"

"I think I just need something to eat."

"Well let's go."

Moments later, when they entered the lobby holding hands, a couple of truckers were seated on the couch near the coffee table. They had beers in their hands, waiting for the six o'clock hour that was only five minutes away. Both truckers stopped drinking, startled by their appearance. One of them got up. He placed his beer bottle on the coffee table. The other one watched, continuing to sip on his beer. The trucker staggered over to the middle of the lobby, where James and Theola stood side by side.

"What you niggers doing in here? The rear entrance is outside and around the back. Don't you know this place is for truckers only?"

The man was muscularly shaped and stood six feet tall. His biceps bulged from his brown t-shirt. He stood taller than James and Theola. He stared with no expression directly into their faces. They were in complete dismay at this trucker's actions. Theola was outraged for being approached just for walking into the establishment and then being called out of her name by someone she didn't even know. She had forgotten she was hungry.

"There aren't any signs outside that say truckers only!" exclaimed Theola.

James was shocked. His heart dropped to the pit of his stomach as he tried to control his fear. James continued to observe the trucker, but he did not move. The trucker was stunned at the comment. He stepped closer to them. At that moment, James placed himself between the trucker and Theola. They both stood taller than him in the middle of the lobby floor.

The trucker glanced over James, facing Theola. He spoke directly to her. He almost fell, just trying to stand up. "You almost tall as me fo a nigga girl. But that won't stop me from knocking your black ass to the floor. You understand me?"

While both of them ignored James, he still stood firmly in the middle of them, focused on the trucker.

"Look mister." The trucker motioned down at James. "We don't mean any harm or disrespect ta ya, but…"

"Your intimidating mannerisms don't phase us one bit. Carry your drunken carcass back over to that couch and sit back down!" Aggressively, shouted Theola.

Amazed that Theola said another word, James cringed where he stood.

Anxiety gripped his heart so tight, that if Theola had said another antagonizing word, he would have died on the spot from fear alone. But James stood his ground and waited for a blow to his face to come. It did not. Instead, the trucker staggered again, trying to maintain his balance.

The trucker turned his head to address his buddy sitting on the couch. "Hey Markus. We have some up-piddy niggers in here. What are we going to do about it?"

"Well I guess we're just gonna have to shoot 'em!" Markus tried to stand up from the couch.

James turned toward Theola. Extreme panic emanated from his entire face. Theola didn't flinch or indicate any utterance of fear. She kept her eyes on the trucker. James mimicked her appearance and watched the two trucker's movements. After Markus took another gulp of beer, he put his bottle on the coffee table. He stood straight up and made two steps forward. He tripped over a leg on the coffee table and fell. The bottles of beer followed Markus to the hardwood floor, shattering into pieces. The other trucker went to help his buddy up. He tripped over his own feet and fell beside Markus. Sarah heard the ruckus and hurried into the lobby. At that moment, the two truckers had picked themselves up and were staggering toward Theola and James.

"What are you boys doing?" asked Sarah angrily.

"We were going to take care of these niggers for you. They seem to have lost their way," said one trucker.

"No you won't, Bruce! I guess I let you boys have one too many beers. You're drunk. James and Theola are my welcome guests. I only asked you boys to watch the lobby and let me know if any one came in until I got dinner ready. Not to try and beat anybody up."

"We're sorry Sarah. We thought we were doing you a favor. We didn't know you served niggers at your place," said Markus, being held up by Bruce.

"If you boys feel like that, you can just leave!"

"Noooo, we're hungry. We will eat first and then leave," spoke Bruce. He was still holding Markus to keep him from falling to the floor.

"Then come on into the dining room, all of you."

"You gonna let them niggers eat with us?" asked Markus.

"Markus you're half the size of Bruce but twice as fat. Trust me, they don't eat white people. Now, do you want to eat or not?"

Bruce and Markus both sighed.

They all headed toward the kitchen. "As soon as I get sober, I will come back and clean that glass up," stated Markus.

"That's what you should have them darkies doing while we eat," added Bruce, following Sarah.

"Enough talk. I will get the glass later. You boys sit down and eat."

Sarah pointed for Bruce and Markus to go toward the kitchen. James and Theola walked in last, keeping an eye on them the whole time. Markus and Bruce stumbled their way into the dinner area. Soon, everyone was seated.

"You all go ahead and just wait for a few moments. I'll place a sign on the front door to let people know I'm in here if they need lobby service. I'll be right back."

Theola and James continued to watch Bruce and Markus. Markus was starting to fall asleep at the table. Bruce was still angered over the words Theola had spoken to him.

A few minutes later, Sarah was back. She served her truckers first. Then she went to Theola and James and placed their plates before them.

"Forgive their arrogant behavior. They just had one too many beers. I'm so sorry."

"Not yo fault Ms. Sarah. Ya ain't got nothin' ta be sorry fo."

Sarah left and went to the kitchen to get more food. Theola was still angry. She was so upset that when food was placed before her, she didn't touch it. James reached over and stroked her long black hair, then touched the side of her face gently with his hand.

"The next time ya gotta death wish, would ya please let me know so I can make peace with God, because I know you have already said yo prayers fo ya ta say something so stupid!" James pulled his hand away from her face. "Ya just stood there and said, God, take me, please. I didn't have a clue that ya were ready ta leave this earth so soon with our baby on the way. Please don't do that again. We have a child we would like ta see grow up."

Theola realized James was right. "I was hungry. He caught me at a bad time."

James managed a small grin. "Let's eat."

They dug into their meals and thought nothing more of the two drunken truckers.

Sarah continued to serve the truckers. She brought them more beer. "This is the last beer you get from me today. This one is just to wash down your supper. You two made fools of yourselves tonight and I know you Bruce, you let it be or you can never stay here again. They are young kids. They don't know where they are going to end up."

"I know where they are going to end up with that attitude."

"Bruce open your heart. They are poor and without a home. They work for me. So don't go busting up my help. Please."

Markus was so drunk that his head fell onto his plate after he had finished his dinner and drank his last sip of beer.

"Ok Sarah, for you. But you better teach that nigger girl some manners or she will get them killed."

"I'll take care of it. Now you boys finish up and go on back to your rooms and sleep it off." She glanced over at Markus. "I see Markus already has a head start on you. Tomorrow is a new day."

Bruce said no more. He finished his dinner and helped Markus from the table. They went back to their rooms and let the incident with Theola and James slide.

They all watched the truckers leave. Sarah walked over to James and Theola. "I'm sure they won't bother you anymore. You two go on and get some rest. James, you have a big day tomorrow. Be here, both of you, in the lobby at six in the morning. Theola, you'll mine the desk. James, I'll drive you to the bus stop."

"But…"

"Don't worry James at that hour in the morning very few people are around. And very few white people ride the bus."

"Yes ma'am." James spoke a little nervous.

"I'll see you bright and early in the morning."

"Yes ma'am," they both responded.

James and Theola went back to their rooms. Sarah was disturbed over the entire incident. She hoped that the truckers were so drunk that they wouldn't remember what took place. But she knew she had to keep an eye on Bruce. She cleared the living room of beer glasses and prepared the kitchen and dining area for another day.

Chapter 19

The Argument

When Theola and James reached their room, James was a little on edge from the situation that Theola had caused.

"Theola I'm nervous 'bout all dat. They may not let it rest and come afta us."

"They won't!"

"How can ya be so sure? Dat trucker coulda killed us and nothin' would have been said or done about our deaths. It still could happen."

"Those truckers deserved every word I said."

"I agree. But ya have ta control yo temper, please. Let white people say and call you what they want to."

"You can let them say what they want to you, as for me!" Theola's tone raised, "I refuse to be called…" Theola paused and relaxed. "It's going to be alright James. Let's say a prayer right now and let God handle our problems."

"Say a pray. Why?" James was still furious.

"So God can help us through our situation."

"I don't need God ta help us. I need you ta stop insultin' white people so we can have a life."

"God can…"

"God can help you shut up!"

"Don't talk to me like that!" Theola walked away from James.

He realized her sincerity in wanting to be an equal in the world. But she had to be realistic. Leave God out of it and learn her place in society. He tried to calm her down.

"Look Theola, I was just as church goin' as you. But do ya believe everythin' the preacher said about God this and God that? He was talkin' in riddles half the time."

"You mean you weren't listening half the time."

"I waz listenin'."

"Well don't believe the preacher James. Do you believe your own mother? She has tried to teach you to trust in God."

"I know Theola. Let's say fir kicks and giggles, I believes in God. I'm down here' and He's up thar. Thar are millions of us on this earth. What make ya thank He will hear yo prayer or mine?"

"He loves us all. He created us and we are His children. No prayer is less important than another. He hears all our prayers equally. And no father turns his back on his children."

"Then ya don't know my Dad at all." Theola shook her head. "You pray Theola. I'm gonna ta sit here in this chair and worry."

"Suit yourself James." Theola knelt down beside the bed. James sat in the chair and watched her. "You sure you don't want to get on your knees and pray with me?"

"You go rite ahead Theola. My faith in God ain't as strong as yo's rite now."

"You do believe, don't you?"

"I don't know what I believe Theola. But don't let me stop ya."

Theola placed both hands together, her elbows on the bed and she bowed her head. She began to pray.

"Dear God in heaven. I realize we have not been the epitome of righteousness, for we have sinned severely. I'm with a child and without marriage. We have defied our parents and their way of thinking. We've had hatred form in our hearts against people we don't even know. So I'm asking you dear God, to forgive us for those sins. Our hearts are in the right place. We mean to do the right things, but somehow, they just don't come out the way we want them to. I am asking you dear Lord, to guide us, keep us safe from harm and let James's first day at work be a wonderful day. Let his day be so wonderful, dear God, that only he will know that you could have created an environment of such tranquility. Watch over my parents, my sisters and my brothers. Please let them find it in their hearts to forgive me. In JESUS' name, I pray. Amen."

James got up from the recliner. Pulled her up from her knees and hugged her tightly.

"That was a beautiful prayer. Let's hope God heard you."

Theola didn't want to go to bed angry. She gave James a lasting kiss.

"Let's get some rest now."

They both undressed. James turned out the light on the end table. Moments later, they were fast asleep.

CHAPTER 20

Henrietta's Restless Night

Two thousand miles away, James's mother couldn't sleep. She was awake at the kitchen table while the rest of the family was in deep slumber. She went to the icebox to get some milk and make a cup of hot chocolate. The cardboard container of milk slipped from her hand and splattered across the floor. The noise woke her daughter. She saw the kitchen light on and went to see who was there.

"Mother what are you doing in the kitchen at this hour? What time is it anyway?"

"It's nine-thirty. Why don't you go back to bed?" Henrietta knelt down with a cloth to clean up the spilled milk.

"No Mother. I would like to know what is troubling you. And let me clean this mess up for you."

Henrietta got up from her knees and found a kitchen chair to sit in. Rena got another cloth from the kitchen drawer to wipe the milk from the floor.

"This is unusual for you to be up at this hour of the night unless you are troubled."

Henrietta just stared at Rena, who was cleaning the floor. "I'm fine."

Rena picked up the empty carton and placed it in the trash. She finished cleaning the floor and placed both clothes in the sink.

"What's troubling you mother?" Rena started to wash the clothes.

"Don't do that. I'll wash them tomorrow on the rub board along with other dirty clothes."

Rena left the clothes in the sink. She sat across from her mother at the kitchen table. "What's Daddy going to say about no milk for breakfast?"

"I'll fix some powdered milk. He doesn't care as long as it's white and fresh."

"Tell me what's wrong Mother. Why are you so depressed?"

"It's your brother. He's been gone for days and not a word. Your father sleeps like a baby. He doesn't even speak of him. It's almost like James never existed. But I'm really concerned about him."

Henrietta got up from the table and walked to the sink to wash the milk from the dishcloth.

"Leave the clothes Mother until tomorrow, as you said. Don't worry about James. James can take care of himself. Besides, that girl he ran off with is very aggressive. She'll push him into doing what he needs to do, even if he doesn't want to. Look… she got him to run away. I would have never thought he'd have the guts to do that. So don't worry Mom. James will be alright."

Henrietta sat back at the table and touched Rena's hand. "You know honey, you're right because I'm going to ask God to send his angels to watch over him."

"Yes ma'am. You do that." Rena was nonchalant. It didn't change the sad expression upon Henrietta's face. "I care. Just not about the situation he is in. He made a choice. Let him live with it Mom."

Henrietta just bowed her head and removed her hand from atop her daughter's hand.

"You know Mom, I have been, meaning to talk to you and Daddy."

Henrietta raised her head. "About what baby?"

"I'm ready to go off to college now. I have been out of school for almost a year, not doing anything. I'm ready now to make that commitment to a career."

"Well that's wonderful baby girl. I'm so happy for you. I know your Dad will be happy too. We'll tell him in the morning. Have you thought about where you want to go?"

"I want to go to Xavier in New Orleans."

Henrietta was surprised at her choice. "Why so far away?"

"So Daddy won't play a part in my life. I want to be on my own. The only reason why I stayed away from college this long is because I was worried about what he would think and how he would react if I went far away. But I realize now, I have to start thinking about Rena Ann Taylor and what I want out of life."

"Good for you Rena. I'll support you every step of the way."

"Thanks Mom. I've called Cousin Jake and Bonnie to see if I could stay with them while I'm going to school in New Orleans. They've agreed. I heard student loans aren't too hard to come by, especially if you're low-income. And I can work in the evenings to have some kind of spending change."

"Sounds like you have given this some thought?"

"Yes ma'am, I have. I'm ready to get on with my life. I am nineteen years old and I want to live my life to the fullest."

"I hope you will baby girl."

"I will. I promise Mom."

"Ok, give me a hug sweetheart. Off to bed with you."

"Yes ma'am."

Rena embraced her mother and went back to bed. Henrietta went to the kitchen sink and retrieved the dirty dishtowels. She made one last wipe to clean the milk up from the kitchen floor. She held the clothes in her hand

and sat back down to the kitchen table. When she put the dishtowels on the table, she placed her hand together and prayed for James and his girlfriend.

"Dear God in heaven. I am but one of your many children. But please hear my cry. I have but one son. I have tried to teach him well. But he is sometimes strong-willed like his father. There are many dangers and pitfalls in this world that I don't even know. So I have not taught him everything. Lord. I beg of You to watch over my son and Theola. Guide them through their trials and tribulations. Don't let them fall by the wayside with nowhere to turn. They are young and they are innocent. All they need is a chance at life, dear God. Please shine the light before them and lead them all the way.

In Jesus name, I pray. Amen."

Moments later she found herself in tears, she dried her eyes, placed the dish clothes back in the sink and went back to bed.

CHAPTER 21

James's First Public Bus Ride

*T*he morning came quickly for James and Theola. At five o'clock, the sun had not begun to shine. They met Sarah in the lobby at six o'clock sharp.

"Right on time. Alright Theola, I'll be gone about an hour. If anyone comes in for breakfast, tell them the kitchen is closed until seven." Theola nodded. "Ohhhh Theola, I took the liberty of placing some crackers by the register in case you got real hungry before I got back."

"Yes ma'am. Thank you."

"And if anybody wants to register, you know what to do? Dust and kept the lobby straight."

"I got it Sarah. You can go."

Sarah turned to James. "Ok. Alright Mr. Taylor, let's ride."

James followed Sarah to the car. He was excited and scared. James got in the back seat. It was only ten minutes to the bus stop the way Sarah drove. Sarah glanced in the rearview mirror from the driver's seat for a second. She noticed sweat beads had formed on James's forehead. His fear was something he had to get over on his own. She cranked the car and hit the road.

Sarah tried to calm him as she drove down the road. "James don't be afraid. Just do the best job you can. Make me proud. Theola is depending on you. So is that baby."

"Yes ma'am. I will do my very best at workin'. I will. But dat is not what I'm worried about."

Before James could hold a deep conversation, Sarah was already at the bus stop.

"Here we are James."

There were five Negroes standing there, three young men in their twenties, one older gentleman in his fifties and one old lady in her late sixties. They stared hard when James got out of the car with a white woman as the driver. Ms. Sarah pulled off. The gawking continued. James found a spot where he could stand alone. The old Negro woman dressed in a solid gray dress with a black hat upon her head and a huge black purse that could have held everything you might need away from home, walked up to James.

"Young man. I know you think here in Chicago that white folks are liberal and all that, but that may be on the surface. They still kill Negroes like you for even looking hard at a white woman, let alone riding in the car with one all by yourself."

"Ma'am, she just helpin' me and my girlfriend out. I'm gonna be married in a few months. I don't want dat white woman. Right naw, she just lendin' me a hand."

"I hear you boy. But if you ever want to marry that girl you say you got, you better stop riding up here with that white lady. There's an older white man who should be getting here in just a few minutes. If he had seen you with her, your days would have been numbered. I know you don't know me. But I have lived in these parts for some years now and I can tell you who the backstabbers and the straight shooters are around here. You can mark my words or you can do what you like. But don't say you were not warned."

"But ma'am, I'm eight miles from this bus stop."

"Son, if you value your life and don't want to be eight feet under and helping the grass grow, you'd better mark my words. You want some kind of future with your family. You better find another way to get to this bus stop."

"Yes ma'am." James sighed and said no more.

Minutes later, an older white gentleman was dropped off by what appeared to be his grandson. James glanced in the old man's direction and then found another spot away from the crowd to be alone. Not long after the old man got there, the bus pulled up. The old man got on first, as always. Then the rest of the Negroes got on. The old woman got on before James. James sat near the front. The bus driver, an elderly white man and another younger white male stared at James. The old woman walked up and nudged James on the shoulder. James followed her to the rear of the bus.

"You never rode a bus before, boy?" asked the old black woman.

"Not with white people on it."

"Let me school you on a few other things son. Negroes never sit close to the front of the bus."

"But why? Thays plenty room?"

"I know son, but other white people will be getting on. They don't sit in the back of the buses. That's where the Negroes sit. Sit in the back, got it?"

"Yes ma'am."

"If you don't, that's another beating. If you know what I mean."

"Yes ma'am. Well I'm not lookin' ta git beat up. Thank ya fo takin' the time ta tell me these thangs. I'm from Louisiana and never been ta another state. My girlfriend and I run off from home. This is all new ta me."

"Well son, the only thing I can tell you is trust no one. Not even the ones who seem to be your friends. Trust no one."

"Yes ma'am." James thought for a moment. "Ma'am, could you tell me why that old man rides the bus if his grandson can drop him off anywhere he wanna go?"

"That's Mr. Bladwell. The man is almost seventy years old. He has been doing this for 30 years. He sits as chairman of the town's community. He and several other white men, like that one sittin' up front with him, watch what Negroes come in and out this town. Most Negroes ride the buses. He likes to ride the buses to make sure we stay in line. Those of us who are fortunate enough to have our own cars get the same treatment. Some white men follow them around too. They are called the KKK around here. But don't say that out loud."

James leaned over to whisper to the old woman. "My Daddy mentioned the KKK to me. But I thought I would never run into one."

"They everywhere boy. You just stay in line and they will think you are a good nigga."

"Why do they follow us?"

"So when a Negro gets out of line, they know who they need to take care of. If you know what I mean?"

"Do they shoot Negroes instead of lynching them?"

"You got one right boy," the old woman smiled. You do know something."

James didn't say another word. He confirmed his suspicion about the North. It wasn't any different from the South, just bigger buildings, more people, more guns and less rope. James sat back in his seat. He noticed Mr. Bladwell eyeing him in the rearview mirror of the bus. James ignored the stare and watched out the window at the places where the bus stopped. The buildings in the town of Chicago were worn, but well-kept. The streets were clean this morning. A half-hour later, James was nearing his workplace.

"Post office stop!" yelled the bus driver.

"Well dat's me," James spoke to the old lady. "Thank ya fo yo advice."

The old lady had no expression on her face. "You welcome and be careful son."

James gave a slight smile and got off the bus.

Chapter 22

The Post Office Job

When James got off the bus, he scanned the area. The post office was not a very large building, but it was all gray brick. The flag flew high from a very tall pole that towered over the post office building. There were little shops, clothing stores and food markets nearby. There were not many people moving about, just the merchants who owned the stores. They were making preparations for the day. Some owners were changing their *closed signs* to *open signs* in their windows. After a quick glance around, James stepped toward the post office. When he entered, no one was around. James stood at the counter until someone arrived. A tall, slender man appeared at the front desk in a light grayish blue shirt and shorts with a black strip down the side of his clothing.

"Can I help you boy?" asked the slender man.

"I am looking for the manager."

"That would be Mr. Robert Hunter. Is he expecting you?"

"Yes sir."

"Hold on then and I'll get him."

The slender man went in the back of the building. A few minutes later James noticed a medium height, dark haired white man with a mustache at the front of the desk.

"I'm Robert Hunter. How may I help you?"

"Mr. Burt told me ta tell ya that he sent me."

"Ohhhh yes. Burt told me he would be sending me some extra help. Come on around." Mr. Hunter stated with delight.

At the end of the counter, there was a part you could raise up and walk right into the back of the post office.

"Come into my office."

James followed Mr. Hunter. The slender man stood and watched them walk away. When they were out of sight, he immediately ran to tell the others about the new man coming on board.

James entered his office. "Have a seat. What's your name again? I'm terribly sorry. I'm not good with names until I get to see you regularly."

"That's ok Mr. Hunter. I go by just 'bout anything."

"No, no you don't." Mr. Hunter spoke firmly. "That's not my style. I don't play favoritism. I treat everybody with respect, regardless of color. If they don't like it, they can find another job. Everybody who works for me understands that. And I don't expect you to take anything off these guys around here. You demand your respect. They will treat you with it."

James perked up after that little speech. James adjusted himself in his seat to sit straighter in his chair and he looked Mr. Hunter in his eyes, instead of glancing away.

With enthusiasm James bellowed, "Yes sir. My name is James Taylor." He felt pretty good about what Mr. Hunter had just said.

"All I expect from you James, is hard work and to try and get along with the rest of the fellows. We work as a team. The public is our customer. We try to put their best interest first, not ours. I want you to know that I can count on you when I call you to do a job. I want you to be like fire. I know if I touch fire, I'll get burned. I want to know that if I call on you, the job will get done. Do the job to the best of your ability, nothing more, nothing less. That's all I ask."

"Yes sir."

"Some of the guys come in at seven. Some come in at eight. Which do you prefer?"

"Seven."

"We work eight-hour days with a forty-five-minute lunch since you have to walk to a local store or deli."

"Yes sir."

"Very well. You will be paid twenty-five dollars a week. You can buy life insurance and health insurance with that. It can come straight out of your check, so you will never miss it."

"Does the health insurance pay fo babies?"

"Sure. You got a baby coming?"

"Yes Mr. Hunter. And I can sure use that health insurance and this job."

"Alright. James, is it?" James nodded. "I'm going to let you work with Joe Jansen. He is one of the best men I have. He is the personnel supervisor of all the men on the floor. He won't mind teaching you the ropes. I'm not going to lie to you. You might run into some opposition among the boys because of your color. There is one other Negro male who works here. His name is Lee Roy. I'm not going to tell you anything about the guys to bias you in one way or the other. You will have to feel them out for yourself."

"Yes sir."

"Be at work on time, do your job well and rewards can follow."

"Yes sir."

"Do you have any questions for me?"

"No sir." James stood from his chair, extended his right hand with a smile on his face. They both shook hands.

"Alright then. Let's get started."

James followed Hunter out of the office.

"Joe!" yelled Mr. Hunter down the hall.

Joe came running from a distant office to Mr. Hunter's beckoning call.

"Yes sir, Mr. Hunter," said Joe.

"Joe, this is James Taylor." Joe and James shook hands. "Today is his first day. I want you to show him the ropes of sorting mail to the right mailboxes for today. We'll increase his duties as he learns more. For right now, introduce him to the other fellows."

"Yes sir."

"Go with Joe. He'll help you get signed in. Welcome aboard." James smiled and shook his boss's hand again. Mr. Hunter left and went back to his office.

"Come on James. I will introduce you to Margaret. She does payroll and Rosalind is the file clerk. Sandy is our administrative clerk. She handles the forms for our health and dental insurance. Then I'll introduce you to the fellows."

"Great!" James walked behind Joe.

"This is my office." Joe pointed to a room as they passed by. James took notice and kept walking.

James was feeling ecstatic. He seemed to be welcomed so far with open arms. He just hoped the rest of the fellows would fall in line. James and Joe soon reached the administrative office. James noticed three women at a glance when he entered the room. Margaret sat by the back door, Sandy's desk was at the front and Rosalind's was across the room, near the file cabinets, next to the windows. Rosalind had four huge file cabinets behind her. Sandy had one file cabinet beside her desk. Pictures of the President and his chain of command were on the walls. Sandy glanced up and noticed the two of them standing before her desk. The other two girls stared as well.

"This is James Taylor everyone, new guy on board. I need you all to get him administratively set up to work. This is Sandy." Joe pointed. "That's Margaret and Rosalind."

James watched carefully and tried to learn the names of the ladies immediately.

"I'm going to leave you with Sandy and the girls to get your paperwork done. Come back to my office once you're finish.

"Please sit down Mr. Taylor," smiled Sandy. James responded and waited to answer questions.

James spent about an hour with Sandy. He stood to leave. "You're done with your insurance papers. You need to see Rosalind now for payroll."

Rosalind observed James from head to toe as they came toward her. "Sit down. Fill out these two sheets. Then you can see Margaret."

James began to write. Minutes later, he went to Margaret's desk.

"Just sign this and you can go." Margaret observed James as he wrote his signature.

"Is dat all ladies?"

They all nodded. Sandy smiled. James left to meet up with Joe.

"Now we got two niggers in the Post Office. What is this world coming to?" Stated Rosalind.

Sandy didn't say a word. Neither did Margaret.

James arrived at Joe's office. "Hey Joe, I's finished with my payroll papers, insurance forms and stuff. The ladies was very kind. What's next?"

"Let me introduce you to the guys. Then we will get busy with the job. We got five walkers and seven drivers for the city. The walkers are local. The drivers are on the outskirts of the city. We all wear the light blue uniform with the strip down the side of the pants. So if you like to dress, get used to wearing your clothes just on the weekend."

"Ok, that's fine." James was delighted. Now, he didn't have to worry about what to wear.

"Let's get you fitted for a uniform and them we will meet the other guys. We will charge you for three uniforms and they will come out of your first month's check." James nodded. "Right now, they are probably collecting their mail. Let's check on them."

They walked up on Charlie, Lee Roy, Bart, Jacob, and Mike in the mailroom collecting packages and letters for their bags.

"Hey guys. This is James Taylor. Our new recruit. Today is his first day." They all waved and shook James's hand with a slight smile on their faces. Then Joe introduced him to the drivers. They were getting their mail also. "This is Mark, Tucker, Dick, Frank, Jim, Ed and Alex."

"Hi ya'll." Stated James.

They gave him a hearty welcome as well.

"Well James, you have just met all the fellows. Now let's get your hands dirty."

"Ok Mr. Jansen. Let's do it."

"Call me Joe. I'm not your boss."

"Ok Joe."

James and Joe went about the duties of instructor and student for the rest of the day. James thought Theola's prayer for this wonderful day had been answered. But he soon dismissed that thought and he also hoped her day was just half as nice as his.

CHAPTER 23

Theola's Close Encounter

Theola was managing the motel lobby wondering how James's day was going. Bruce was coming through for breakfast. Sarah was on her way back from dropping James off. When Bruce entered the lobby, Theola observed Bruce headed her way. Her heart sank.

"I don't smell breakfast cooking. Where is Sarah?"

With a stern facial expression, Theola stood tall and unyielding, not to display the fear that overcame her body. She hoped he wouldn't bring up the issue they had before.

"She had to run an errand. She will be back soon."

Theola grabbed the register book and a pen in an appearance to be writing something.

Bruce walked closer to the desk and leaned across the counter. Theola glanced up. Their eyes met. Theola was nervous but ready for confrontation.

"I want you to know if you weren't workers for Sarah, you and your nigga boyfriend would have no teeth to smart mouth another white man."

Agitated by his words, her fear was overwhelmed by anger.

"Look!" Theola slammed the pen into the book register. Placed both hands on the counter to propel herself toward Bruce. Bruce backed off the counter and stood firm. He didn't bat an eye or flinch a muscle from Theola's emotional outburst. "It's people like you that make this country a difficult place to live in peace."

"You wanna die nigger girl."

Without thinking, Theola grabbed the ink pen and leaped from behind the desk. She held the pen like a knife at Bruces' face. "You may be larger than I am, but I will take this pen and anything that is not nailed down in this lobby and try to take the white out of your skin."

"Do you want to fight me?"

"Oh that's right, one on one would be too equal. You need sheets with holes in them and about five or ten other guys to make it fair."

"You better watch your mouth or I can make that happen."

Suddenly, remembering what James said about vinegar and sugar, Theola calmed herself and went back behind the counter. "I don't have anything else to say to you." She stretched the ink pen toward Bruce. "Would you like to sign out?" Bruce just stared at her. "I told you Ms. Sarah would be back momentarily. You can wait in the lobby or go back to your room, sir." Emotional tension was suppressed, but volatile.

At that moment, Sarah entered the lobby. Not a moment too soon for Theola. Bruce stepped away from the counter. Theola relaxed and continued her duties.

"Hey Bruce, I see you and Theola are getting acquainted again. That's nice. Let me fix you some breakfast. Come on to the diner and let's talk. Where's Markus?" Sarah headed back toward the kitchen. She yelled at Theola. "Did anyone check into the motel while I was gone?"

"No ma'am."

Bruce focused on Theola until he and Sarah were in the dining area.

"Markus is still sleeping. He has a later route than I do today." Bruce was still upset about Theola. "You know she stared me in the eyes and got aggressive with me."

"Oh Bruce, get a life."

Bruce frowned. "She's going to get them killed."

"Sit down and let me fix you some breakfast so you can be on your way. If all you have to worry about in your life is some colored girl staring at you in the eyes, you are a blessed man."

Bruce sat at a table, sensing that Sarah wasn't the least bit interested in how he felt. He sat quietly and waited until he was served. He ate and left without another word.

As the day progressed into the afternoon, Theola continued to greet guests as they entered the lobby for lunch. Theola soon forgot about Bruce.

Sarah came to the lobby after the lunch hours were over. "Bruce is gone on his run. He won't be back for a few days. Theola I'm sorry about Bruce's behavior."

"Don't apologize for stupidity Sarah. It's not your fault his manners need improving. I just appreciate all the help you are giving James and me. By the way, what time are you picking him up from the bus stop?"

"I almost forgot. He should be arriving at four o'clock. Would you like to take the car and pick him up?"

"Nothing would please me more, but I don't know how to drive."

"Well why don't you ride with me. We'll shut down the lobby and be back in time to start supper. On the weekends if you want, I will teach you how to drive and we'll get you a drivers' license."

"Great! I would love to ride with you and get my license one day."

"Three-thirty it is and the weekends are a date," said Sarah.

Theola raced to finish the remainder of her chores and be ready at the designated time.

Chapter 24

Granny and the Ride Home

James was winding down from a good day at the post office. All the fellows seemed to welcome him with open arms, but he did get teased about his southern accent by some of the guys and Margaret, but that was ok.

"Well James it's three-thirty. Your day is almost over. Finish up the last few items. I will see you tomorrow," said Joe.

"Alright," James said with a smile.

When it came time for James to go home, he got on the bus delighted with his performance and his reception from the fellows. He saw that old lady he had met earlier that morning. He sat beside her.

"Misssss… , I'm sorry. I forgot ta ask yo name."

"That's ok Sonny, because I wasn't giving it. But you can call me Granny."

"Well Granny, I had a wonderful day. And my boss ain't prejudice and the other fellows are very friendly."

"Beware Sonny."

"Please call me James."

"Beware Sonny. All those who smile at you aren't your friends. Those might be the backstabbers. I'm not saying that they don't want to be your friend. Just be careful who you make your friends and watch yourself."

"I'll be careful." James sat back in his seat and smiled.

Granny had nothing more to say. He knew the old woman was wise and he would heed her warnings. An hour later, the bus rolled up to the bus stop. James kissed Granny on the cheek. He didn't look to see her expression. He didn't care. He was just grateful for her concern. When he got off the bus, he waited until the bus rolled away before he approached the car.

"How was your first day?" Theola asked.

James said not a word and sat in the back seat. The silence made Theola and Sarah curious.

"Come on James, how did your day go?" Sarah asked, anxiously.

Theola turned around in her seat to address James. He had a bowed head. Theola put her hand on his knee.

"I'm sorry baby. Maybe tomorrow will be better."

James immediately perked up with a smile. "I had a wonderful day! Everybody was very helpful. And all the fellas was polite. They did tease me bout the way I talk. But dat don't bother me none."

"I'm going to slap your face silly once we get out of this car. Why did you let us think you had a bad day? James Paul… one of these days."

"Oh baby, I'm just playin'. But the day went as bright as the sun on a clear day. Thank ya very much fo askin'."

"That's wonderful James," said Sarah.

Once they reached the motel, James expressed his concerns. "Ms. Sarah. I won't be riding with you to the bus stop in the morning unless Theola can ride along with us. If she kan't, I will have to start early enough ta walk."

"What! Why?" asked Sarah, perplexed at the comment.

"I was warned that a Negro man alone with a white woman can be very dangerous, even if it is innocent."

"James that's…"

"No Ms. Sarah. I mean no disrespect. But I would like to live to see my son or daughter grow up."

"Alright James. Suit yourself."

"Thank ya."

"Hun. Did someone threaten you?" asked Theola.

"Let's just say I was warned."

Theola sat back in her seat, puzzled to why James was adamant about Ms. Sarah not driving him to work. She felt someone spooked him. Sarah felt James always over reacted to what people said. But James knew he couldn't ride another day with Ms. Sarah driving him to the bus stop.

Chapter 25

The Baby

From that day forward, James went to bed early and woke up early to walk miles and meet the bus. The job was treating James well, except for occasionally teasing his accent. He soon grew weary of the harassment that was not funny to him. But he took it with a smile, being new on the job. James remembered what Granny had told him. He talked to his male associates about work only and kept his personal life separate. Theola was on time every morning, five days a week, assisting Sarah with the register and cleaning the lobby. This went on for five months until Theola's baby was almost due. More weeks passed until that day finally arrived. Labor pains struck Theola hard one November night.

"James!" screamed Theola, reaching for him.

Startled by her cry in the middle of the night, James leaped straight up out of bed, tripped over his shoes, raced into the bathroom and turned on the light. He placed cold water on his face. He glanced at his wristwatch. It said 3:00 a.m. Then, he looked in the mirror and wondered why he was in the bathroom at three in the morning. He suddenly heard another scream and realized Theola was in labor. He hastened back to the bedroom and placed his shoes on the opposite foot. Theola was moaning on the bed, holding her stomach. James ran three doors down and awakened Sarah. She got up and raced to warm the car. James got Theola dressed in her maternity clothes and shoes. Sarah waited in the car as planned in front of the motel. Soon, James and Theola were coming out of their room.

"It's about time!" shouted Sarah. "I thought you two were going to have the baby in the motel room. Get in!"

James eased Theola into the back seat. He got in beside her. Sarah drove as fast as she could without killing them. They soon arrived at Chicago Memorial Hospital. Sarah raced through the emergency doors.

"There is a lady in labor! Come help, please." She informed a nurse at the emergency entrance.

The hospital staff responded immediately. Theola was rushed to a maternity ward. For twenty hours, she had labor pains until the baby was ready for delivery. James and Sarah sweated the hours until the doctor announced to him that he had a baby girl.

"Can I see Theola now? How they both doin' Doc?"

"Of course you may see your wife now. Your baby girl is doing just fine." The doctor pointed. "Down the hall, room 353."

James and Sarah walked swiftly to her room. "Man, my feet are hurtin' me. Maybe I should ask that doctor if he could take a look at my feet."

Sarah glanced down at James's feet. "Perhaps if you put your shoes on the right foot, it would help relieve some of the pain."

James looked down at his feet and smiled. Sarah started to laugh.

"You know I didn't feel anythin' until just now." James stopped in his tracks and placed his shoes on the right foot.

Once they reached Theola's room, she was a little groggy, but coherent. She raised her hands, one for James and one for Sarah.

"I'm so happy you helped us Ms. Sarah. We don't know what we would have done without you."

Theola had dry lips, her hair was going in four different directions and her entire face gave the appearance of battling a bear. James kissed Theola's hand.

Observing the happy couple, Sarah smiled. "You welcome Theola."

"Thank you dear, for being the man that you are and being here for me."

"I wouldn't da missed it fo the world. Where da baby at? I wanna see what I look like."

"Who said the baby would look like you?" questioned Theola.

"Well, since it's a girl, she may look like you, but with my body," laughed James.

"Oh James," Sarah laughed too.

James looked at Theola and Sarah with a slight glimpse of sadness.

"What's wrong honey?" asked Theola.

"Baby I'm so sorry. I am so, so, sorry."

"James what is it? Please tell me." Theola pleaded.

James peered into her eyes and glanced over at Ms. Sarah. "I guess the only thing ta do is ta come out and say it."

"Tell us please James." stated Ms. Sarah.

James sighed. "I want yawl both ta know I kan't cook."

"What! Is that what that long face is for?" asked Theola. James started laughing. Sarah burst into laughter too.

"Don't worry James. As long as you two stay at the motel, you can always come down and get breakfast or dinner for Theola."

Sarah was still laughing. Theola didn't think it was too funny. James leaned over and kissed her on the cheek. Theola gave a slight smirk and shook her head. James tried to redeem himself with a helpful reminder.

"You know you's eighteen' naw. Sometime this year we needs ta get married." Theola, too tired to answer, radiated with happiness on her face.

Sarah smiled too.

At that moment, the nurse came in with their baby girl.

"She is beautiful," said Sarah.

The nurse tried to hand the baby to James. James placed his hands behind his back.

"Oh no. She's too tiny fo me. I might drop her like a hot potato. I ain't never held a baby befo."

He retreated from the nurse. Impatient with his attitude, the nurse handed the baby to Theola. Sarah noticed Theola's exhausted appearance and she reached for the child.

"May I hold her nurse?"

The nurse nodded with approval. The nurse took the child from Theola and handed her to Sarah. The nurse did not look at Sarah, only the child. Then, she took Theola's chart from the foot of the bed. She didn't completely understand why a white woman would be in the same room with a couple of Negroes.

"Mr. and Mrs. Taylor have you given any thought to what you are going to name the baby?" asked the nurse. James and Theola traded stares.

"Yeah, we gonna name her Billy Jo."

"The heck we will!" Theola looked at James. He was smiling. "Ohhhhhh... another joke."

"Whatcha wanna name her babe?" asked James.

"Her name will be Marilyn Delrio Taylor." The nurse wrote the data on Theola's clipboard. James leaned over and kissed Theola.

Sarah thought to herself, "Someday, this will be me."

The nurse stood for a few moments to finish the chart. "I'll take the baby now. You two must leave and let the mother get some rest."

"Yes nurse." James kissed Theola on the lips ever so softly. The nurse started past James. He leaned to kiss his baby girl. The nurse moved quickly. James missed kissing his baby girl good night. Sarah walked out of the room behind the nurse and James followed her.

"Ms. Sarah. I'm going ta stay here 'till Theola is released from the hospital."

"Very well James. I will gather some extra things for Theola and you, an extra shirt and pair of pants."

"Yes ma'am."

Sarah left the hospital. James went back to the hospital lobby and waited. While sitting on the sofa, he pondered their wedding and where they were going to live now that the baby had finally arrived. Exhausted from sleeping uncomfortably on the sofa that night, he soon drifted off to sleep.

Hours passed, later that evening Sarah came back to the hospital. James was sitting up, asleep, on the couch in the lobby.

"James." Sarah said softly. Not to startle him. She gently tugged at his shoulder.

He blinked his eyes a couple of times to focus on who was speaking to him. His eyes were red. There were tiny little sacks underneath them because of his lack of complete rest. His clothing was wrinkled.

"Ms. Sarah." James was groggy. He yawned.

"James here are some things for you and Theola."

"Thank ya Ms. Sarah." James took the sack.

"James I want you to know that I understand that Theola wants to go back and finish high school. Tell her not to worry. While you work and she goes to school, I will take care of baby Marilyn."

"We kan't even begun to thank ya fo all the kindness you done showed us over the past few months. You bought the baby crib, a supply of cloth diapers, milk, clothes and toys. You've done enough fo us already."

"Don't be silly James. You know me. This will save you the trouble of the baby being with strangers if I watch her. I want to do it. Besides, I'll be getting practice when I have my own."

"Ok. I will let Theola know."

"When did the doctor say he will release her from the hospital?"

"He givin' her two mo days."

"Ok great! She will be out in time for the three of you to spend Thanksgiving dinner with us. So I will be back in two days to pick the three of you up. If anything changes, call me and I will be back here sooner."

"Yes ma'am."

Sarah left. James went to wash up and change his clothing in the hospital bathroom. James felt like the proud father and lucky man to have such good friends as Sarah and Skip.

CHAPTER 26

The Surprise Homecoming

On the same day James had his newborn child, Rena was coming home for Thanksgiving from college. Edward was sitting on the wooden swing on the front porch, catching a brisk breeze of the morning air, half asleep. Suddenly, he heard the yard gate open and in front of his house. Rena came up the steps.

"Rena!" He jumped from the swing and reached out his arms to give her a hug. They embraced. He glanced over her shoulder as they released each other.

"What a beautiful car honey. What is it? A fifty-six Impala, solid red with a gray strip on the side?"

"I don't know daddy."

Edward continued to admire the car. "How were ya able ta buy that?"

"I borrowed it."

"Borrowed?" confused to the fact of what male would let a woman borrow such a beautiful car. But Edward was so glad to see his daughter that he soon dispensed with the questions. But he still remained focused on the car. Rena noticed his curiosity.

"It's not mine Daddy and I didn't steal it. So you can stop looking at it so hard."

"Never mind that baby girl. Let me look at you."

Rena spun around and flung her arms out to the side for her father to observe her appearance. She was dressed in an all-white light jacket, matching skirt, black blouse and black high heel shoes.

"Do I meet with your approval?"

"You done gained a pound or two," jokingly stated Edward. "But other than dat, ya still beautiful as always. I done missed ya so and so has yo Mama."

He turned and yelled through the screen door. "Henrietta! Rena is here."

"Isn't it a little chilly sitting out here on the porch Daddy?"

"It's sixty-seven degrees' little girl. That air feels good. You've been away too long. Even the weather down there done changed ya."

Henrietta was in the kitchen fixing an afternoon snack for Edward. She came running through the house, past the guest bedroom, to the living room, to the outside porch.

Henrietta grabbed Rena around the shoulders and hugged her tight. "Rena we are so happy to be seeing you. We were wondering if you were coming home for Thanksgiving dinner. Why didn't you call?"

"Yes ma'am."

Henrietta stood back from Rena and just admired the way she dressed.

"I would have called, but I wanted to surprise you two."

"You gotta surprise fo us after just six months of college?"

"Yes sir, I do." Rena turned from her father and looked back at the car. "Daniel!" A young man peeked his head up from hiding in the front seats. He waved. "Come on in Daniel!"

He slowly got out of the driver's seat and walked toward the house. Edward sized him up from the moment he set foot outside the car. Daniel made his way to the front porch.

"Hi Mr. Taylor, Mrs. Taylor. My name is Daniel Scott." He reached his right hand out to greet her father.

Edward slowly put his hand into his and quickly pulled it back. Daniel reached to shake Henrietta's hand. She placed his hand down and gave him the same hug she gave Rena. Edward stared at him the whole time, thinking, what kind of man hides in the front seat of a car, a sissy. The young man was fair-skinned, had very straight hair, was six feet tall and had a slender build. He had dark eyebrows, green eyes and beautifully straight white teeth. He had a black mustache that connected to his evenly trimmed beard that covered the lower part of his face. He was dressed in dark blue slacks, a white shirt and a dark blue blazer. His shoes were made of real black leather. Edward watched his every move. Henrietta broke the ice.

"Come on in Daniel. Take a load off your feet. Come in Rena and get the young man some tea."

Daniel followed Rena into the house. The first room they entered was the living room and master bedroom.

"Sit here on the couch and get acquainted with Daddy while I get you something to drink." Rena said.

Rena followed her mother into the kitchen. Edward sat in the recliner next to the sofa and eyed Daniel.

"Ok honey," said Daniel.

Those words coming from another man to his daughter irritated Edward inside and out. He had never let his daughter date a young man or even get close to her when she was growing up. Edward gritted his teeth and for a dark man, veins protruded his forehead. It was obvious a strong feeling of displeasure ruled his physical nature. But he said not a word. Daniel sat on the couch, rocking back and forth as he glanced around the house. He rubbed his thighs, then his legs and he never looked in Edward's direction. Daniel nervously waited for Rena to return from the kitchen. Rena was hoping her mother would approve.

"Mama what do you think of Daniel?"

"I don't know Rena. I just met the young man a second ago." Henrietta reached for the pitcher of iced tea in the ice box. "You have done the exact opposite of what we asked you not to do. You are forgetting about your career."

"Mama he is everything you told me to look for in a man. He's strong, he's supportive of me finishing school, if I so choose. He loves me and he has money."

"Is that what I told you to look for in a man?" Rena just stood in the middle of the kitchen floor. "While you're standing there, get the glasses from the cabinet."

"Something like that."

Rena retrieved four glasses and passed them to Henrietta.

"How about this Rena? Is he your friend, does he help take care of your needs, is he there when you are hurting, does he love you for who you are and not for what you can give him? How about that? Did you remember to look for those values instead of just lust and a lot of money so you can quit school?"

"Oh Mama. You don't understand. If Daniel can take care of me financially, what do I need with school? So he's got money. His daddy owns some gas stations out in Baton Rouge. He gives me things all the time. He said he would take care of me for the rest of my life."

"And you believe him?"

"Yes ma'am. I do. In college, he followed me around like a dog in heat. I wasn't interested, even though he dressed nicely and drove a fine car. I just thought he only wanted one thing, like Daddy always said most men do. But he's not like that. He tried to get to know me before anything physical happened. Believe me, he is a really nice guy. He is all those things you just mentioned and more. We even go to church on Sundays at his request."

"Ok baby girl." Henrietta sighed. You're over eighteen and there's nothing I can do or say to stop this relationship. I just want you to have a better education than I had. I never went to school. I barely read well and my writing, is legible. You know, if it hadn't been for Theola working with me on my vocabulary and reading books, I would still be a lot worse off. I just want more for you, that's all."

"I know. Listening to you read poetry was funny. But I can read and I write, but most importantly of all, I can count."

Henrietta sighed. "Rena, Rena, Rena."

"I will be just fine Mom." Rena noticed the sad expression on her face had turned into a deep depressive gaze. Rena wanted her mother to have empathy for her. "You don't understand Mom. When I was going to school, the kids would talk. They would talk about the color of your skin. We had a saying. If you're brown, stick around. If you're black, get back and if you're white, you're alright. These are my friends who said this. So just to make sure I didn't lose my brown skin tone, I used Nadnola Bleaching Cream to keep my skin color light."

"What?" cried Henrietta in shock. "How could you? I never bought you such stuff."

"No Mama. I got it from my friends who did the same thing."

"I never taught you to be ashamed of the color of your skin."

"No ma'am, you didn't. Society did. White people have everything. Light-skinned people get some things. I want to be in one of those groups. Right now, I am."

Henrietta just shook her head and said nothing further on the matter.

"You know your Daddy was hoping you would come back home and live with us until you got your feet on the ground."

"Look around Mama. Look at this house. It's got four rooms and a kitchen with barely enough room to eat and cook in. Your bedroom is shared with the living room. Right now, Daniel is looking at the bed you and Daddy sleep in because the living room couch happens to be in the master bedroom. The bathroom is so small you have to step in, turn sideways and kiss the wall to sit on the toilet. Then, you have to spread your legs if you don't want your knees touching the wall. My bedroom is so close to the bathroom that I have to let the window up if somebody is taking a squat in the middle of the night. And that's in the summertime. If it's winter, I can't open a window or I would freeze. I have to bury my head in the pillow until the stench is gone."

"At least you had an inside bathroom. I didn't."

"That's exactly what I mean. I don't want to live like you and Daddy. You barely have a front yard to speak of. The backyard is full of chickens and chicken shit. The aroma hits you every time you open the back door. I have had to watch my step when hanging clothes on the line to keep from stepping in that crap. When you told me to get the eggs from underneath the chickens in the chicken coop, I cringed at the thought. When I opened the door, sometimes the hens would fly from the top loaf to get out into the yard, catching their claws in my hair. I ducked from fear, placed my hands over my head and closed my eyes many times to escape getting my hair messed up."

"Why? That was an easy task. All you had to do was lift the chicken gently and reach for the laid eggs. You shouldn't have scared them."

Rena sighed, "Every time I lifted a chicken, it flew into my face, causing me to fall backward to dodge its path and I always fell or stepped into a horde of chicken mess. Not only that, but the grass is constantly beaten down by the chickens walking and plucking the seed you throw out there to them. I hated to feed them. They would always race and pluck my shoes if a grain of corn would fall on them. Then my shoes ended up scratched from being pecked. I'm tired of it all. I'm tired of that stinky chicken smell and this four-room house!"

"Honey those chickens feed you for most of your life."

"Maybe so Mom, but this is not how I want to live. This house itself stands on ten slabs of stone, with two slabs holding each corner of the house and two in the middle for support. The wooden floors creak and you are so close to your next door neighbor that if you spit, you better look first, because your neighbor could catch it. What kind of living is that?"

"It's called living the best way you can with what you have. You and James have lived well in this house for years."

"Did we have a choice? James and I lived in the same room for eighteen years. Look at that closet. It's too small for four people to use the same one. Our shoes were piled up on top of each other. Our clothes didn't even fit in the closet. We hung what we couldn't fit in the closet upon the doors, which obstructed our pathway from one room to the next. Don't get me wrong Mother. You and Dad have done what you know how to do. I have done it right alone with you. I have lived like this for eighteen years. I want more. Anything I do for myself now will be better than this."

Hurt by her daughter's words, Henrietta continued. "At least you didn't starve. You had a roof over your head and clothes on your back. Your Daddy always kept you in the finest of clothes when he made James wear his hand-me-downs." Henrietta poured the tea into the glasses. "Get some ice cubes from the box."

Rena walked toward the refrigerator to retrieve the ice cubes.

"That's because James took that crap. If he had made me wear your clothes, I would have never set foot out of this house. He knew that. I don't want the same things you and Daddy have. You work two miles away from Mr. Charlie's house. The same man you worked for when you were a slave. You still cook and clean for his household after forty years just to get the food and five dollars a day. Daddy still works at the cotton mill. Your lives aren't going to change. No Mom. That's not where I want to be. I have got to have more. I have lived your lifestyle. Now it's time for me to live my own. Daniel is going to give that to me."

"How much more?"

"I want it all. Everything I can get."

Rena passed the ice tray to her mother.

"What?" Henrietta was baffled by her statement.

"That's right Mama. I am already married. I'm Mrs. Daniel Scott and I'm going to take everything he wants to give me. He has already bought me a three bedroom house that sits on concrete and two acres of land. Just for the two of us. I don't have to share nothing with nooobody."

Stunned at the news, Henrietta dropped the ice tray on the table. She plopped down in the chair closest to her, from near faint.

"Are you going to stay in school?"

"No ma'am. Daniel would like me too, but I told him he makes enough money for the both of us. He agreed."

"You're gonna throw your life away for material things. I bet you don't even love that boy. Do you?"

"He gives me things."

"You are willing to take things over happiness and a good education. Is that what I taught you?"

"No ma'am. You taught me love, kindness, respect, and friendship. As long as he keeps me well-dressed and in expensive jewelry, I'm happy."

"Rena you have only been away from us for a few months. Now you have married the first man who promises to take care of you and for all the wrong reasons." Henrietta sighed and shook her head. "Well, you're married now honey. There is nothing I can say or do to change that, but I wish you the very best." Henrietta sighed again. You are going to tell your father?"

"Of course, that's why we are here."

Henrietta had nothing more to say. She rose from the table. The shock the ice tray took from hitting the table loosened the cubes. Henrietta placed cubes in each glass, filled the ice tray with more water, and placed the tray back in the freezer. She passed Rena two glasses and she took two.

"Alright then. Let's serve our men folk."

"Yes ma'am."

Moments later, they both entered the room with tea in their hands. Not a word had been spoken. Rena handed Daniel his tea.

"Thank you sweetheart," said Daniel.

The expression of anger on Edward's face when Daniel spoke those words to Rena would have killed a deer from a mile away.

Chapter 27

The Moment of Truth from Rena

Henrietta handed Edward his tea. Edward took a sip and placed his glass on the coffee table next to him. Then Rena sat on the couch with Daniel. Henrietta sat in the other recliner near the bed.

"Daddy," softly spoke Rena.

"Yes baby girl."

"Daniel and I have something we would like to say."

Edward stood from his chair. Rena and Daniel leaped up simultaneously. Henrietta stayed seated and sipped her tea.

Edward stared at Daniel. Then he looked at Rena. "If you're pregnant …." Edward pointed his hand at Daniel, excitedly. "This boy is gonna marry you."

"I'm not pregnant. But we are married Daddy."

Edward sat back down, overwhelmed by the news. Daniel and Rena sat back down. Edward's emotional disbelief had him dazed and mumbling beneath his breath.

"What are you saying dear? Don't mumble," spoke Henrietta.

"Ya know Rena, I bought a house fo ya. Right down the street from us. Just in case afta ya finished college ya might wanna come back here and teach school."

Henrietta was surprised. Rena and Daniel were shocked.

"What did you say? You bought a house?" Henrietta was flabbergasted by the comment.

"Yes honey. I meant ta tell ya, but it just seemed ta slip my mind. I thought our baby girl might wanna live here with us afta school. Then I thought it might be a nice surprise fo both of ya at Thanksgiving dinner. I guess I'm the one surprised."

"Oh Daddy. I'm sooo sorry. But Daniel and I are going to live in Florida. We already have a nice brick two-story house down there."

"What! Why so fur away? We ain't gonna be able ta come and visit ya. You knows we don't fly." He waited for Henrietta to comment.

Henrietta just smiled at Rena. "That's wonderful baby girl. Are you two going to stay for Thanksgiving?"

Surprised that Henrietta did not argue the distance, he figured Rena must have already told her.

"Yes." said Edward. "Stay for Thanksgiving. Let us git ta know Daniel here. Although what kinda of man hides down in a seat? I sure hope ya ain't no wimp and can take care of my daughter."

"Oh no Sir. Mr. Taylor. I box in my spare time. No one will hurt your daughter with me around."

"Uh huh, tape boxes," muttered Edward.

"Yes, Mr. and Mrs. Taylor, I would be delighted to stay. I want us to get to know each other very well. I love your daughter. I will take excellent care of her."

"Oh, so ya can speak more than one sentence at a time," said Edward sarcastically. "Then tell me what kinda man slumps in the front seat of a car if a woman tells him ta?"

"Excuse me, Sir."

Edward spoke louder and more aggressively. "I said boy. What kinda man slumps in a car? A sissy with no backbone who hides in the front seat of a car because a woman tells him ta, he can't be too much of a man. If ya not man enough ta face me when ya come ta my house, then you're a coward, boy!"

"That's enough Daddy. That was my ideal. I wanted to surprise you. Don't blame Daniel."

Daniel stood. Edward stood. Daniel confronted Edward eye to eye. "I'm man enough to take care of your daughter. I love her. I will provide for her every need. Just because I dress well and don't act like a gangster on the streets doesn't mean I can't defend myself or protect your daughter, my wife. And Sir, staying here to get acquainted with you will be my pleasure, Dad."

Edward flinched at the words he spoke and sat back down. Edward reached for his tea from the coffee table and took a sip.

He didn't look at Daniel anymore. "Don't call me dad, boy." Daniel sat back down. "Ya don't know me like that. I sure as hell don't know you. So don't even form yo lips ta say dad. Don't even let it be a thought. Don't even…"

Henrietta interrupted… "I think he understands Edward."

"I understand sir. Sometimes I wonder myself if I am good enough for your daughter." Daniel turned to Rena. "But as long as I live I will dedicate my life to making her happy."

"Love you babe." Rena kissed him on the cheek.

"Sir I would be honored to stay and get to know her family."

Edward had a smirk on his face. "I need somethin' stronger than tea. Do I have a bottle in the kitchen old lady? I knowed I promise not ta drink in the house, but dis calls fo a good stiff one."

Henrietta ignored Edward. "That's wonderful Daniel. Rena will just fix up her old bed. The two of you can sleep in there. You can sleep in James's bed and Rena in her own."

Henrietta and Edward stared at each other without a smile.

"But Mom, we're married."

"I know Rena honey. But this is going to take some getting used to. So please accommodate us this visit."

Rena smiled and said no more. But she whispered in Daniel's ear. "This will be our last visit." Daniel nodded in agreement.

Edward appeared depressed. His only daughter no longer belonged to him, but to another.

Chapter 28

Spreading the Word

While the Taylors and guests were getting acquainted, a different celebration of a newcomer was being held a thousand miles away. Sarah, Theola, and James were on their way from the hospital. Theola and James were in the back seat.

Minutes later, they arrived at the motel. James helped Theola get out of the car. Sarah took the baby. Sarah went ahead and opened their door. James and Theola followed slowly. When James and Theola entered their room, one side had been decorated with pink wallpaper. One-half the walls were bordered with pink and yellow balloons. The crib sheets had beautiful flowers of all different colors. A huge dresser with a vanity mirror was draped with white and pink crepe paper. James and Theola were astonished when they entered the room. Sarah placed the baby in the crib.

"If you need anything, let me know. Theola I know I said no to using the kitchen after eight, but please feel free to warm bottles as necessary."

"I won't need to warm bottles. She will get everything naturally." Theola smiled. "This room is beautiful."

"Ms. Sarah ya didn't have ta do all this. We coulda managed."

"I know I didn't have to. I did it because I wanted to. Now you get Theola into bed. I will bring some supper down later."

"No Ms. Sarah. Ya ring me. I will come git it. Ya done enough."

"Very well James. I will call."

Theola made her way to the bed and tried to get comfortable. Sarah left to fix dinner. James checked on his newborn. He gazed at his baby girl and touched her tiny feet.

"You know Theola, I thank we done a pretty good job. She is cute. A full head of hair and a set of lungs ta match."

"You've heard her cry?"

"I watched her fo the past three days in the nursery. When she got hungry, she let the nurses know. Believe me."

"Ohhhhh… Ahhhhh…" Theola grunted.

James walked over to the side of the bed. He sat gently down beside Theola. "Ya know, love of my life. I don't think I realized how much I do love ya until just rite now. This is the first thing in my life I done helped ta create and I like it. The things we have been through seem all worthwhile after lookin' at our child."

Theola smiled. James leaned toward her and kissed her on the cheek.

"Yes, God has blessed us well. When are we going to officially jump across the broomstick?"

"What dat mean?"

"You know? Your Mama didn't tell you?"

"Know. What?"

"The way Negro people married themselves a long time ago before they had churches and ministers. They would say a few words, kiss and jump over a broomstick. That meant they were officially married in the eyes of each other."

"Ya pullin' my leg?"

"No I'm not James. Your mother and father never told you that story?"

"No. I don't thank my Mom and Dad thank very much of the marriage they are in. But no matter Theola. Right now, I do feel very lucky ta have ya. Any day ya pick is fine with me ta jump over the broomstick."

"Well as soon as I am able to walk normally, we will pay a trip to the minister."

"Two days before Thanksgiving and I have more than any man could ever ask fo. I just want to say, I love ya both very much and I will try my very best always ta be yo rock, yo anchor, yo everything that ya can always lean on. I love ya both baby."

They kissed passionately. Then she gently pushed him away. "I love you James. But the doctor told you…"

"I know, I know. No hanky panky fo the next six weeks."

"That's right."

"Of course, I will honor the doctor's words." He kissed her on the forehead, got up from the bed and paced the room. "While you were in the hospital, I had been thanking. I decided ta go ta work for Ms. Sarah in yo place on the weekends. With the extra money, I can continue ta pay her off and bank the check at the post office so we can move from here and get an apartment in town with a little more space fo the baby and all."

"James are you sure?"

"Yeah I'm sure. I'll be moppin' the lobby and kitchen, movin' furniture around, stuff like that after I come back from the post office. Plus I won't be that far from you. I can take my breaks in here with ya and Ms. Sarah promises ta check on you two during the day."

"Ok James. I hate feeling in need of other people's services. I like doing things for myself."

"I'm not other people. I'm your man." James grinned and raised both arms to flex his muscles. "Well ya got all the help ya need. James Paul Taylor is at yo service ma'am."

"Don't make me laugh or my stitches will burst." They suddenly heard a small whimper from the crib.

"Uh, oh. I thank she wakin' up. You got some milk ready fo her baby?"

"The breasts stay ready James. Bring her over."

James was a little hesitant. He ever so gingerly picked up Marilyn and handed her to Theola.

Marilyn began sucking right away, quenching her appetite. "Man, she musta been hungry. Can I do that when I get hungry?"

Theola laughed gingerly. "You do do that."

Oh yeah. I forgot ta tell you." James smiled. "Just before ya went in the hospital, my boss said if I keep up the good work, in another year, he would give me a raise. All the more reason to save our money fo dat apartment."

"We need a car first. So we can get around."

"Don't worry about that babe. I'm way ahead of ya. Ms. Sarah has a friend of a friend who sells used cars. She's gonna ta talk ta him about sellin' us a car."

"You mean one we'll be able to afford."

"You know Ms. Sarah, she wouldn't have it any other way."

"James I want you to know I still plan on going back and finishing high school."

"I know Theola. The car will be fo ya ta go ta school. Ya can drop me off at work. Ms. Sarah has already said she'd be glad ta watch the baby while you went ta school and I went ta work."

"That lady is wonderful."

"I know. Dat's why we will let her know after Christmas, dat the money we saved will eventually lead ta our leavin' here. That way, she will have plenty of time ta find additional help."

"Speaking of the holidays James, let's call your Mom and Dad and let them know they have a grandchild. It will be a nice Thanksgiving surprise for them."

"You're right. It will be a surprise." James sarcastically commented. "My Dad will hang up the phone." James shook his head. "No way Theola. My parents could care less."

"It's almost Thanksgiving. Let's let them have a wonderful Thanksgiving too and spread the word to my sisters about our joyous new buddle of life. Besides, I know my father has disowned me. But my sisters and I are very close. This is their only way of knowing where I am and what I'm doing. They can keep me posted on Dad's feelings. So when I graduate from law school and we have a beautiful granddaughter to show him, maybe he will have a change of heart and accept me back into his life. I love my family James. I never meant for this to happen the way it did. But I wasn't going to give my child up either. So please, let's call your family for Thanksgiving."

"You know Theola, ya have a way of breaking me down. Alright, we'll call my parents on Thanksgiving Day. This way, maybe, they will be in a festive mood."

The baby sighed as Theola fed her. They both watched her nourish, delighted about the arrival of their newborn. James just hoped his parents would feel the same way.

Chapter 29

The Surprise Phone Call

A couple of days passed. Sarah had cooked a grand Thanksgiving dinner with turkey, ham, mashed potatoes, rolls, cakes and pies. Drinks lined the kitchen counter with beer, wine and liquor of all kinds. After Sarah, Skip, James and Theola blessed the table, they passed food around and filled their glasses. Merriment was throughout Sarah's home this day as they ate well and enjoyed each other's company.

"James have you ever had a beer, wine or booze of any kind?" asked Skip.

"We try to stay away from such distractions," stated Theola.

"Oh Theola relax. Let James at least try a beer." Sarah said.

James looked at Theola, who shook her head. "I'll try some Skip."

"Great!" Skip passed James a beer.

James took a sip. "Hmm, I like this."

"Miller is my favorite James."

Theola just shook her head. Sarah sipped her wine. She said not a word, realizing Theola's discontent.

The baby's bassinet was by Theola's chair. Marilyn was sound asleep. Skip only had the holiday off. They all ate until they were full and enjoyed a pleasant conversation among themselves. Sarah and Skip were a little intoxicated. Now it was time to relax and enjoy the rest of the evening.

"Thanks Ms. Sarah. Dinner sure was good." said James.

"We'll help you clean up," said Theola.

"Oooooh no. That won't be necessary James and Theola. I will help Sarah clean up," said Skip.

"Yes James. You and Theola go and take care of that beautiful baby of yours. Thank you for joining us for dinner. Skip and I can handle things from here." Sarah gazed into Skip's eyes. Skip lovingly gazed back.

"Yes ma'am." said James.

Theola and James smiled and left the dining area. James carried Marilyn still asleep in her bassinet. They went back to their motel room. Marilyn was placed back into her crib. Theola sat on the bed. James started to get undressed.

"It was nice of Skip and Ms. Sarah to invite us to Thanksgiving dinner."

"Yeah, I had a nice time too," said James.

"I'm feeling grateful. Let's call your Mom and Dad now James. To wish them a Happy Thanksgiving and tell them the wonderful news."

"What news?"

Theola shrugged her shoulders. "About the baby."

"Alrite, but I don't think they will be too happy ta hear from me."

"Just call please." James picked up the phone and dialed. Marilyn started to whimper. Theola picked her up from the bassinet. She held Marilyn in her arms while sitting on the side of the bed and rocked her back and forth.

A few moments later, Theola was listening to a pleasant conversation between James and his mother.

"Mom it's me. James."

"How wonderful son to hear your voice!" Henrietta was excited. "It's been seven months since we heard from you. I've been so sick with worry. How are you doing son?"

"Mom, I got some good news to tell ya. I'm a dad and you're a grandma. I don't mean ta sprang it on ya dis way, but I don't know how else ta say it."

"Son, you know I love you. That's wonderful. I couldn't be happier for you. How is Theola doing? And the baby?"

Edward and Rena had a look of shock on their faces when Henrietta said, *Baby*.

"They both doin' great Mom. Things are going well fo us rite now. How's Dad and Rena?"

"Son they are both right here in the living room. We have just finished Thanksgiving dinner and we are just sitting here talking. Rena brought her husband with her from college. We are just getting to know him a little better too."

"Husband? Rena got hitched?" James was surprised.

"Yes she did." Henrietta sounded a little disappointed. "Would you like to speak to your father?"

"Only if he really wanna ta speak ta me."

"He does son. Hold on." Henrietta beckoned Edward with her right hand. Motioning him to come take the phone, while she held the phone in her left hand and spoke softly to James.

Edward looked at Henrietta, shaking his head and silently saying *no* from across the room.

Henrietta's facial expression and stomping of her foot forced Edward to start walking. Rena and Daniel sat silently and observed.

"He's coming right now. Hold on sweetheart."

Henrietta stretched the phone to Edward. She silently whispered to Edward. "Be nice and find out where he is."

Edward snatched the phone from Henrietta's hand. "What in the Sam hell do ya thank ya doin'? Runnin' away with that gal! How could ya? Why did ya call after all these months? I bet ya stuck somewhere and need some money. Well, I ain't givin' ya none. Ya ain't never gonna amount to a hill of beans. So ya can just…" Before Edward could finish his sentence, the phone went dead.

"Why did you hang up James? You didn't tell your mother where she could reach us."

"My father got on the phone. I know mother forced him ta. He never had much ta say ta me when I was at home. Now he's gonna start lecturin' me on what I done wrong. I am on my own. I don't have ta listen ta dat man. So I'll call them back later and ask Mom not ta let me speak ta Dad."

"James you should honor your mother and father despite their misgivings."

"Well I'll honor him from three thousand miles away." James looked at the phone. "Shut the hell up, Dad!"

"Nooo James."

"Don't *'nooo James'* me. You don't know!"

"Know what?"

"In my entire life, my Dad, he has never called me his son."

"Never?"

"Never! He never said, *'Son, can ya get me a drink of water.* Or *son, will you get me dis* or *son can you get me dat* or *I love ya son.'* It's always a *boy. Boy do this, boy do that, com'mere boy…* like I was someone else's child."

"But James…"

"Just stay the hell out of it Theola!"

"Don't curse at me James Paul. We don't need to raise our child hearing curse words."

"Theola you're pushing it. Marilyn didn't understand a word I just said." James paced the floor to calm down.

"I know that. I'm stopping you before you make it a habit."

James thought about what he said and how he said it. "I'm sorry Theola. I only curse when I get upset. Dat man can make me sooo mad. I already have a deep resentment fo him. I don't know if I can ever forgive him fo all the unfair thangs he done ta me throughout my life."

"I will help you work on it James. That's what wives are for." Theola smiled.

"I don't wanna work on it, ever! As far as I'm concerned, he don't exist."

"James...I can understand how you feel."

"Let's drop the subject Theola. I don't wanna talk about him anymore." James raised his right hand in the air, motioning for silence.

Theola grew angry. She placed Marilyn back in her crib and stood in James's face.

"Don't you ever raise your hand to me like I'm some kind of child to be hushed when daddy has spoken! We are a team. This is not a dictatorship!" The baby started to whimper. Theola lowered her voice. "I love you James, but if our relationship is to work, we must work together. That means communicating our concerns, whatever they are."

James nodded his head in submission to her words. He spoke calmly, "If ya want this ta work, then let's not ever brang up my father."

Theola took a deep breath and sighed. "Let's change the subject. I know something more pleasant we need to talk about."

"And what might that be?"

"Don't we need to get married?" Theola smiled.

"Well I have already talked ta Ms. Sarah. She said she knows a preacher who will marry us fo five dollars. All we have ta do is git a marriage license. I'll take care of dat first thang next week. Ms. Sarah and Skip said they would be our witnesses."

"Great! Sounds like you have been on top of things."

"Of course. Now let's get some rest. I'm kinda tired."

"It's a little early in the evening to be going to bed."

"I didn't say I was goin' ta sleep."

"I'll be right there as soon as I check on Marilyn," spoke Theola.

Theola was delighted that James was serious about their lives and wanted things to be right between them. Theola kissed her newborn with much delight in her heart. She turned out the light for this night and greeted her man with cheer.

Chapter 30

Words for Edward

s lights went out in Chicago, a conversation lit up in Louisiana. Henrietta verbally attacked Edward for not being cordial to their son.

"You don't have but one son and you treat him like crap. You don't give him the time of day. You didn't give James a chance to say two words before you jumped down his throat! What kind of father are you?"

"The kind dat don't give a shit what happens ta dat boy, because he ain't mine!"

Rena and Daniel looked at each other and decided to walk outside on the porch.

"You know I have just about had enough of your lies. You are the only man I have ever been with in my life. I have given you nothing but love. Our son has done his very best to give you the same. He has tried to seek your approval on everything he has done and all you did was criticize him for his efforts."

"Dat's enough out of ya Henrietta!"

"That's your boy whether you like him or not. And as far as I am concerned, you probably have more children out there in the street than I care to name on both my hands."

Edward softened his tone. "What ya talkin' 'bout woman? You knows me."

"That's right. I know you too well. I know you have been sleeping around on me Edward Lee. But that's alright because God is just to the unjust."

"Now leave God outta it. I ain't been sleepin' round on you. Who told ya such a thang?"

"Don't you worry your handsome head over who told me. I know, so just leave it at that."

"Oh com'on Henrietta, honey. Ya know ya the only one fo me. Besides, I married you. Not them other women who be chasin' me. Ya da one I lay down with at night."

"You mean some nights."

"Well sometimes I be out and get my head bad with the boys and go ta sleep where I is. Ya know that Henrietta, honey. Now come on over here and give me a kiss." Edward pointed to his cheek.

"Kiss yourself. I think you will get more enjoyment from it."

"Now you stop talking like that Henrietta or I'll…"

"Or you'll what… leave me. Ha! Don't make me shout, Halleluiah! I'm too good to you Edward. No other woman will put up with your nonsense." Henrietta sat back down. "Call the children back in the house. We are wasting precious time bickering, when we both know the truth. Let's enjoy their company while they are here."

Edward had nothing more to say. Edward called Rena and Daniel back into the house. They sat back on the couch. All were silent until the phone rang. Henrietta quickly answered the phone, hoping James had called back.

"Hello," Henrietta spoke anxiously.

"Mrs. Taylor, this is Deborah Delsin. I know it's Thanksgiving Day. It has been months since we have called you. We were wondering if you have heard a word from our sister. We were just hoping that for this holiday, they might have called."

"You are in luck today. Good news. They are doing fine. You all are aunties now."

"She had a baby?" spoke Deborah. She realized now why Theola had to leave home.

"Yes. I didn't get a chance to find out if it's a boy or a girl, but everyone is just fine."

"That's wonderful. I will tell the rest of my brothers and sisters of the news. Thank you so much Mrs. Taylor. Did you find out where they were?" Before Henrietta could get a response… "Uh-oh, my sister is giving me a signal. My parents might be coming. I must go now. I will call again soon. Thanks again."

"You welcome, goodbye."

"Who was dat?"

Henrietta was still angry over their conversation about James. "No one you need to be concerned with." She glanced at Rena and Daniel with a smile. "Would you two like a piece of my lemon pie?" She got up from her recliner and headed for the kitchen.

"I would love some," spoke Daniel.

"I just bet ya would," mumbled Edward.

Everyone ignored Edward's comment.

"I would love some too Mother."

Rena and Daniel followed Henrietta into the kitchen. Edward was left in the living room alone.

Chapter 31

The Promotion

As time passed, the days were good to James and Theola. They even found a nearby church to go to on Sunday mornings. After they were married there, James stopped going, but Theola took Marilyn every Sunday morning. Life was good except for James being criticized about his accent at the office.

"Honey the men at work make fun of da way I talk, especially Lee Roy. And I don't like it."

"Then let's do something about it. Listen to the way I talk, then try to speak the same way. I will correct you when you revert back to your southern accent. And try to read some of my poetry books from class. Your Mom really took a special liking to the poetry I used to read her."

"Let's skip the poetry and keep it ta English."

For two years, James worked hard at getting rid of his accent, pronouncing his words clearly and increasing his vocabulary. Theola kept her promise and corrected him at every given moment. James also worked hard to pay off Ms. Sarah. He got promoted at his job. He bought a used 1947 Tucker Torpedo car to get around in. Theola finished high school. Now it was time for them to move on. One Saturday evening, as they played with Marilyn on the floor in their motel room, James and Theola were discussing when would be a good time to leave.

"You know Theola, I like the idea of you staying home and taking care of the baby. Besides, I'm doing pretty well at the post office. I have enough money saved to live in a two-bedroom apartment for a year or until more promotions come my way."

"Or I can get a job in the daytime and go to school at night."

"I would feel more comfortable with you staying home with our child."

"You mean permanently?"

"Yes. Or at least until she gets some age on her. Maybe six years old or something like that."

Theola leaped from the floor. "What about my dream James? What about my family? Am I just supposed to let all that go by the wayside because we have a child now?"

The change in conversational tone drew Marilyn's attention from her toys to her parents. But she still sat quietly, playing with her dolls.

James stood from the floor. "Theola you saw how hard it was for you just going back to high school and studying at night for tests. If it hadn't been for Ms. Sarah, we would have struggled a lot more than what we did."

"You took care of the baby at night while I studied. Is that it James? You're tired of taking care of your own daughter while I go to school and try to better myself. I made a promise to my parents and to myself that I wouldn't just be another housewife, barefoot, pregnant with one child in my arms, while another child was on the way."

"What's wrong with being a mother? What's wrong with you being there for our child rather than some woman who didn't birth her and could care less if your daughter's nose is clean? A babysitter wipes our child's nose only because she is getting paid to clean it. Don't get me wrong. It was different with Ms. Sarah. She loves us too. But every babysitter isn't babysitting for the love of the child. It's the love of the money."

"Then we just have to work our schedules to the point where we are the only ones who take care of her James. I'm not throwing away my dream!" Theola eyes were tearful when she glanced over at Marilyn. She had stopped playing with her toys to watch Mommy and Daddy. Her eyes were very sad too. Theola softened her tone of voice. "James we can do this together sweetheart. Just work with me baby." Theola walked over to give James a soft kiss on the lips. Marilyn smiled. "Just work with me baby, please."

"Alright Theola. You go to college at night. I'll watch Marilyn while you go to school and study." Theola screamed a little and wrapped her arms around James's neck. Marilyn went back to playing with her toys.

"I won't let you down baby. I promise. I'll study hard and be the best lawyer I can be. You'll see. All I want is a better life for our children and us. That's just not going to happen with you working two jobs and barely making ends meet James."

"Well the first thing we need to do is find a nice apartment for us. Then we'll know how many classes you can take for college, judging from the rent. And don't think every time I get a promotion, you take more classes."

"Ok babe."

"Next, we need to let Ms. Sarah know we'll be moving as soon as we find another place to stay. That way, she can find some other help to replace us."

"I'm going to miss her James."

"Yeah, me too. But we have got to move on. I saw some real nice apartments closer to the college."

"Once we move, I'll have to let my sisters know our new phone number and address."

"Of course. I knew you would. I know you all talk at least once a month. Let's get some rest. We will let Ms. Sarah know first thing in the morning."

As the night settled in Chicago, James and Theola snuggled together for another sensual evening, while Marilyn slept quietly in a crib.

Chapter 32

James and Theola Move On

s the sun rose for a new day, Theola and James were excited about their plans. They told Sarah at breakfast of their intentions to leave.

"I'm happy for you two. I'm still working on Skip. He has given me some really good times. But I realize my heart wants it all. Maybe I want too much?"

"Nooo, Sarah. You just have to find a man with that same dream," said Theola.

"Maybe I should be thankful for what I got."

"Oh no Sarah. Don't stop wanting your dream. Your dreams define who you are. If you give up on your dream, then your dream will die. But just keep praying to God for guidance. He will answer your prayers."

"Well that sounds like awfully good advice from someone younger than me."

"Yes ma'am. My mother and father are church *going* people. I try to tell others what they tell me when things just aren't going the way you plan."

"Well you just keep on telling people that. I've got to run into town. Just be sure you don't leave for good without saying goodbye. I'll see if my sister is willing to come back and work for me now."

Three months later, James and Theola moved from the motel to an apartment in town much closer to the college. Things were still going well for them. They stayed in touch with Sarah. Now it was time to get in touch with Theola's sisters.

"Now that we have our new phone number, I'll call your mother and let her know what it is."

"Deborah and Konee should be in college by now. Why can't they call you direct Theola, instead of going through my mother?"

"Because they still live at home. Daddy wants to make sure the riffraff of a college campus didn't get to my sisters before they graduate."

"You mean like me."

"I didn't mean it like that."

Feeling that he had somehow *short changed* Theola, he thought he would make it up to her. "I know. You know honey, the fall semester is going to start in September. That's two months from now."

"I know sweetheart."

"You go ahead and start looking at the classes you want to take. It appears the rent is only eighty-five dollars a month. You can take at least two classes this semester."

"Great honey. I hope you get more promotions. The more I can take at once, the sooner I can get my degree and start helping with the rent and other things."

James didn't want to burst her bubble and said nothing negative. Theola and James went to the college to get a school catalog. Theola scanned thoroughly the classes she thought she would need before James made it back home and parked the car. She continued analyzing the book, while James tended to their two-year old.

Chapter 33

Does Hard Work Pay Off?

James worked even harder as the weeks rolled by, hoping for another promotion in the coming months. But one day, he went to work and things just weren't quite the same. As soon as James walked through the door to his workroom, James's supervisor was waiting for him.

"James come with me to my office." said Mr. Hunter. James followed his boss.

James felt butterflies in his stomach. He couldn't have imagined what he had done wrong. Many thoughts were racing through his head.

"Sit down James." James took the chair in front of his boss's desk.

"James how long have you worked here?"

"A little over two years, sir."

"And I want to say you have done an excellent job." James took a deep breath. His heart came back from the pit of his stomach. It slowed to its normal rate. "I want to change your job and place you in another area. If you do as well there as you have done with every other job I have given you, I'll give you another promotion within a year. You think you can handle that?"

"Yes sir." James stated confidently and nodded in acceptance of the responsibility.

As other office workers passed by the boss's glassed-in office, they noticed James's joyfulness. When James came out, he was smiling from ear to ear.

"What's going on James?" asked one of the guys.

So excited, he told him what the boss had said.

"That's great James. Keep up the good work." said the other guys.

James was so enthused that he worked twice as hard and did other things he normally wouldn't have done if he hadn't been so happy. He helped others sort mail and washed the mail trucks. All the other workers noticed his exuberance, especially Lee Roy. Pretty soon, the other employees were talking amongst themselves about James's quick promotions. His overzealousness was irritating some of the other workers.

James went home that day, exploding to tell Theola the good news. "Honey!"

"I'm in the bathroom!" Theola was on her knees, giving Marilyn a bath.

"It's five o'clock. Why are you giving her a bath now? It's nowhere near her bedtime."

"Honey, I've been with her all day. We played in the park for a couple of hours today. I tried to get dinner before you got here. She laid a big one in her clothes before I could get her to the bathroom."

"Ohhh, sorry honey. But stand up. I got some good news."

"Babe, I'm bathing Marilyn. I can wash her and listen to you at the same time."

"When I got to work today, the boss said I was doing such a great job that he was placing me in a new position. If I do well there, he will give me another promotion within the year."

"That's wonderful honey." Theola continued putting soap on the baby's bottom.

"You don't seem to be excited about it. What's the problem?" said James aggressively.

Theola stood Marilyn up so she would not slide down in the bath water. Theola jumped up, hands dripping with water and soap. Standing taller than he, she stared straight down into James's big brown eyes.

"James do you see me busy here?" Theola said aggressively.

Marilyn started crying. Theola lowered her tone. "I'm trying to give our daughter a bath. Give me another minute. Go in the kitchen, grab you a beer and I'll be in there in a minute."

James, disgusted with her nonchalant attitude, didn't say another word. He went quietly into the kitchen. Theola kneeled back down to Marilyn, kissed her, sat her back down in the tub and explained what she and Daddy were doing.

"Sometimes Marilyn, Daddy and I get a little upset and we try not to yell, but sometimes we do." She kissed Marilyn again and they hugged each other. With a smile, Marilyn placed bath soap all in mommy's hair from wrapping her arms around her head.

Moments later, Theola came into the kitchen. James was sulking over their confrontation and sipping his beer at the table. Marilyn walked over and laid her head on Daddy's lap. James, pleased by his daughter's affection, placed his beer down. James rubbed his daughter's head with great pleasure. A certain calm came over him. He picked her up and held her out in front of him.

"Did you have a good day with Mommy?"

"Yes Daddy."

James sniffed his daughter's neck. "Hmmmm… You smell good baby girl. Mommy did a good job on bathing you."

Marilyn nodded.

He kissed both her cheeks and placed her back on the floor.

James got up from the table and walked over by the stove. Theola was stirring mashed potatoes and boiling corn. James wrapped his arms around her waist and gave Theola a loving kiss upon her neck.

"I'm sorry honey. I was so caught up in what had happened to me today that I just wanted you to drop whatever you were doing and focus your attention on me. Our baby girl comes first. Just tell me when I start to act like that again."

Theola forgave quickly and kissed James on the cheek. "I've got dinner ready. Are you ready to eat?"

James nodded. "You know honey. I've been thinking. With another promotion soon, you can perhaps take as many as three classes this semester. If you don't think it will be too much of a strain."

"Are you kidding James? Our daughter is two and a half, she plays by herself beautifully with her toys. She is hardly any trouble at all as long as she is fed and occupied. I could probably get some study time in during the day while Marilyn takes her nap. This is great James. I love you for helping me to try and complete my dream."

"I love you. You are my life, along with that little girl right there."

James turned and Marilyn was gone. "Hey, where did she go?"

They both ran into the living room. There she was, playing with her dolls quietly to herself.

"See what I mean?"

"Ok honey. This semester you go ahead and take three courses." Theola hugged James again. "Ok I'm hungry. Let's eat. Hmmm, smells like meatloaf?"

"You guessed right. I'll set the table right away."

"Ok. I'll show Marilyn how to style hair on her dolls."

James grabbed his beer and went into the living room with Marilyn. Theola laughed and set the table.

CHAPTER 34

The Gathering of Minds

Meanwhile, that afternoon in Joe's bar, where some of James's peers met every evening for a beer before going home, they gathered once again. They were all sitting at a circular table enjoying their beers except for Lee Roy, who was in the bathroom.

"What are we going to do about James?" asked Ed, an average white male with brown hair and a toothpick in his mouth.

"I know. I have been thinking about it," said Frank, sipping on a bottle of beer. "If we have two Negroes in our organization, next there will be three and four and then we'll be overrun by them."

"So what are we going to do?" asked Ed once again.

"We can't go against him. If we do and our boss finds out, James can file a racial complaint. Then we may be frowned upon by Mr. Robert Hunter, the equal opportunist." Frank stated with sarcasm.

"Ok…"

"Ok, so we get Lee Roy to do it," said Frank.

"Get Lee Roy to do what?" questioned Ed.

"Take James down."

"How?" asked Ed.

At that moment, Frank noticed the men's bathroom door opening. "Shhhh. Lee Roy is coming back. Just follow my lead," said Frank.

"Ok."

Lee Roy, a medium-height, bulky-sized Negro male with nappy hair and a mustache to accent his face, sat back in his chair and grabbed his beer.

"James told me he might be up for a promotion," said Frank.

"That can't be. He's only been here a couple of years," said Joe, another drinking buddy. He too, was an average white male with dark hair and brown eyes.

"Hey Lee Roy. It took you eight years to get your first promotion. James is almost working on his second in three years. What do you think James has over you?" said Frank. "It can't be your color." Frank, Joe, and Ed laughed.

"Yeah, you're the same color as he is. What about that Lee Roy?" said Ed, taking another swallow of beer.

Lee Roy just sat there taking gulps instead of swallows. He thought about what they were saying. He had now finished his third beer. "You know you fellas are right. What he got over me?" Lee Roy was slurring his words. "I do just gooda job as James or anybody else who work there. Why is he getting promoted so fast?"

"You know Lee Roy, I think maybe you should start watching James. See what he is doing. He could be sucking up to the boss." said Ed. Frank and Joe nodded their heads in agreement.

"Yeah! That's probably it. He is sucking up to the boss." said Frank, now leaning over his fifth beer bottle.

"You fellas are right. I'm gonna start watchin' James. I'll… I'll… find out how he's getting the boss's attention."

"We behind you all da way Lee Roy." said Ed, with bloodshot eyes and working on his seventh beer. Joe was so drunk he just nodded at every sentence.

After drinking their eighth and ninth beer, James's peers had decided to keep an eye on him for his remaining days at the post office. All three men were stone drunk at two o'clock in the morning. They had passed out in the bar. The bar manager, knowing their routine on Friday nights, let them sleep the night in the bar.

Chapter 35

The Diaper Change

James had just finished dinner and Theola was getting ready to place Marilyn down in her room for the evening.

James watched her when she placed Marilyn into her crib for the night. James kissed her as she lay peacefully in her bed. Then he whispered into Theola's ear.

"When you finish laying Marilyn down, I'm going to apologize for how I acted this afternoon when I came home."

Theola turned and spoke softly to James. "Oh yeah. Just how are you going to apologize?"

"Go ahead and sing the baby to sleep. Meet me in the bedroom."

"You have a deal. I'll be right there." smiled Theola.

James left the room. Theola covered Marilyn with a light blanket and tucked the sides underneath the mattress. "Let's close our eyes sweetheart and say our prayers."

"Okay Mommy. Now I lay me down to sleep. I pray the Lord my soul to keep. If I die before I wake, I pray the Lord my soul to take. Amen." Marilyn opened her eyes to see that Mommy was smiling.

Marilyn smiled too and waited to hear Mom's lovely voice.

A couple of minutes later, Marilyn was sound asleep. Theola kissed Marilyn on the forehead and tiptoed from her room. She left Marilyn's door slightly ajar so they could hear her from their room if she cried. James was just coming from the shower when Theola entered the bedroom.

"Now James. I'm ready to hear about your day, if you still want to tell me."

"Nooo, I don't want to talk anymore today. I just want to apologize."

Theola laughed. "Alright James. Give me a chance to take a shower. I'll be right back."

James laid back in the bed, two hands behind his head, pleased about his day at work and his loving family. He felt like the king of his castle. While Theola was taking a shower, James heard Marilyn whimper. James tiptoed in her bedroom to see if she was awake. From the dimness of the night light James peeked through the door and to his surprise, he saw the whites of her eyes peering through the crib bars.

"What's wrong honey?" James smiled, knowing a response was not coming back. "I know Mommy just fed you."

As James walked toward her, tears fell. "Now, now, let's not cry. Let's check your diaper if you're not hungry."

James removed her plastic cover panties from her bottom. "Oooooweeee, man! No wonder Mommy was scrubbing your bottom after the big one you had today. How can something so little and so cute stink so bad? I bet you laid this big stink bomb when Mommy walked out of the room. No wonder you woke up with all this crap sticking to your butt. I would have woken up too. Let's get this stuff off of you. James was trying to hurry before Theola came from the bathroom. James started to loosen the safety pins from both sides of her diaper.

"Ohhhh, wait a minute. I need a clean diaper and a wet cloth over here before I do this. Right?" James looked at Marilyn. She smiled. "You're a good baby… yes you are." James glanced around the room to where Theola would have kept the cloth diapers. He spotted them on top of the dresser with a clean towel and Vaseline. "Hey, I see them little girl. Now you stay right there. Daddy will be right back. James went to the kitchen to wet the cloth. Marilyn flopped around and kicked her legs as James had loosened the safety pins on her diaper.

Only minutes passed until James returned.

"Daddy's back now. Ohhh no!"

James saw boo-boo everywhere, on Marilyn's sheets, her legs and her pajamas and Theola would be getting out of the shower soon. James took Marilyn's blanket and placed it and her on the floor. He hurried to clean the mess from her bed. James took the baby's towel and wiped her bed. He picked Marilyn up from the floor and placed her back into the crib. He soon wiped her bottom and pajamas. He put a clean cloth diaper underneath her and soon placed her plastic cover panties on her. He took the soiled diaper and cloth towel and threw them into the baby's hamper. He had baby poop all over his hands. He wiped his hand on the bottom of his pajamas. He picked Marilyn up and placed her upon his shoulders to rock her back to sleep. Tired though she was, the removal of her soiled diaper was all she needed to fall back to sleep. James was pleased. He laid her back into her crib very gently and kissed her forehead. James, in his haste to get back to the bed, tripped over Marilyn's blanket and fell to the floor. He wanted to shout but did not, hoping the fall didn't wake her. He sat still on the floor for a moment to see if he might hear a whimper. He did not. He gave a silent sigh and got up. He placed the blanket he had just tripped over on Marilyn. Sound asleep, he kissed her again. He tiptoed on his way out. He left the door slightly cracked to hear Marilyn if she cried again. Once clear of the baby area, he immediately raced back to bed and pulled the covers up to his waist. He patiently waited for Theola to return.

Moments later, Theola emerged from the bathroom. James beamed with delight. Theola ran from the bathroom door and jumped into the bed, naked. The lights were soon dimmed.

"Honey, what's that smell?" asked Theola. "I thought you had already taken a shower before me."

"Marilyn," replied James.

And quiet fell upon the Taylor's home for the evening.

Chapter 36

Going to Church

Saturday morning came as usual for the Taylor's. When the sunlight struck the windowpane, Marilyn woke up right away.

"Maaamy," called Marilyn.

"I'm coming baby."

Theola raised her head from James's chest and pulled herself from his arms while he slept. Once Theola reached Marilyn's room, she was standing in her crib. Marilyn reached her arms toward her. As Theola picked her up, she noticed poop on her pajamas and bed. In James's haste, he forgot to place the safety pins back in place before he put the plastic diaper back on her bottom. Theola laughed and hugged Marilyn.

"I ready for break-fuss mommy."

"As soon as I get you all clean little girl."

Moments later, James walked into the room rubbing his eyes. He kissed both his women.

"Oh Theola...today we'll run down to the university and get a schedule of classes to see what you would like to take for the fall semester."

"Today is Saturday. Do you think they are open?"

"We could go find out. Maybe they might have a schedule in the hall of the administrative office or the lobby. I don't know, let's just go see."

"Great honey. Then I'll get some breakfast and we can go afterward. Oh, by the way honey, our across-the-hall neighbor invited us to go to church with her on Sunday."

"That nosey old bitty. Every day I come home from work, she is standing at the door watching me come in. Like I'm her son or something."

"Oh honey, she means well. She's sixty-five years old, so what else is she going to do with her time? But I would like to take her upon her offer and go to her church. We need to go to church as a family and thank God for all our blessings."

"Honey, you know on Sundays I like to watch my football games. If her church is like our Baptist Church used to be, they start at eleven and don't get out until four."

"I don't know honey. Mrs. Fenceroy didn't say how long church lasted."

"Well you and Marilyn go to church tomorrow. If you two get home before the start of the first game, then I will consider going to church. But if you get home after the first quarter starts, then you can forget it."

"Babe how can you base going to church on a football game?"

"Dear the weekend is all I have to relax. I work hard during the week and on the weekend. I like to spend Saturday's and Sunday's doing what I like to do. And going to church is not one of them. I just want to sit in front of the television, with a nice cold beer and enjoy the Sunday football games. Is that too much to ask sweetheart?"

"Your Mom raised you in the church."

"That's right. And for eighteen years of going to church, I figure I done my time. I don't need church no mo."

"You mean anymore."

"No, I mean no mo, because that's how I feel about it."

"I'm not trying to push you James. I just thought if you went, that you may hear something from the pastor that would bring you closer to God."

"Right now, I'm as close as I care to be. Can we drop the subject? You and Marilyn are welcome to go with the old bitty. I don't care."

Theola dropped the conversation. She went to the kitchen and started breakfast. After eating, they went to the university and found a fall schedule. Theola studied the curriculum after they came back home and picked her classes for the fall semester.

Chapter 37

The Same Symptoms

Two months later, one month before fall registration. This particular evening when James came home, Theola appeared depressed as she held Marilyn sitting on the couch.

"James I have something I need to tell you."

"What is it honey? Why the gloomy look on your face?"

"I missed my period."

"Well, choose another period to take the class you want." James headed toward the kitchen to grab a beer.

He stopped in his tracks. "Please tell me you are speaking of a class you wanted to take, but it was booked up already. Please tell me that."

"Sorry honey, but it's not that."

"But how can this be? We have gone almost two years without another child. As often as we have sex, I thought we couldn't have any more children. What happened Theola?" screamed James.

"James don't yell at me. I don't know. I'm just as baffled as you are."

"Baffled! That's not the half of it. I thought you were being careful. Didn't your mother tell you how to count days or some kind of rhythm thing or something like that? Are you sure you are pregnant? Maybe you just happened to miss one month or something by accident because of stress with your classes?"

"James this is what I went through when I was having Marilyn. I've been feeling nauseous and hungry almost every two or three hours. I just didn't want to tell you until I was real sure."

"And are you sure now?"

"I'm sure honey. I've got the same symptoms as I had with Marilyn."

"Theola do you know what another baby is going to do for us? It will reduce those classes you were thinking about taking. We need to get a three-bedroom apartment. This two bedroom won't be big enough. Our lifestyle has already changed with one. Now it's about to be two. What kind of life are we going to have with two children?" James paced the floor. "I didn't sign up for two children! Theola."

"James calm down. Let's think about this rationally."

"Yeaaah. Let's do the abortion thing."

"My God! James. How can you say such a thing? God has watched over us this far. He has provided us with shelter and food when we didn't have a dime in our pockets. Do you think God will bless us more if we destroyed one of his miracles? If we are having another child, it's because He wants us too."

"Then why were you looking depressed when I walked in, if God wants us to? And you said it. Does that mean you aren't really sure?"

"I mean, since we are having another child, God wants us to have another one. And I wasn't looking depressed. I'm nauseous."

"But Theola, how are we going to make it? I have only budgeted for the three of us and your classes."

"We have to trust in God James. And besides, I can just take one class. The other classes will just have to wait."

"Fine. Then all of the classes should wait!" James angrily spoke.

"Why?"

"Because Theola, you don't know what kind of strain the baby will have on your studying or my working."

"What kind of stress can there possibly be? Marilyn is wonderful, she's quiet and she's plays by herself."

"It worked well with Marilyn because you started when she was two and she played quietly on her own. So you think a newborn is going to play quietly? Theola I just think we need to wait before you start a new semester."

Tears formed in Theola's eyes. "No James. I can handle it. We have at least seven months before the baby is born and the classes are already paid for. I can still finish these classes before it's time to have the baby."

"No! Theola."

Theola, furious from his words, burst into tears. "Why are you trying to smother my freedom of education?"

"Smother your freedom of education!" James toned his voice down. "I'm trying to smother these debts. Nothing would please me more than to see you become a successful attorney. Then I could brag about my wife to all my friends."

James smiled, paused and gently touched Theola's cheek. Moved by his affection, the tears slowly faded away.

"But honey, it's not you that I'm worried about. It's me. I don't know if I can handle another child and all our debts too."

James walked to the kitchen to get the beer he never got before he heard the news.

Theola followed him. "Honey if we just plan our lives around two children, we can make things work out. I know we can."

"Theola you're a dreamer. I'm motivated by the facts that come in the mail every month and between a second child, your classes, paying the rent, the car note and trying to eat, we aren't going to make ends meet!"

"Alright James. I won't schedule any more classes for this year and finish the ones I've started. We'll see how our dollars run with two children in the household before I start anything new."

James sighed, "Alright Theola."

"Hey, I just had an idea. Why don't we ask Ms. Sarah if she could watch the children for us during the day."

"What! That woman is running a motel, not a babysitting service."

"James I just can't watch my dream of becoming a lawyer fade away. I have to try every possible way I can think of to accomplish my goal." Tears started to fall from her eyes once more. "I want my father to love me again."

Empathy overwhelmed James. "Ok baby. You call Ms. Sarah and see what she will do. I guess it won't hurt to ask."

Theola leaped toward James. She wrapped her arms around his neck and kissed every inch of his face. He wiped the tears from her cheek with his hands.

"Ohhh thank you, thank you, thank you. I love you."

"Yeahhhhh, yeahhhh, yeah, only when you get what you want."

Theola raced toward the phone. She dialed. James drank some of his beer. He placed the bottle on the kitchen table and went to play with Marilyn in the living room.

Minutes later, James could hear bits and pieces of the conversation. James had Marilyn up on his stomach while he laid flat on his back, tossing her gently on occasion, into the air and catching her. Moments later he heard Theola hang up.

"Well honey, what did Ms. Sarah say?"

"She said she couldn't do it. Not that she wouldn't love to watch Marilyn, but her prayers had been finally answered. She was getting married to Skip in a month. He finally decided to settle down. They will be starting their family soon after their marriage. As a matter of fact, she is three months pregnant. The reason we didn't know, is they were going to do it quietly and then celebrate with us later. They are going to buy a little house with the white picket fence she has always wanted. She was glad I called. She said since we know now, we are invited to go with them to the justice of the peace."

Theola spoke as if she were in a daze.

"That's wonderful honey. The prayers you would always say for her finally came true. Did you tell her that you were happy for her?"

"Of course I did." Theola sounded almost tearful.

"Then why the solemn look?"

"I guess I'm just thinking of myself. What am I going to do?"

James placed Marilyn on the blanket to play by herself. He got up from the floor, grabbed Theola around the waist and pulled her toward him.

"Oh honey, just wait and see. I didn't say never to take your classes again. Finish these three classes, but after that, no more for a little while. Let's see how our schedules and money are after the baby is born. Once we see what we have to do in order to make things work for all of us, then that's what we'll do. I promise."

James gently pulled Theola's head down toward his lips and kissed her forehead.

"Oh sweetheart, I know you're right. That's what we'll do."

"So as of right now, you are about two months pregnant?"

"Something like that."

"Tomorrow you go see the doctor. It's free. The company insurance is paid in full. So let's make sure it's a baby we have and not gas or indigestion."

"Alright, I'll do that."

"What's for dinner?" James smiled reluctantly.

Theola worked up a smile and went into the kitchen to get dinner ready.

James turned and picked up his baby girl. He looked her in the face. "You know honey, you are about to have a little baby brother or sister.

What do you think about that?" James rubbed his nose to her nose and she laughed. He twirled her around and gave her a lasting hug.

Minutes later, Theola called for James. "Let's eat honey. Dinner is on the table."

James placed Marilyn on his shoulders and rode her into the kitchen. They ate dinner quietly, not saying very much. Marilyn glanced from her mother to her father on occasion. They both smiled at her when she looked at them. When dinner was done an hour later, James went to bed while Theola gave Marilyn her evening bath. She was tucked in as usual with a silent prayer and a song until she was asleep. When Theola got into bed, the phone rang on the bedside end table.

"Hello," said Theola.

"Hey sister, it's me, Konee."

"Hold on. Let me pick the phone up in the living room. I don't want to wake James."

Theola laid the phone down easily on the night stand, got up from the bed and walked into the living room. She sat on the couch and picked up the phone off the end table.

"I'm back."

"This is my monthly check-in call. I'm downstairs in the living room. I'm sorry to call so late. Mother and Father just went to sleep about an hour ago. I wanted to be sure not to wake them from calling you. How are you?"

"Konee I'm pregnant. I'm trying to go to college and I'm pregnant."

"Again?"

"What am I going to do?" Theola broke into tears.

"Hey sis. You know God is the answer to all our problems. The child you are about to have is a blessing for you and James."

"But what about college?"

"College will come when it is time." Konee paused. "I heard a noise upstairs. I've got to run. Hang in there sister. College will come and your children will be proud of their mother."

The tears turned to sniffles. "I love you Konee. I feel better already."

"Love you too sis, bye."

Theola hung up the phone. She wiped the tears from her eyes and smiled. She thought perhaps God did want her children to be proud of her one day. Theola felt relief that Konee was right and went back to bed. James had hung up the phone on the end table and was sound asleep. He tossed and turned during the night, wondering how the bills were going to be paid. Theola felt his grief and said a quiet prayer for the entire family, asking God for guidance. Soon, James came to a rest. A calm expression came over his face after her prayer. Feeling at peace, Theola soon matched James's slumber.

CHAPTER 38

Envy and Jealousy Arises

James had a great concern for their lives, but he also wanted to be sure that Theola was pregnant with their second child. The next morning, James took Marilyn and Theola to the doctor's office.

"I'm going to go to work honey. Call when the doctor is finished. I'll come back and pick you two up."

"You don't have to do that James. We can catch a bus."

"No sweetheart. I'd rather feel safe knowing that you two have made it home alright."

"Ok, I'll call you."

James kissed Theola and Marilyn on their cheeks as they were seated patiently, waiting for the nurse to call. Marilyn waved to Daddy, bye-bye. James blew her a kiss.

James drove fast, but safely to make it to work. When James got to the post office, Frank, Ed, and Lee Roy were waiting for him at the front door.

"James!" yelled Lee Roy. "What's happening man?"

"Hey brother. I got some heavy news laid on me when I got home yesterday."

"You don't say. And what was that?" asked Lee Roy.

James forgot his golden rule of not letting his family affairs be known to his peers, but he felt he needed to speak to another man about his situation.

"My wife and I are going to have another child."

"That's wonderful man. Are you happy about it? Or was this something unexpected?" asked Frank.

"Let's just say it wasn't on our schedule right at this particular time."

"Oh, I see. Well, if you're happy, I'm happy for you. If you aren't happy, they have doctors who take care of little problems like that," stated Lee Roy.

"Oh no man. My wife would pitch a hissy fit if I even mentioned that word."

"Man who got to feed it. Women think they can just get over on a man like that. Says it's her body. She just uses her baby to hold over your head. She probably doesn't want it any more than you do. If you are a good man, she will zap you with that child support so fast, it will make your head spin. She knows what she is doing man. You the sucker," said Lee Roy.

James's expression was slightly puzzled. He wondered where that comment came from. Theola was his wife, not some woman he got pregnant off the street. James soon realized he was talking to someone who didn't respect women very much.

"Well look Lee Roy, Frank, Ed, I have got to get started working here. I'll catch you guys later."

"Ok man, later." said Lee Roy. Frank and Ed waved.

Lee Roy smiled and walked closer to Frank and Ed. "Looks like James has been a little busy."

"Man, James and his wife are having another child," said Frank.

"I'll bet he's laying that guilt thing on our boss about he's black. Got all these babies and he needs more money to support his family." Said Ed.

"Right, right," said Lee Roy. "The boss is going for the baby story. That's why he's giving him all the raises."

"Our boss isn't that easy," said Frank.

"Oh yes he is. He will bend over backward to help anybody who needs it," said Ed.

"Well, what I need to do is start having some babies," said Lee Roy.

"Man are you crazy? You just can't use the same line as James. Then the boss will know you are up to something. You got to think of something else or find a way to discredit James," stated Frank.

"How am I going to do that? He's always at work on time. He does what the boss says and then some. Where am I going to find fault?" asked Lee Roy.

"You just have to start watching James Lee Roy. If you watch him long enough, he will mess up something. Then you let the boss know," said Ed.

"Yeah, Lee Roy. And if he doesn't mess up, we can help him mess up." Frank smiled.

Lee Roy looked at Ed. He was smiling. Then Lee Roy started to smile.

On this day, Lee Roy watched James like a hawk. After three hours, James got a call from Theola. James alerted his boss that he needed to go to the doctor's office and pick up his wife and child. His boss agreed. James left and forgot to check out. Lee Roy noted the error and wasted no time in alerting his boss of James's mistake.

CHAPTER 39

Is James in Trouble?

Minutes later, James was at the clinic, happy to see his wife and child comfortably sitting in the lobby waiting for him.

"Hey honey. What's the verdict?"

"I won't know for a week."

"Well let's get the two of you home so you can get some rest. I'm going back to work after I drop you off."

"Thanks honey. You are such a sweetheart."

"You two are my life now. I mean, possibly you three." Theola and James grabbed Marilyn by the hand and strolled to the car as if they were a happy family.

James drove them home and went back to work. Once James entered the building, he went to clock back in. When he realized he had forgotten to clock out, James immediately went to the boss's office to explain what he had done.

"Mr. Hunter, I forgot to check out. I will work late to make up for the time I missed."

"That will be fine James."

Mr. Hunter realized James was being scrutinized by his peers. But he felt it was not his position to tell him.

Chapter 40

New Born Stress

Weeks later, James performed above and beyond his duties at work. He had learned that hard work paid off in this organization. He was still watched carefully by Lee Roy. It was hard for Lee Roy to find fault, but he had to if James was to lose his job.

Seven months later, James and Theola were in the hospital with a newborn. Sarah held on to Marilyn while Theola was in the hospital.

"Mr. Taylor you have a son," proclaimed the doctor.

"Wow! A baby boy. Great! May I see Theola now?"

"Yes and she is doing fine. But the boy was almost nine pounds. We had to cut Theola slightly to get him out. So she has some stitches and will need a few days of bed rest when she leaves the hospital."

"Thank you doctor. She will get her rest."

James raced toward Theola's room. Theola was smiling as she held their son in her arms. "Here's your boy". James took him gently from Theola and rocked him slowly in his arms.

James beamed with joy as he boldly proclaimed… "Your name will be James Paul Taylor Junior."

James and Theola couldn't have been happier. When the doctor released Theola and James Jr. from the hospital, Theola was bedridden for the next few days. James stayed home for two days to assist Theola in her recovery. By the second day, James was getting a little weary.

"Theola are you feeling any better yet? I can't keep getting up with Junior in the middle of the night. I'll be too tired when I start back to work. I've been off two days. I feel I have worked harder here at home, than I do at the post office. I start work tomorrow. I want to be rested."

"I'm feeling a little better James. It still hurts a little walking around."

"I'm going to work tomorrow. You think you can manage at home by yourself?"

"Do I have a choice?"

"I just don't want you injuring yourself and taking longer to heal."

"I'm being careful James."

"Well I'll get up with James Jr. still, until you feel you have your strength back."

"That's sweet of you. I'll take you up on that offer."

That day, James had gotten up with James Jr., fixed breakfast for Theola and Marilyn, washed the dishes, washed the dirty clothes and prepared lunch. By the time night fell, James was extremely tired. He tried to go to bed early, but James Jr. was not cooperating. He woke up every three hours, hungry, during the middle of the night. James found it hard to sleep. Theola got up with James Jr. each time he cried. He noticed Theola was limping to the children's room. She was still hurting from the stitches she received. She made her way to the kid's room, retrieved James Jr. from the crib, walked back to her bed, breastfed him and then walked back to his crib.

"Honey I see your pain. The next time James Jr. wakes up, just call me. I will get him and warm him a bottle of breast milk from the frig."

"Thank you honey." Theola wiped the tears from her eyes with her hands.

"Are you taking the painkillers you got from the hospital?"

"I'm trying to deal with the pain. I don't like taking medicine if I'm breastfeeding."

After three hours, James Jr. cried again. Theola woke James. "The breast milk is on the second shelf in the refrigerator." He stumbled his way to the kitchen, placed a pan of water on the stove to warm it, got a bottle from the refrigerator and placed it in the pan. He went into James Jr.'s room and got him before he woke Marilyn again. Minutes later, James Jr. was sucking on a warm bottle of milk. James burped him, placed him back into the crib and peeked in on Marilyn. Getting into bed, he looked over at Theola. He thought he was gazing at an angel as a ray of sun from the morning dawn broke the crease in the blinds and shone a glimmer of light upon her face. James smiled and soon drifted off to sleep. Minutes later, the five o'clock hour hit. James tried to pull the covers over his head and ignore the alarm.

"Wake up honey." cried Theola.

James groaned. Still sleepy and disoriented, he slowly rolled the covers back over his body. He went to the bathroom, shaved, showered and cologned. When he walked out, Theola was sound asleep. He heard not a word from James Jr. or Marilyn. But he dared not go into their room and kiss them goodbye for fear of James Jr. waking before his time. James dressed and went to work without disturbing a soul.

Chapter 41

Don't Leave Me

James had put in a hard day's work. When he arrived home, he noticed Theola lying in bed, Marilyn playing with her dolls and James Jr. lying quietly on their blanket in the middle of the floor. James went into the kitchen and saw nothing on the stove.

James was furious. He stormed into the bedroom to give Theola a piece of his mind. "This morning I was so sleepy, I almost fell asleep at the wheel and I am only twenty minutes from work. This is not working out honey. And look at you. You're at home all day, the children playing and no dinner. What have you been doing?"

"Baby it's only been a couple of days since I came from the hospital. It still hurts to stand for a long period of time. That's why nothing is cooked." Theola paused. Her attitude changed to that of being more aggressive. "And why are you so upset. You fixed dinner for the past couple of days. Why is today an exception? You weren't this bad with Marilyn."

"I went to work today. That's the difference! It's been almost three days now and you're still claiming to be in pain. I think you would like me to work all day and pamper you and the children all night."

"You got up with James Jr. last night because I was in pain. Did you think the pain would go away before sunrise this morning?" James just stared at Theola. "It's only been two years since Marilyn was born. I just don't remember you whining this much."

"Whining! Let me see you try working and staying up half the night. I'm waiting on you, Marilyn and James Jr. I'm tired! And besides, Ms. Sarah was there to help out, if you recall. She kept Marilyn for the first year until you were back on your feet and finished high school while I went to work."

"Well Ms. Sarah isn't here now. It's just you. If the situation were reversed, I wouldn't have a problem waiting on you, because I love you that much."

"Don't try to use that psychology bull crap on me. I may not have a few semesters of college under my belt like you do, but I know when I'm getting played. I didn't ask for any of this you know."

"That's right! You didn't ask for me to love you, you didn't ask for your children to be born and you didn't ask for me to be weak after giving birth. You didn't ask for any of those things James. But guess what? They're all a part of life and living life as it deals you the cards. You don't have to own up to any of your responsibilities. You can walk out that door right now, James Paul and I won't think ill of you. I'll just know that you were tired."

"Theola I know my responsibilities. It's just that I've been at work all day. Now I have to come home and wait on you and the children. I'm exhausted."

"Tired, huh? You're tired of waiting on your own family. You're making the ultimate sacrifice by putting your time and efforts into your family. Well I get the picture. As long as things suit James and his needs, everything is fine. But when you don't get things going your way, it's a problem. You only took care of the children and me for a couple of days by yourself and now you're whining. Why don't you just go? Get out! This way you don't have to worry about anybody but yourself."

James was angered by her words. He noticed Marilyn from the corner of his eye. She had walked to the bedroom door. Marilyn's expression of sorrow broke his anger. He decided not to yell back. James adjusted his tone of voice, trying not to let his temper rise any more than it had.

"Theola I'm not going to argue with you. I'm tired. I'm pulling Junior's crib in here by you and placing Marilyn's blanket in here too. I'm going to sleep on the couch for a couple of hours. Forget any kind of dinner for me. I'll make myself a sandwich when I wake up. Any objections?" James started moving toward the living room. "Ohhh, but don't forget to feed your children, Mrs. Too Hurt to Move."

Infuriated at James, Theola gave him a stare that could have pierced the heart, if it had been a dagger. Displeased by his attitude, but remorseful for not being able to help, she tried to reason with her husband. "James I would wait on you, if I could. I would have dinner ready for you, if I could. I would love you tenderly each night, if I could. But all I can give you right now is my affection."

"Bull!"

James left the bedroom after placing the crib in the room with Theola. Marilyn had been silent, but saddened by watching her parents fight. James Jr. just lay quietly asleep on his blanket.

"James!"

He ignored her voice. He left the bedroom and went to lie on the living room couch. Hours passed. James woke up at about eleven o'clock that night. He took a double look at his watch. Indeed, it was eleven. He arose and went into the bedroom. He found an empty room. He searched Marilyn's and Junior's rooms. No one was in the house. James panicked for a brief moment. He dashed to the window. The car was still in the parking lot. It suddenly dawned on him that the only other person that came to mind was Sarah. He quickly called.

"Ms. Sarah is Theola and my children with you?"

"Yes James."

A sigh of relief came over his heart. "May I speak with Theola, please?"

"I gave her one of the motel rooms. She and the children are asleep. Why don't you get a good night's rest and call before you come over? Theola told me what happened. Why don't you let her stay here? I'm a housewife now. I have someone else to manage my motel business. I can help Theola until she is back on her feet and you can rest at night. She is more than welcome to stay here until she is feeling better. Tell you what? Why don't you come by the motel tomorrow? We'll all sit down and talk about it."

"Thanks Ms. Sarah. I'm relieved that Theola is with you. We don't mean to be an inconvenience to you."

"James you and Theola are like family. You're never a bother for those you love. That's what friends are for. See you tomorrow." Sarah hung up the phone.

James went to their bedroom and rested peacefully, knowing his family was safe with friends. However, Theola had a restless night. She was alone in a motel room with two children. James Jr. was asleep on her chest, while Marilyn lay asleep on one side of the bed. Theola's pain from childbirth still haunted her, but not as much as James acting as if his family was a burden. Was this going to be what the rest of her life was going to be like? She looked at both her children with a smile. But she knew she needed James to accomplish her goals, not to mention how much she loved him. The hours passed and the uncertainty of James upholding his responsibilities plagued her mind, until her eyes became heavy and Theola fell quietly asleep.

Chapter 42

Being Nosey

The dawn came quickly for James. Even though he rested peacefully, he did not rest well. The family he loved so dearly was not at his side. He dressed quickly and went to work.

"Hey James," yelled Lee Roy. "How are things working out with the newborn? Is he sleeping nights for you?"

"I don't have to worry about that. My wife handles the children."

"Three days after giving childbirth. She's good. Ed's wife gave natural childbirth and it took her a whole week to get back on her feet. Ed resembled a zombie that whole week." Commented Lee Roy.

"My wife is strong and young. She is doing just fine, thank you. Now I've got some work to do. If you will excuse me?" James started to walk away. Lee Roy placed his hand in the center of James's chest to stop him from leaving.

"You got bags under your eyes man. You take care of the children at night, don't you?" James just stared at Lee Roy's hand in the middle of his chest.

"Move your hand man." James replied aggressively.

"You better tell that woman of yours who's the boss or you'll be doing all the work, all the time. She'll be watching you work while she lays on her ass." James slapped Lee Roy's hand from his chest.

"Mind your own business Lee Roy. Stay out of mine." James walked off before Lee Roy could speak.

Lee Roy watched him walk away. "I've only just begun," he muttered to himself. Lee Roy knew James was taking care of the children. With James being restless and tired, he will surely make a mistake sometime soon. Lee Roy inconspicuously stalked James all that day. To Lee Roy's surprise, no errors were noted. Before James got off work, he called Sarah and told her he was headed in her direction.

Fifty minutes later James was pulling in the driveway of the motel. Sarah was outside waiting for James. She greeted him with a hug once he got out of the car.

"Ms. Sarah. Excuse me, I guess it's Mrs. Sarah-Skip now." James laughed.

"Yes James, it is and I am quite happy."

"I'm sorry Theola and I couldn't go with you to the Justice of the Peace, but we have had our own issues. Where's Skip? Is he here too?"

"Not right now. He's on the road."

"And your baby? This will be the first time I have seen her."

"She's in the motel lobby with your wife."

"I'm ready to bring my family home."

"And Theola is ready to come home. But don't go in there demanding what you want. Tell her how you feel and gently encourage her back home. She's hurting too James. Strong tactics will not get her back. Theola is a strong woman, but the wrong emotions can bring anyone down."

"Yes ma'am. I did come to apologize. A guy at work just made me realize how stupid I acted the other night. Don't worry Mrs. Sarah. I love her and I'll take care of my family no matter how difficult it gets. Last night made me realize they are my life."

"Well alright James." Sarah smiled.

James kissed her on the cheek. "Thank you for all you've done for us. It's my turn now."

They both walked into the motel lobby. Theola was on the couch watching Marilyn, while James lay on a pallet of blankets, napping. Nikki, Sarah's daughter, was also asleep in the crib. Theola watched when they both entered the room. James had a solemn look on his face.

Sarah observed both of them. "I'll be in the kitchen if you two need me. Before I go James, take a peek at my little Nikki."

James walked over to the crib and glanced at Sarah's daughter.

"She is beautiful Ms. Sarah. Just like her mother."

Sarah smiled and went into the kitchen. James reached out his hands to Theola. She grabbed both his hands. He pulled her slowly from the couch. Marilyn watched as the two of them stood over her, embracing each other. Marilyn enjoyed her parent's happiness and continued to play with her toys.

"Theola I want you and the children to come back home."

Theola slowly walked away with her back to James. "But…"

"Please let me finish. Last night, when you left me, a few things Sarah said about what friends are for, like being there when you are needed the most, made me think. And today, at work, one of my coworkers said something totally foolish. That also made me realize what a jerk I was being."

Theola turned to face him. "James…"

"Let me finish. It's my responsibility to take care of my family no matter how tired I get. You need me now and I didn't realize how much I needed my family until I was alone last night. Theola I love you and the children. I want you to know that this won't happen again. And I will always be there for my family no matter how hard times get."

"I love you too James. And I will always be there for you, no matter how tough the situation may be. Just at this very moment, my health isn't the greatest. All that I ask is that you give me two more days to get back on my feet and I will be there for you."

"Honey you can have two more weeks if you want. Just come home."

Theola realized his sincerity. They both embraced and kissed each other for a few moments. Sarah came back into the lobby and saw them kissing.

"Now that's much better," said Sarah.

They both turned when Sarah spoke. "Sarah we'll be leaving now. Thanks very much again."

James gathered Marilyn's toys and blankets. He went to place them in the car. Sarah picked James Jr. up from his blankets, he remained sound asleep. Theola grabbed Marilyn by the hand and they walked to the lobby door.

"See Theola, I told you things would work out. James always struck me as the kind of person that doesn't drop his responsibilities in someone else's lap. You picked a good one Theola. Hang on to him."

"I intend to Sarah and thanks again."

James had already placed their things in the car. Theola slowly walked to the passenger side. Sarah followed. James took Marilyn and buckled her in the back seat. When Theola drew near, he opened the passenger door. Theola gently sat down in the car. Sarah handed James Jr. to Theola after she was buckled in. Sarah kissed Theola on the cheek. Sarah stepped back from the car. James started the engine.

"Maybe someday soon Theola, we can get together for lunch and talk about our little secret," said Sarah. Theola smiled and nodded her head.

"Where is your daughter?" asked James.

"She is still asleep in her crib."

"Well Ms. Sarah, thank you again for everything. You have a beautiful daughter. Tell Skip we hope to catch up with him too."

Sarah, delighted they had reconciled, waved as James pulled off and drove down the lonely dirt road once again.

"Theola don't you ever walk out the house without telling me where you are going, please. I worried for hours until I realized there was only one place you could be. Our differences are our differences and no one else's."

"I just didn't want to burden such a tired man any more than I had to."

"Theola if you are going to run off every time we have a disagreement, then you may as well stay with Ms. Sarah. A family doesn't function only when everything is fine. You know you are a family when you stick together to work out your problems."

"Look who is the preacher, now. Did your mother tell you that?"

"As a matter of fact, she did. And my mother was right. We, you and I, have to work out our differences, not run to our friends or our family to work them out for us. I realized what I said last night was wrong and I apologize. But we must communicate and agree upon a solution. Do we understand baby? I love you and I think we will be in this together for the long haul."

Theola sympathized. "I love you too James. I promise to work out our differences and not to run away again."

"Good."

"Just one more question Theola."

"Yes dear."

"What was the little secret Ms. Sarah mentioned?"

Theola didn't respond and gave a slight grin. James got the hint from her reaction and said nothing more. They drove quietly home.

Chapter 43

James's Submission

One year passed, James put forth every effort to watch James Jr. and Marilyn while Theola went to college. The nights were hard. James would come in from work and Theola would leave out for class. They would kiss as one came in the door and the other went out. Dinner was already ready when James got home. James fed the children and bathed them before they went to bed every night. He read to them and told them bedtime stories. Marilyn would fall fast asleep listening to Daddy read since James didn't pray and couldn't sing. James Jr. was too young to realize what time it was and wanted to play with Dad until ten thirty at night. By this hour, Theola would be walking through the door.

"Honey," James listened as Theola locked the living room door back. "Can you watch James Jr. now? I have got to get some sleep. I have to be at work by seven."

"I know James. If you would just give me a chance to place these books down, I will be right there."

James played with James Jr. in the master bedroom. James Jr. laughed while Dad tickled him on the bed. Theola came from the living room. James stopped immediately from playing with James Jr. and held him up. "Here, take him honey."

Theola leaned over the bed and reached for James Jr. James fell back on the bed, exhausted from working all day and taking care of the kids all night.

"This isn't working out honey." James was resting on the pillow. Theola paced the floor with James Jr. to get him to fall asleep.

"What do you mean James?"

"I'm tired, even before I get to work and we haven't made love but twelve times in the last twelve months."

"Well we have both been very tired James."

"I didn't realize college was going to reduce our sex life. If I had known that, I would have said, hell naugh, you kan't go to school."

"What!"

"I'm just teasing Theola." James laughed.

"Don't tease me. I'm tired too."

James noticed James Jr.'s eyes were finally blinking shut.

"Shhhh, Theola. Stop all that talking. I think he is falling asleep." Theola continued to pace the floor. "That's all he wanted was his mommy. A few more minutes honey and I think he will be gone."

Theola said not a word and managed to smile. A few minutes passed and James Jr. was ready for the crib. Theola went to place him in the same room with Marilyn. While Theola was gone, James stripped. He threw back the bed sheets and lay on top of the cover in his shorts only. When Theola walked back in, she noticed James's position.

"Not tonight honey. I'm tired."

"That's what I have heard for the past thirty days." James's temper flared. "We have got to stop with this once-a-month crap! It's been school, it's been the kids and it's been school papers due." James paused. "When is it going to be my turn?"

"Shhhh, not sooo loud. Look, James…" Theola stated with an exhausted voice.

James interrupted. "Don't 'look James' me! We have barely touched one another in almost a month. Surrrrre, we peck each other on the lips as we pass each other going out the door. But something has got to give Theola and it's not me. I'm trying to do my part. Now how about you?"

They heard a whimper from the children's bedroom. "Shhhhh…" They both listened silently for another sound.

"I don't hear anything. Come on Theola."

Theola didn't care. She was tired and angry. Fussing with James was the last thing she wanted to do when she came home.

"I thought you were tired?"

"Not for this."

"Alright James, come on!"

James didn't care about the attitude this time. He pulled the covers back on her side. Theola undressed and got in bed. She was callous and stern emotionally. James realized she was playing hard to get. But he gently kissed her face and body continuously. He soon wore her hardened heart down. Theola relaxed from her rigid body and became like a rag doll in James's arms. The lights went out. They rested peacefully for this evening.

Chapter 44

Lee Roy

The alarm soon went off. James jumped straight up in bed, knowing it couldn't be the five o'clock hour already. Theola didn't move. James arose and got dressed for work. A half-hour later, James was ready to walk out the door. He kissed Theola on the cheek. She didn't move. James tiptoed into the kid's bedroom and kissed the children goodbye. He slowly walked to the front door and eased out. James arrived at work, sleepy. He could barely keep his eyes open as he walked through the door. He tried not to let anyone know of his fatigue, but his body motions screamed lethargy.

"Hey man, your eyes are red. You stay up late or were you banging it all night long?" laughed Lee Roy.

James didn't want to hear language like that so early in the morning. "Man get out of my face. None of your damn business!"

"Ohhhhhhhh, a little testy this morning, are we? Don't worry brother. Man, my face is out of your face." Lee Roy started to walk away, but he turned to make one more comment. "Just don't fall asleep on the job. The boss doesn't like that."

Sleepy and tired, James angrily stared Lee Roy down until he was out of sight. James went to sort the mail and fill the mail trucks for their daily route of delivery. Lee Roy went to find his buddies Frank and Ed.

"Hey Frank," shouted Lee Roy. Frank was processing bulk mail for delivery.

"Yeah, what?"

"James is a little testy this morning. He wouldn't exactly tell me what was wrong. Do you think you can find out something?"

"I don't know Lee Roy. You know he stays pretty much to himself."

"Maybe we can get him to come to the bar with us this evening, get him a little sauced and maybe he'll start talking?" asked Lee Roy.

"I don't think he will go for that. You know he goes straight home after work. You have been watching him for over a year now. Has he done anything to warrant his dismissal from the job?"

"Nooo, I can't find fault with him anywhere."

"You know the boss is thinking about giving him another raise."

"What! How soon? Maybe we can put a stop to it Frank. Did Margaret tell you that?"

"Lee Roy you know Margaret tells me everything. That's why I take her out to lunch every now and then. She may be the best payroll clerk you have ever seen, but she can't help but tell me everything. Her mouth never stops running. You know that. By the time lunch hour is over, I have eaten mine. She has to wrap hers up and bring it back, because she couldn't stop talking long enough to eat."

Lee Roy burst out laughing. "Yeah man. But why is the boss going to give him another raise? He has only been here almost four years and is about to get a second raise. It took me eight years to get my first one."

"I don't know man."

"Well it ain't gonna happen!" aggressively spoke Lee Roy.

"I told you the boss could be sympathetic to a man with kids. Or James could be shining his shoes. I don't know Lee Roy, but you sure don't need another Negro trying to take what you rightfully deserve."

"Yeah you're right. He's taking the money that should be coming to me." Lee Roy thought for a moment. "You know Frank. I'm going to fix him and fix him good."

"Ok Lee Roy. Whatever you do, I'm with you all the way," smiled Frank.

"I'm going to find out where he is right now. I will set him up to fall so hard, he won't know what hit him."

Frank patted Lee Roy on the back and pushed him slightly out the door to get a move on finding out where James was in the post office.

Lee Roy searched around and spotted James through the thick glass windows that surrounded the boss's office. James had his back to Lee Roy. Robert Hunter was sitting on the corner of his desk, speaking to James. Lee Roy stared at the thick glass. He couldn't hear a thing. He tried to follow their lip movement.

"James I just want to congratulate you on the fine job you have been doing over the past four years. Every supervisor you have been under has given you nothing but praise on the excellent job you have performed."

"Why thank you very much sir."

"I have always been one to believe that an employee should know all the jobs of his co-workers just in case he may have to fill his shoes for any reason. And you didn't wait to be asked. You volunteered. You have offered suggestions in certain areas of the post office that have even benefited the customer."

"I was just trying to consider what I would appreciate as a customer, sir."

"Well keep up the good work. In a few days, you will be getting another assignment from one of the supervisors and I know you will do well."

"Yes sir."

"I told you all I ask of my employees, colored, white or anybody, is to do your job well and the rewards will find you. As a gesture of your excellent efforts, you will receive an additional fifty dollars in your pay a month."

"That's wonderful sir! Thank you sir." James jumped up from his chair, excited. "I sure can use it."

"Well it's already in the administrative office for processing. You can check with Margaret or Sandy. They can tell you where they are with the processing."

James shook Robert's hand and left the office, smiling. Lee Roy followed him. He came up behind James. "Hey man. Do you want to come over to the bar with me and the other boys and have a beer?"

"No thanks Lee Roy. I have to get home. My wife is waiting for me."

"Do you always do what your wife wants you to do?"

James ignored the question. He walked away in a hurry to find out when his extra raise would be in his paycheck before he had to leave. Lee Roy just stared at him with squinted eyes, a frown upon his face and envy in his heart.

After a long and rewarding day, James returned home only to find Theola at the door waiting with books in hand and the children in the middle of the floor playing with their toys. James and Theola kissed each other as she walked out and he walked in. He wanted to tell her the good news, but he would wait for a better time for her to listen. They barely saw each other during the weekdays. But the weekends were filled with love and affection. He would tell her then.

Chapter 45

Another Surprise on the Way

When the weekend arrived, James told Theola the good news. She was thrilled that James was excelling in his job. Things were going well at work and at college. Four months passed, James and Theola couldn't be happier. But one day, James came home expecting to go through his normal route with Theola and instead, he came home and found Theola not waiting at the door. He was concerned. There was no movement in the house. Suddenly, he heard a disturbing sound coming from the bathroom. He raced quickly through the living room to see what was wrong. To his surprise, Theola was on her knees, her head bowed, both hands gripping the toilet seat and James Jr. and Marilyn were watching.

"Honey what's wrong? Was it something you ate? Have you been doing this all day?"

Theola turned her head slightly to acknowledge James, but only more fluid started to flow from her lips.

James quickly ushered the children into the living room. "Marilyn, I want you to watch your little brother while I take care of Mommy."

"Yes Daddy," responded Marilyn.

James dashed back to the bathroom. He heard the toilet flush. Theola was just getting up from her knees. James wet a towel in the sink and handed it to Theola. "What is it honey? Is there something I can get you?"

"How about some crackers, watermelon and sardines?"

James' heart sank. He let the lid down on the toilet and sat on it, holding his head in his hands.

"Ohhhh, noooo, ohhhhh noooo. Please tell me you're not what I think you are?" Theola wiped her lips with the cool towel and dapped her forehead. Her hair was all over her head, sweat dripped from her brow and her blouse was drenched from perspiration. "With that kind of request for food, it can only mean one thing."

"Yes honey." Theola was exhausted. She appeared almost faint.

"Come." James stood up and reached for her. "You need to lie down before you fall down."

James took Theola by her waist and escorted her to the bedroom. He lovingly eased her onto the bed and helped her lay back to rest herself. He sat beside her.

"We are not going to get rid of this one either, are we?"

"James you should know me by now. These children are a part of us. If we hurt a gift of life, then our lives aren't worth living. God created what I have inside me. The baby wouldn't be there if it wasn't His will."

"Then is it going to be His will to add a few extra dollars to this house? You know I just got a pay raise three months ago. That pay raise gave us change at the end of the bills. Now we have another child on the way. Do you know how many children we will have after this child is born?"

"I can count James."

"Theola our pockets can't hold another child." James got up from the bed and paced the floor. "Shooooot, I'm twenty-three years old, working on my third child." James laughed.

"You said you wanted a lot of children."

Yes, but I had no idea what it takes to raise them. The time, money, food, clothes, toys…I just thought all I had to do is just have them and the rest would somehow take care of itself."

"This is your dream James. Now it's your reality. You were going to be working at a cotton mill the rest of your life. I was going to be barefoot and pregnant all the time. It looks like your dream is coming true. At least now you have a better paying job and one that recognizes your efforts, rather than your skin color."

"That's right Theola. And do you think I'm going to continue to get raises when I have to take off to take my wife and children to the doctor or rush home if you and the children are sick?"

"People have families James. Things happen and sometimes it's the father who needs to take care of the children."

"Why are you being so stubborn about everything Theola?'

"Not stubborn, determined."

"Why do you always have something to say after I have made a comment?"

"I'm opinionated."

"And you always have to have the last word."

"Closing points to a discussion," smiled Theola.

"See what I mean. Stop trying to be something that you're not!" James lashed out of frustration over the baby. "You're not a lawyer!"

Theola remained calm. "Not yet. James if we are ever to rise above what people think we are and how people think we should act, we have to perform the way we should be. I consider myself a smart individual. No better than you or anyone else. But nevertheless, an individual in my own right and a smart one, I might add."

"Theola the world isn't ready for smart Negroes."

"That's where you're wrong James. The question is, is the world ready for Negroes to be the individuals that they are? There are some brilliant minds out there. But they are just too afraid to express them for fear of being cut down. We've been trained that we are inferior people James, so we act like the dumb Negro that can't even tie his shoe unless he's told."

"Theola…"

"Here me out James. You've known me for a long time now and even more so in the past four years. I've been taught to strive for my desires. To be the person that God created me to be, not some pre-trained animal that doesn't have the good sense to get out of the rain unless I'm told."

"Theola I can respect what you are saying, but the fact of the matter is, I'm the breadwinner. If I don't work, nothing gets paid and nobody gets fed."

"James we have to be willing to make sacrifices along the way. No one said it would be easy. But my success is our gain. I'm becoming a lawyer to benefit others as well as our own family."

"I don't see it happening Theola."

"James we have to envision the future in order to change the present. I don't want my children to struggle the way we have. I don't want them to grow up wondering why they can't eat in a public restaurant or use the same public bathrooms as their white peers. There has to be a change."

"And you're going to make that change?"

"With every breath I take and every move I make, I will fight against the injustice of this society."

"And what about all the children we are having?"

"I will teach our children to be self-confident and to believe in themselves. Our children will have a purpose too. Maybe they will be by our side to see that change occur and be a part of it. Maybe they will follow in our footsteps and make a difference in their lives and others. I don't know James, but I do know that God wants them here."

"Theola I'm looking at the facts. And the facts say with a newborn, not only will we be back to no money left at the end of the month, but I'm borrowing money from Skip and Ms. Sarah just to keep us afloat. I owe them money."

"What! Why?"

"Remember three months ago, I had a flat tire?"

"Yes."

"The new one cost fifteen dollars and I borrowed it from Skip. Remember last month the air conditioning went out?"

"Yes."

"I borrowed twenty-five dollars from Ms. Sarah to get it fixed. I couldn't let you and the babies ride in the heat. And remember six months before all that happened, the car was burning a lot of gas and cutting off at stop lights?"

"No."

"Well it was. So I had to get a major tune-up. That cost thirty-six dollars and fifty cents and I borrowed that from Skip."

"Is there anything else James?"

"Yeah, I borrowed all that money just so you can stay in college. They let me pay them back when I can, being the gracious people that they are. Your college leaves me with no savings, so I borrow."

"Don't go there James. If you hadn't wanted to have sex, we wouldn't be having another baby right now."

James walked closer to the bed and stared her in the eyes. "Ooooh! What am I supposed to do, become a priest? I don't think so. I can count the number of times we have had sex in one year! We barely get together on the weekends because the children have our attention. That's ridiculous. I'm a man. My needs are more than just once a month or whenever we can fit it into our schedule. So don't *you* go there!"

Theola sympathized. "I know. But it seems almost every two years, when we have sex, a child is conceived. We just have to deal with it James, the best way we can and with God's help."

"There you go again. You think God is going to give us the money we need to raise our children?"

"We've made it this far with God's help. Don't start talking about God in a negative way James or just to prove to you He is God, He can remove His umbrella of love and mercy from over us and let things really hit us hard."

James walked across the room and got in Theola's face. "Umbrella of love and mercy? Ha! I'm the one who has been placing food in our home, clothes on our backs and busting my butt at the post office. Why can't I talk about God in a negative way? Is God the one who is letting you have all these babies?" Theola just shook her head. "You seem to think having babies is a good thing and all we are supposed to do is take care of them. Then what you need to do is find the book that says, *how*. Ask God *how*, when you don't have lots of money, enough space, food or clothing for your family to live. How are you supposed to take care of them? How Theola? Just tell me how? How are we going to make it with three children and three hundred dollars a month and you in college?"

"James I don't see how you can say things about God when your mother raised you to love and believe in God."

"She did, but I didn't say I believed her. I only did what she told me to because I love and respect her."

"Alright James. I will not argue with you about your beliefs. That's between you and God. But why didn't you tell me you were borrowing money?"

James walked to her bedside and sat beside her. "Theola, my job is to take care of you and the babies. You are to stay home and take care of the kids and the house. Not to worry about the financial matters."

"But I need to know these things James. So I can help anyway I can."

"And what are you going to do, quit college?"

She paused. Theola bowed her head. She was hurting inside. But she quickly raised her head and stared James in the eyes and made her proclamation. "I'm going to finish the classes I've started and there will be no more classes until the baby is at least three."

"Hallelujah!" James jumped up from the side of the bed and clapped his hands. "You are finally making some sense."

"If God wants me to be a lawyer, then I will be one eventually."

"That's the way it looks to me right now. Our chemistry is so good girl that it's like butter and sugar in a bowl of hot oatmeal, we just go together naturally. God wants you to be a baby making machine. I mak-em and you bak-em."

Theola tried not to crack a smile. She held on to her solemn look. "That's not funny James."

Theola sat up on the side of the bed. Tears formed in her eyes. James walked over and sat beside her. He placed his arm around her shoulder. "Theola I'm trying to support you and the children the best way I know how. I just want the very best for you and the children. If I had to work three jobs to support our family, I would because I love you and the children just that much. But what I don't want is to be the way my dad was with us."

Theola sniffled. "And how was that James?"

"My dad used to ration my mother with the food."

"What?"

"Yeah. That's right. My Mom, if she saw we were running out of milk before the end of the month, instead of a full glass at breakfast, we would get half a glass. If that milk wasn't lasting, she would water down some pet milk to stretch having some kind of milk until the end of the month."

"Why?"

James wiped the last small tear from her eyes with the thumb of his hand.

"Because he didn't want to give her an additional thirty-five cents to get another gallon. He felt if he did that, then she would ask him for more money during the month to get more food."

"Why James?"

"He always said he wasn't trying to fill us up. He just wanted to stop the hunger pains."

"Come on James. You're kidding?"

"Not only that, Mom would buy enough pork chops in a pack to feed the family. Dad would get two and one for each of us. If my sister and I wanted more, my Mom would cut hers in half and split it between the two of us so we would have enough meat."

"Did he care about that?"

"No. It was my Mom's loss, not his."

"Didn't your sister complain?"

"Yeah, but that complaint he ignored because he didn't want her to get fat and lose her beautiful figure. People always told him how lovely she looked. So he wasn't about to lose his compliments over seconds at the dinner table."

"Were you all poor?"

"You know what, that's the clincher. My father was not a poor man. He worked at the cotton mill and he made good money. They paid by the number of bales of cotton you would band and made ready for shipment. Dad was quick with bailing cotton. He worked sometimes on Saturday's just to get the overtime pay. He would get a check of two-hundred dollars or more a month."

"Soooo, why did he ration food?"

"He was stingy with his money. However, he had to take care of the family, but with little money as possible. He would check the grocery list to make sure Mother didn't buy any snacks for us. So she would take the little money she had from cleaning Mr. Charles's house and buy snacks separate from the grocery bill so he wouldn't know."

"That's a shame James."

"She would hide ice cream, donuts and cookies in the kitchen."

"Didn't she think he would ever find that stuff?"

"Oh no. Not Dad. He never came to the kitchen unless Mom called him for a meal. She waited on him hand and foot. Dad never lifted a finger to get a drink of water or a plate of food for himself. Mom handed him everything. He could be standing right next to the refrigerator and he would call my Mother from the living room to get him some cold tea or a glass of water from the ice box."

"That's awful James. Did she do it?"

"Yes she did. And she did it with a smile. She loves my father." James paused. He thought. "That's why I made a promise to myself that I would never treat my woman that way. I want a wife, not a slave. I want to provide for my children. I want to provide for you in every way I can. But what I don't want is to place you on a budget or stop you from doing the things you want to do to better yourself. I love my children. I don't mind having more. As a matter of fact, I like making them whenever we can. But, the fact is, the babies are placing a strain on our financial situation."

"Now that you have explained the rationale behind not having them, I can see your point. You're right James. I'm glad you talked it over with me. I guess I am being sort of selfish. College will have to wait until we are able to provide for both our family and school without the financial stress."

They both smiled and kissed each other with much love and passion.

Marilyn and James Jr. walked and waddled into the room. James turned and saw the children. He got up from the bed and gently picked them both up. He kissed them both.

"How would you two like for Mommy to be home at night to read and sing you to sleep Marilyn. And...tuck you into bed James Jr.?"

Marilyn smiled and nodded. James Jr. looked at his sister and responded in the same manner. James placed them both back on the floor.

"See honey," James pointed at the children, "They both want you to be home at night."

Theola just stared at James with a slight smile.

"Let's let you get some rest. I will see if I can't find some watermelon, sardines and what else?"

"Crackers."

"Yeah, crackers. And I'll feed the children whatever you have fixed for dinner." James picked up James Jr., grabbed Marilyn by the hand and took them both into the kitchen. Theola rested her head on the pillow. Tears began to flow again. She loved her children, but her dream of becoming a lawyer would have to wait. The longer she waited to get her degree, the more her father's heart would harden against her. She turned her head to the pillow and continued to cry silently.

CHAPTER 46

The Conspiracy

That same evening, Lee Roy, Frank and Ed were at their favorite bar, lining up beers, but this evening, Sandy decided to go to the bar with them.

"Hey Sandy. It's been a while since you went to the bar with us. What's the occasion?"

"Oh nothing Ed. I just decided to break up my usual routine of going home, feeding my face, walking the dog and going to bed. I just figured for tonight or until I get bored again, I'll have a few beers with you guys. Maybe shoot some pool."

"Great! Are you still the pool shark we remember you to be?" asked Frank.

"Try me." Sandy had confidence in her voice.

They all got up with a beer in their hands and found an empty pool table. They played for a couple of hours. The more the men drank, the more they talked. Sandy was still on her first beer while the guys had finished their fifth. The men became more talkative after the beers kept coming. Sandy was winning all the games.

"Hey Lee Roy. Have you decided what you are going to do about James Paul Taylor?"

"Yeah Ed. Since he's so hard-working, I'm going to have to help him make a mistake."

Sandy couldn't believe her ears. But she kept shooting the balls on the table while the guys kept talking.

"What's your plan Lee Roy?" asked Frank.

"Tomorrow he will fill the mailbags and place them in the appropriate trucks for delivery. When he finishes the mail bags and places them in the trucks, I'm going to try to help him and then switch the bags. By the time the drivers get to their destination and deliver the mail, they will realize they have the wrong mail for their routes. So much time will have elapsed that it would take a whole day to get the mail sorted right. The drivers will come back to the post office complaining they had the wrong bags. The mail will be delivered late or the next day and it will be all James's fault."

"That's ok, but it doesn't sound like something that would get him fired," said Ed.

"Sounds pretty good to me. What do you think will get him fired Ed?" asked Lee Roy.

Sandy missed her shot.

"It's your turn Lee Roy," said Sandy. She stepped from the table to let Lee Roy shoot.

Ed sipped more beer and continued to talk.

"Lee Roy I heard James is going to get a special assignment," stated Frank. I can find out what it is."

"But if you can mess up that assignment in addition to making him seem like a total fuck up, then he will be fired for sure," stated Ed.

"So go ahead and switch the mailbags?" asked Lee Roy.

"Yes. Do that tomorrow," said Frank.

Lee Roy missed his shot. "It's your turn Sandy."

Sandy got back on the table, not speaking a word about what they were talking about. "In three shots I'll have you Lee Roy."

"Give it your best shot Sandy." Lee Roy staggered, leaning on his pool stick.

"Yeah, go ahead and take him out. I want to take you down anyway," stated Frank.

Lee Roy and Ed stood to the side to finish their conversation, continuing to finish their beer bottles.

"Another round!" yelled Ed to the bartender.

"I'll find out what the special assignment is Lee Roy and I'll let you know," stated Frank.

"Thanks Frank. You're a good buddy. I'll start working on the mishaps for our friend tomorrow."

They all observed Sandy knocking her last ball into the side pocket.

"By the time we are through with him, the boss will be kicking him out the door," laughed Ed. Lee Roy smiled. Frank had a smirk on his face.

"Eight ball in the corner pocket," called Sandy.

"Ohhh now she's about to clean your clock Lee Roy," said Frank.

"Good. Now I can finish my beer." Lee Roy placed his stick back in the rack and put both hands on his beer. Frank grabbed the rack and positioned the balls on the table.

"Now you can take on a true pool shark," stated Frank. "Shoot!"

Sandy positioned herself in front of the cue ball and gave aim. Bam! Balls fell everywhere when Sandy busted the rack. She proceeded to run the table in low balls on Frank. Ed and Lee Roy got their fresh cold beers from the waiter and watched as she cleared the table without missing a shot.

"Next!" Sandy shouted.

"Oooooooweeee, she sat the shark down," stated Ed. Lee Roy stood snickering.

Ed put down his beer. He spat spit in one hand and rubbed both hands together. He picked up his pool stick and rubbed it too. Ed set the stick against the wall and began to rack.

"You're not going to do to me what you did to those other two wimps over there," said Ed.

Frank and Lee Roy laughed. Sandy smiled. When Ed finished racking the pool balls, Sandy positioned her stick on the cue ball again, and bam! She started all over again, clearing balls off the table with Ed. Frank and Lee Roy continued to laugh.

CHAPTER 47

The Conspirators in Action

While James's peers drank their night away, he was performing his duties as a father and loving husband.

When Theola fell asleep early after dinner, James prepared the children for bed. He bathed them and read a bedtime story to bore them to sleep. Minutes later, James went to bed and fell into a deep slumber. Soon, another dawn peeked through the window of the Venetian Blinds to awaken James from his night's rest. Not long after his eyes were open, the alarm clock rang, from bell to bell, until James reached over to shut it off. He rubbed his eyes, yarned, peeked at Theola, still asleep and slowly rose from the bed. He tiptoed to the children's room to see if they were awakened by the noise. They were also still asleep. James dressed and went to work, thinking all was well.

"Hey James," Lee Roy spotted James coming through the front door. "How are you doing this morning?"

"I'm fine man. But you don't look so good with those bloodshot eyes."

"I'm fine. Hey, do you need some help filling the trucks with the mail this morning?"

"Naugh Lee Roy. I got it, but thanks for asking."

James thought this a little strange, for he had been filling the mail trucks for months and Lee Roy had never volunteered to help. But James soon dismissed the thought and went to sort the mail for the trucks.

Lee Roy went to find Ed. Four rooms down from James, Ed and Frank were processing the bulk mail for delivery. Lee Roy entered their workroom immediately closing the door behind him.

"Frank," spoke Lee Roy. Did you find out anything about the special assignment for James?" Ed continued to work.

"Not yet Lee Roy, but come back after lunch today. I will know something then."

"All right Frank. Hey, Ed." Lee Roy waved at Ed.

Ed waved at Lee Roy. Ed waited to speak to Frank, feeling Lee Roy was far enough away that he wouldn't hear the conversation. "Why are you helping Lee Roy get rid of James? We don't like either one of them niggers. We should be getting rid of them both so it can be all white postal workers here."

"Don't you see Ed? If we get Lee Roy to get rid of James, it can't be called prejudice. Our hands are clean."

"But we don't like Lee Roy either."

"Ed, Lee Roy is our token nigger. If we keep him around, we can use him to get rid of all the other niggers that the boss hires."

"How did James get in here anyway?"

"I heard James had a friend to help him through the door. The boss hasn't gotten rid of him because he does a good job at whatever he is given. A lot better than Lee Roy."

"Why don't we get rid of Lee Roy and keep James since he is the better worker?"

"Whaaat! No way. We already have Lee Roy trained in our way of thinking. Look how he fell for the crap we gave him. You see, James is quiet and keeps to himself. Lee Roy is not motivated to do more than necessary.

James outshines us all and we really don't know that much about him other than he's a family man. Naugh, it would be too much to try and train another nigger to do what we say. We'll keep Lee Roy."

Ed nodded his head and continued sorting his bulk mail.

Frank followed suit. A few hours later, not long after lunch, Lee Roy was looking for Frank. Frank was speaking with Sandy in the administrative office. Lee Roy spotted him and entered the room.

"Excuse me, Sandy. Frank, what's the word?" asked Lee Roy as he approached him.

"I heard he is getting the assignment today. Do you know where James is?" questioned Frank.

"Yeah, he just finished his lunch. He was eating in the sorting room."

"Ok, keep an eye on him right now and let me know if he goes in to see the boss."

"Why?" questioned Lee Roy.

"James is to get the assignment today. When he goes in to see the boss, you and I are going to observe them through the window. When James leaves out, you see if you can dig any information out of him. I will go in to see the boss and see what I can't find out about what he told James to do."

"Can't you just ask?"

"Robert is a fair man. I don't want him to think I'm being nosey. He might think I'm trying to set James up for a fall. Especially if something happens after I just questioned him about something he gave James to do."

Sandy couldn't believe what she was hearing. She fiddled with paperwork on her desk and just listened.

"Alright Frank. I'll keep an eye on James and let you know when he goes to see the boss."

"Good boy Lee Roy. You know this is for your benefit. You don't need any other competition holding you back from promotions you should be getting, right?"

"You damn right!" Lee Roy left the administrative room pumped up. Sandy just shook her head slightly.

"Frank what are you doing? Why are you trying to destroy James's reputation as a good worker?"

"Are you kidding Sandy!" Frank pounded his fist on her desk. Sandy jumped, startled by the abrupt blow. "We got two niggers in the post office and that's just one too many for me!"

Margaret and Rosalind were down the hall gathering more forms.

"I didn't know you hated Negroes that much. You always seemed so kind to Lee Roy."

"Honey, that's just to keep Lee Roy exactly where we want him. That's dis-liking any other nigger coming in here thinking they can get promotions over Lee Roy and the rest of us. As long as he thinks other niggers are his enemy, he'll always be the only one of them to work here."

At that moment, Lee Roy came rushing back to the administrative office.

"Frank! James just went into the boss's office."

"Ok, let's go Lee Roy." Frank looked at Sandy and winked an eye. Sandy had no expression. She felt a little uneasy about what was about to happen to James. She knew somehow she had to try to warn him. She sat there and thought.

Soon, Lee Roy and Frank were near the boss's office. They could see everything and hear nothing. They observed James and their boss. Their eyes focused on both men closely.

"James the reason I asked you in my office is because I want you to do a very critical and important job for the post office. The only reason I'm giving it to you, is that I am quite confident that you can handle the job."

James smiled. "Thank you very much sir."

"James just this morning I received this letter…" Robert handed the letter to James. While James read the letter, Robert continued with the briefing. "James this letter is placing me on an alert to watch out for four huge priority mail packages coming into this post office for delivery to certain places in Chicago."

James quickly glanced up from the letter and handed it back to Robert. "Yes sir."

"I am counting on you to deliver these packages within a few days. When they come in, Sandy will log them as Special Delivery and then have them sent to the mail room to await you to deliver them."

"Yes sir!" James spoke with enthusiasm.

"Good. The exact date is unclear, so keep an eye out for them. Once they arrive, I will depend on you to get them where they need to go."

"Sir?"

"Yes James."

"Are there any more obvious markings or emblems. Or are there specific destinations, something other than priority mail to let me know I have exactly the packages you want me to deliver?"

"Ohhhh, there is. I'm glad you asked. There are six triangles in a circle. The triangles are red and the circle is black. The markings will be on both sides of each package." Robert paused. "Good thinking James. I had forgotten about the special markings."

Frank and Lee Roy observed the entire conversation from a distance in the hall.

"Yes sir."

"Now do you have all that?"

"Yes sir. I have."

"Do you have any other questions?"

"No sir. I don't."

"Alright I'm counting on you James not to let me down."

"Yes sir. I won't." James rose from his chair and shook his boss's hand. "Thank you for your confidence in me."

James left the room and proceeded down the hall to alert Sandy to let him know when the packages arrive. Lee Roy slowly followed, not to alert James of his presence. Frank went immediately into Robert's office to try to get a glimpse at the paper Robert had shown James.

"Mr. Hunter, may I speak with you for a second?"

"Yeah Frank. Give me a minute. I just have to run to the can. I'll be right back."

"Take your time sir. I'll just sit here until you return."

Robert Hunter immediately left the room. Frank watched until his boss was out of sight. He quickly glanced into the hallway, right and then left. He spotted no one. Now was his chance to find the paper that Robert showed James. Frank had noticed where he placed the paper. Frank picked it up and began reading, glancing up every now and then to see if anyone was coming. Frank quickly read the letter and sat in his boss's guest chair.

Shortly after Frank sat down, Robert returned. "Now what can I do for you Frank?"

"I was just wondering if you had reconsidered joining the Wildcats Bowling Team on Thursday nights? We sure could use you sir."

"Now you know I don't bowl Frank."

"It doesn't matter. I know that. We have good bowlers. We need you just to have some kind of handicap."

Robert walked to his chair and sat down. He grabbed the letter from the center of his desk and placed it in his hot item box. Frank observed his action. "Thanks for asking, but I'll pass. Now if you don't mind, I have some matters I need to take care of."

"Well if you change your mind, let me know. It's never too late." Frank left Robert's office. He paused in the hallway and came right back. Frank poked his head in the door. "By the way, we have a couple of single girls on our team, you being a single man and all."

"Thanks Frank, but I can find my own girls." Robert continued to work, not even noticing Frank standing in the doorway.

"Yes sir...suit yourself." Frank left the office this time.

He was now eager to find Lee Roy to learn what he had found out from James. He only walked a few feet down the hallway. He saw James and Lee Roy in a conversation. Frank walked slowly up to them, not to arouse suspicion.

"Hey Frank." Stated Lee Roy.

"What are you guys up to?" asked Frank.

"Nothing," stated James. "I got to go and finish my duties. I'll see you two around." James walked off to his mailroom. When James was out of sight, Frank was anxious to know what Lee Roy had discovered.

"What did he say Lee Roy?"

"He didn't tell me anything. He didn't even tell me he had gone in to see the boss."

"No matter Lee Roy. I got a look-see at what the boss showed James."

Frank had Lee Roy's full attention. "What did you find out?"

"That piece of paper we saw was a letter from the Postmaster. They wanted special packages delivered soon to certain places in Chicago. Four packages will be arriving here in a few weeks and the packages are to be delivered immediately."

"Then all we have to do is intercept those packages and make sure James doesn't see them."

"That's right. Hunter must want James to deliver them as soon as they get here. The packages will go into James's division first.

"How are we going to get them without James's knowledge?"

"What we have to do is find out exactly when those packages are going to arrive. Divert James's attention somewhere else and hide the packages until James gets into trouble for not delivering them."

"But how are we going to find out when those packages are going to arrive?"

"Margaret has friends in high places, even though she is a payroll clerk. She knows people, people in important places. I can take her out to lunch, pick her brain and see what she can find out for me."

"That's wonderful Frank. If you find out when the packages are coming, I'll do the rest."

"Deal."

Frank went to the administrative office to find Margaret. Not long after he got there, he invited her out for lunch. Being secretly in love with him, she accepted Frank's invitation.

They left at noon for the local Dan's Bar and Grill across the street. While they sat waiting for the waitress, Frank was eager to start with the questioning.

"You haven't invited me to lunch in a long time Frank. Why now?"

"Can't a man invite a pretty woman to lunch when he wants to?"

"So why did you invite me?"

Frank laughed. "Come on Margaret. You know I think you're the greatest."

"Ok, let's cut through the small stuff. What is it that you want to know? Every time you invite me to lunch, our conversation ends up being about a favor."

"Why do you think all I want you for is information?"

"We've been out together three times this year and this is the fourth time in eight months. If I'm the greatest, I think I would have made it in the little black book that you keep in your back pocket."

Frank gingerly reached down and touched his back pocket to see if his book was still there. "Now, now, Margaret, why would you say something like that?"

"I know you show all your buddies whom you are dating this week and every other week."

"Alright Margaret. Enough about me. Let's get to the meat of things. I need to know what the Postmaster has coming through our post office that is so important and what day it's to arrive."

"That kind of information is going to cost you Frank."

"You got it babe. Name your price."

"You pay for lunch this time."

Frank smiled. Margaret forced a grin. "No problem. Order anything on the menu."

Frank patted her hands and waved for the waitress to come and take their order. Margaret knew Frank was up to something, but she didn't know what. However, before she delivered such vital information to this callous man, she knew she had to find out how it was going to benefit him. They stayed to finish their lunch, while Lee Roy followed James around the post office.

Chapter 48

The Backstabber

Lee Roy was envious of James's flawlessness in his work. So he decided to give James a hand in making a mistake.

"James," called Lee Roy. James was placing mailbags in the trucks. "Can I give you a hand?"

"You finished all your work man?" James continued putting mailbags into a truck. "You know how the boss doesn't want anything to fall through the cracks. He prides himself on prompt and accurate deliveries."

"I'm finished James. Trust me man. I wouldn't be out here trying to assist you if I had work to do."

James thought this a little strange, but he ignored his gut feelings, thinking he might finish faster with a little assistance and could finish some paperwork that needed to be done before he went home.

"All right. Well, you see how I got the bags. They are positioned from left to right on the ramp very close together?"

"Yeah."

"Well hand them to me that way one at a time. Because the way the bags are positioned is the exact location that each particular truck is pulling out to a certain section of town."

"That's a great idea."

"Yeah. This way, after I sort by town, I place the mailbags according to the area the drivers are going to. This ensures they are on time to their particular routes with the correct mail."

"Ok James. I'll pass the bags and you tuck them in the trucks for delivery."

"Deal."

James jumped from the ramp, stood beside a truck and awaited Lee Roy's mailbags. When James's back was turned to position the mailbag in the truck, Lee Roy would take a mailbag from another position, hand it to James and then slide another bag over to make it seem as if he were staying in the same order James had staged the bags. They continued to work at a steady pace until all the mail trucks were loaded.

"This is the last bag James."

James stored that bag in the last truck.

"Thanks Lee Roy. You know, I think I got through at least thirty minutes faster than if I were doing it by myself."

Lee Roy smiled, "You welcome James, anytime."

"Well, I got to go James. If you need some assistance anytime, please let me know."

Lee Roy went back to the lounge and waited for Frank to return from lunch. When Lee Roy left, the mail truck drivers were reporting. They all spoke to James with a warm greeting and salutation. James watched and waved as they drove off.

Lee Roy could hear Margaret. Margaret and Frank laughed as they came down the hallway. When they entered the lounge, Lee Roy was pacing the floor. They noticed his apprehension. So did Sandy eating her lunch.

"What's wrong Lee Roy?" asked Frank.

Lee Roy paced the floor, rubbing both hands together.

"I've never seen you like this Lee Roy. What have you done?" asked Sandy.

"Yeah Lee Roy. What have you done?" Frank intervened. Margaret just observed, not really concerned one way or another.

"What you see is a pace of success." Stated Lee Roy, proudly.

"What do you mean?" asked Sandy.

"James was loading the mail trucks and I switched mailbags. Mail that was supposed to go to Aurora, will now go to Buck town and so on and so forth."

Sandy was perplexed by the conversation. She recalled the other night at the bar. Thinking they were just in a drunken stupor, she didn't take them seriously. "Why would you want to send the mail to the wrong town? The drivers would be late delivering the correct mail to the right house. Not to mention, James will be in big trouble."

Frank smiled. Margaret laughed. "You said it Sandy. James will be in big trouble." Frank turned to Lee Roy. "How long ago did you do the switch?"

"About twenty minutes ago."

"Then the mail trucks should be back here within fifteen or twenty-minute intervals after they realize they have the wrong mail."

"But they all won't be back at the same time, meaning that all the trucks will have to wait until the other trucks arrive just to ensure the mail is on the proper truck," stated Sandy.

"You're right sweetheart," smiled Frank and Lee Roy. Sandy just shook her head. Margaret left to go back to the office.

"But Lee Roy, James will never trust you to do anything for him again," stated Sandy.

"I will plead to his good heart that it was all a mistake. He has no reason to doubt me. He should be forgiving. Besides, I hope he gets fired. Then, I won't have to worry about his feelings."

"Let's be back at our jobs when those trucks roll in and the boss starts screaming."

Frank shook Lee Roy's hand and Lee Roy exited the lounge. Frank was on his way out, he turned for one last word to Sandy.

"Tell Margaret don't forget I paid for lunch. She'll know what I'm talking about."

Sandy just nodded her head slightly. Frank turned and walked back to his room. Sandy paused in deep thought before she headed back to her office. She couldn't believe this was actually happening.

Was she going to do the right thing? How could she alert James or her boss of what was going on? If she did tell someone, would she be in trouble? Would she be fired or even harassed by Frank and anyone else who felt like he did? Sandy bowed her head and contemplated what she would do as she walked back to her office.

CHAPTER 49

Chaos in the Post Office

As time passed, the mail trucks were delivering their cargo. James was in his office working diligently on paperwork he needed to finish before he left for home. But thirty minutes later, you could hear Bob screaming coming down the hallway.

"James!" Bob shouted. "James!"

James heard the screech of his name and ran immediately from the sorting room. "What is it Bob? What's wrong? Why are you back so soon?"

By this time, Robert and all the employees who had worked that day were in the hallway.

"I got the wrong mail in my truck."

"What? How can that be? I sorted the mail as I always have and filled it in each truck for each section of town as usual?"

"Well, I don't know what you did this time, but I got the wrong mail in my truck."

James had a flashback of Lee Roy assisting him.

"Surely there is a good explanation for the mix-up?" stated Robert Hunter.

By this time, Harry had come into the hallway. "I'm glad you are all here. I got the wrong mail in my truck. What happened James?"

Ted followed Harry. "What happened James? I also got the wrong mail in my truck."

James appeared angry and turned around to find Lee Roy in the crowd. He spotted him standing next to Frank. Robert knew this couldn't have been all James's fault. He knew James was a perfectionist.

"James," called Robert.

James's eyes shifted to his boss. "Yes sir."

"Did you do anything different this time when you loaded the mail than you normally do? Was there any change in your normal routine?"

James thought for a moment. He turned to Lee Roy. He thought Lee Roy might step forward and say it was his fault, because he helped him with the mailbags. Since Lee Roy didn't, James kept silent. He didn't want to blame the situation on Lee Roy and it seemed as if he was shifting the blame to someone else. Lee Roy stood by Sandy and Frank when the questions were asked. He was very nervous, thinking James might name him.

Sandy was hoping James would tell the truth about what happened and save her from her conscience.

James turned from the crowd and addressed his boss. "No sir. I did the bags the way I usually do."

Sandy sighed, her head dropped in disappointment. Lee Roy exhaled a deep breath he was holding and smiled in the very same motion. Frank grinned. He was assured now that James would not talk about what happened between him and Lee Roy for fear of noncohesion among the employees.

"Alright everybody, get back to work. You men get your mail sorted out. James, come into my office."

The crowd disbursed. They walked away talking amongst themselves about what had just happened. James felt terrible. He hoped this incident would not stop Robert from letting him perform the special job he had already assigned him. Robert walked into his office first. James slowly followed. Robert walked around to his seat and sat down while James stood before his desk.

"Close the door James."

James did as Robert instructed. James started to sweat. Robert leaned forward in his chair and intermingled his fingers. His voice was stern but calm.

"Do you realize what you have done? The mail will be hours late. The postmen, your co-workers will be getting home late to their families, because you didn't pay attention to what you were doing. Or at least, that's the way it appears." Robert paused, he thought for a moment. "James you have been working here for a few years now and in my days as your supervisor, I have never known anything like this to happen."

"Yes sir." James responded. Remorsefulness was in his tone.

"James I don't know what happened today, but I do know that you are better than that or I would not have given you that special assignment. And because I know you are just that good, I'm not going to take the assignment away from you. But whatever went on today, don't let it affect your job performance again." Robert paused. He stared at James. "Do you want to talk to me about what just happened?"

James bowed his head and thought for a moment. "No sir. I will get it straightened out."

"See to it James. I trust you will."

"Yes sir. It will not happen again." stated James with confidence.

"Now get out of here." James started out the door. Robert called to him. "James! You realize you have to stay late and help those trucks deliver the right mail to the correct part of town. Call your wife. Don't be thoughtless. Let her know what happened. But I want those trucks back on the streets within an hour."

"Yes sir."

James left the room and went straight to the administrative office to remind Sandy about the special packages he was looking for. He wanted to make sure he didn't miss that assignment. After he left Sandy, James knew only one thing could have happened and that was Lee Roy. It was not necessary to track Lee Roy down. James just decided to cut Lee Roy off completely. Their conversations would be related to work and work only. No more assistance would come from anyone. James went back to the sorting room to call Theola. He knew she had to be at school at a certain hour, but tonight, he had to work late. He picked up the phone and dialed, hoping she would understand once he explained everything. The phone rang twice.

"Hello."

"Theola I have some bad news." James's tone was remorseful.

"No baby. What happened?"

"It's not enough time to explain now Theola. I have to work late. I'll be home in about two hours."

"James what are you talking about?" Theola was angry. "I need to be going to class in an hour. I count on an hour to study at the library before I go to class. Now you are going to take that away from me. If you're late, I will barely make it to class on time."

"Honey listen, something came up and it can't be helped. It's just for today. All I can promise you is I will do my best to hurry."

Theola lowered her tone, realizing that some circumstances can't be helped. "All right James. Please do."

"Honey, call Ms. Sarah. See if she wouldn't mind watching Marilyn just for tonight and see if Skip could take you to class?"

"Good idea. I will give her a call. Love you, see when you get home."

James hung up the phone, relieved that Theola was not terribly upset.

Chapter 50

Confronting a Friend

As soon as James placed the phone back on the base, Lee Roy walked into the sorting room. James's anger overwhelmed him. He ran up to Lee Roy and grabbed him by the collar.

"What happened Lee Roy? I gave you explicit instructions on how to pass me those bags. How could you have messed me up like that?"

Lee Roy pushed James back. "Get off me man! It was an accident. What did the boss say? He didn't fire you did he?"

"You wish. Is that why you messed me up? You want me fired?"

"Nawh man. I saw this beautiful girl across the street. She waved. I waved back. I tried to keep the flow coming to you. I guess I grabbed the wrong bags by accident. Anyway, I came to say thank you for not ratting on me about helping you today."

"Don't thank me Lee Roy. As far as I am concerned, don't ever come to me about anything. You just stay the hell away from me. Got it!"

James stormed out of the sorting room to assist the mail carriers in putting the right mailbags in the right trucks. Lee Roy smiled just when James left the room. Lee Roy went to find Frank. He went down the hallway to the administrative office. Sandy was sitting at her desk. Frank was standing at the front desk.

"Hey Frank. I just left James. He is really angry at me. He will never let me do anything for him again and Bob is not going to fire him."

"No matter. We still have the special job James has to work with," stated Frank calmly.

"But how are we to get our hands on the important packages coming in?"

"I'm working on that now." Frank looked at Sandy. "The packages are due in a few weeks. I need you to find out the exact day so Lee Roy and I can divert the packages from James's area. Talk to Margaret. She's supposed to be getting the information for me."

"But Frank, that's mail tampering." Sandy stated.

"We aren't going to open them. We are just going to misplace them for a few hours, ok?" Frank leaned over and kissed Sandy on the cheek. Sandy smiled. Frank smiled. Lee Roy grinned and left the room.

"Ok Frank, for you, I will do it. I'll get the information from Margaret."

"That's my girl Sandy baby. It's about time for you to be getting off. Would you like for me to walk you to your car?"

"No thank you Frank. I can manage." Sandy smiled. Frank put three of his fingers to his lips, kissed them and then touched Sandy's forehead. Sandy mustard a grin. Frank left the room. Sandy was unphased by Frank's gestures of affection. She always felt she wasn't his type.

Sandy now knew how they were going to discredit James. She knew she couldn't let James fall for someone else's hatred and spite. How would she help him? If word got out, it would be known it was her. If she did nothing, her conscience would haunt her. What would be her plan of action? Sandy would ponder for days and have many sleepless nights whether or not to inform her boss of the conspiracy against James. But she decided to confide in one of her associates.

Chapter 51

Friendship

ne morning in the office, Sandy appeared sullen. She wasn't her usual happy-go-lucky self. Margaret noticed the depressed expression on her face.

"What's wrong?" Hesitant to discuss the situation, Sandy said nothing. But Margaret persisted. "Sandy you don't look quite yourself today. Is something wrong?" Margaret waited for a response. Sandy gave no response. "We've been working together too long not to notice that something is wrong. Now tell me what is troubling you."

Still pondering the issue, Sandy decided to give in. "Margaret I know of a situation where one of our co-workers is trying to discredit another co-worker."

"What? Who? Who? Tell me. My ears are wide open." Margaret's curiosity was greatly aroused, but she was mostly upset because Sandy knew something she didn't already know. "Who is it Sandy? Who is doing what to whom?" Sandy went silent again. Margaret screamed. "Who?" Margaret realized she was being overzealous and reduced her tone. "Tell me Sandy, please."

Sandy pulled a chair to Margaret's desk. Sandy placed an elbow on top of her desk and placed her chin in her hand. Margaret leaned closer to Sandy because she thought she was going to whisper.

"Margaret Lee Roy wants to destroy James Paul's reputation and possibly get him fired."

Margaret sat straight up in her seat. "Oh Sandy…you are talking about two Negroes. I thought you meant one of us." Sandy was shocked but tried not to appear phased by her comment. "Why should we care about what two Negroes want to do to each other? They could kill each other for all I care."

"Margaret I didn't realize you felt that way about Negroes."

"Oh, I put up a good front for our boss because he doesn't like prejudice. But hell honey. What's a nigger going to do for you. He will never be over you. He will always be beneath us. So we don't have to like them, please them, treat them with respect or nothing. Shoot, forget about it. Don't worry your little head over some niggers."

Sandy played along. But she realized now she was probably alone. More than likely, Rosalind felt the same way. "You're right Margaret. How stupid of me. Why should I care about a negro?" Sandy paused. They both smiled and went about their daily chores. When Sandy's back was turned, Margaret stared at Sandy as if she thought Sandy cared what happened to James.

Suddenly, Sandy turned to remind Margaret about Frank and she caught Margaret's stare. "Oooooh Margaret, huh, Frank said he needed some information from you."

"Yeah, I got it honey."

"Great. All Frank wanted to know is if you had it. I guess he'll get it from you later."

"Alright Sandy."

Margaret went back to processing papers and making copies. Margaret felt Sandy was unreliable. Plus she didn't mention to her that she was receiving the special packages. Margaret waited until Sandy left the room.

Margaret immediately got on the phone with Frank. She alerted him that Sandy would be receiving the packages and logging them in when they arrived. She let Frank know of Sandy's concern for James.

"Margaret we must not let Sandy spoil our plan. Tell her the entire plot."

"What?" Margaret was confused.

"Tell her everything. If James finds out, we will know where he got the information from."

Margaret followed Frank's instructions and alerted Sandy to the entire plot. Margaret watched her expression as she told the story. Sandy seemed emotionless versus being delighted that the office was trying to get rid of an unwanted Negro. But Margaret continued her story until Sandy had heard it all.

CHAPTER 52

Sandy Tells James

Sandy knew she had to alert James to what was going on without giving herself away as a snitch. She pondered the night. The next morning, she saw James in the hallway at a distance. Sandy looked at her watch. It was seven o'clock. She scanned the area to see if the two of them were the only ones around. They were. She approached James.

"Hey James. If you have a minute right now before you start work, I would like to speak to you about your insurance forms."

"Sure Sandy. Give me a minute to stop by my section and I'll be right there."

Sandy turned and glanced back at her office. James went to his. When she sat down at her desk, she took a glimpse at the clock on the wall. It was three minutes after seven. Sandy got up and paced the floor. She knew Margaret would be arriving at 7:15 a.m. Just in case Margaret came in earlier, Sandy got some of James's papers from the file cabinet ready for him to sign. She sat back down at her desk. Eight minutes after seven, James walked into Sandy's office. Margaret trailed him coming through the door. To Sandy's surprise, she quickly pulled James's papers in front of her.

"Hey Sandy, what papers did I need to sign?" asked James, walking through the door. Margaret went straight to her desk and sat down. She placed her things on top of her desk while she observed James and Sandy. "Morning, Margaret."

Margaret nodded her head at James and began to flip the papers that were on her desk.

James turned back to Sandy. "Oh, I needed you to sign these health insurance papers for the added coverage for your newborn."

"Oh sure Sandy. Where do I sign?" James leaned over to Sandy's desk.

Sandy pointed at the paper, "Right here where I have the X." She looked at Margaret out of the corner of her eye. Margaret continued to listen and occasionally glanced over in their direction.

James finished signing his name. "Thanks Sandy for doing the paperwork so fast. I really appreciate it with me expecting another child soon."

"Oh, you're welcome."

James paused on his way out the door. "Ohhh Sandy, let me know when those Special Delivery packages arrive. I just can't afford another incident like yesterday."

Sandy nodded. James exited the administrative office. "I made a note of it James."

Sandy glanced at Margaret to see if she had heard what James said. Then she glanced back at her desk. Margaret let James leave and she raced over to Sandy's desk.

"Why are you taking care of his stuff so quickly? You are supposed to tell him it will take two to three weeks."

"Well he needed it right away." Replied Sandy.

"Sandy if you start doing things quickly for him, then he will come to expect it. We don't do nothing for Negroes fast. Also, you won't tell him when those packages come in." Margaret had a frown on her face.

"Right Margaret. It won't happen again."

"I will keep you posted on any changes in our plot. I will check with Frank now." Margaret walked out of the office.

Sandy went back to completing forms and filing paperwork. Her attempt had failed. But thank goodness it did, because Margaret would have let Frank know right away.

How would she warn James now? Perhaps she could write him a letter. No, that wouldn't work. He would be curious and might start asking questions to the wrong people about where the letter came from. Perhaps she could leave him a note on his car asking him not to tell anyone of the information he found out. No, that wouldn't work. What if she was spotted by someone in the office placing the note on his car? She could call him at home. No, that wouldn't work. She didn't want anyone, not even James, to know it was her who had called to warn him. Nooo, Sandy was going to have to wait her time and hope for an opportunity to reveal what was about to happen. The only problem was, James's time was short. The packages would be due in six months or less and James had no clue what he was in for. For the days to follow, James continued to put forth an excellent effort at his duties. Lee Roy continued to watch him and Frank persisted with his interrogation of Margaret on a weekly basis to make sure the schedule hadn't changed for the packages.

CHAPTER 53

Theola's Plan for the Children's Future

ach day, James would come home and find Theola sitting on the couch with a plate full of crackers before her. She always appeared pale in the face.

"Another bad day honey?" James kissed her on her forehead.

"This one is a little different than the last two. I wasn't as nauseated as I am with this one."

"Well babe, just be grateful it doesn't last the whole pregnancy. Where are the children?" Theola wiped her face with the towel on the coffee table.

"Marilyn is playing with her dolls and James Jr. is still asleep in his crib.

"Is dinner ready? I'm starved." James escorted Theola to the bed.

She sat gently on the side. "Yes dear, but it's only a few pieces of fried chicken. I've been too weak to stand on my feet and do a lot of cooking. The smell of food makes me sick."

"It's ok honey." James sat down at her bedside. He gazed at her pale face. "You lay down. I'll get little James and Marilyn something to eat." James stood up, and Theola leaned back against the pillow. James dropped the house shoes from her feet and placed her legs on the bed.

"Thank you baby. I really appreciate that." Theola closed her eyes. James leaned over to kiss her on the cheek. He sat back down on the bed beside her. He watched her for a long time. Theola felt his eyes upon her. She opened her eyes and saw his stare. "What is it honey? I know I look like a wreck. I'm sorry I'm not much help to you right now, but I feel sooo bad."

James smiled at her. He paused. "Theola this is our third child. I have watched you go through this twice before. I just want to say that I don't understand what you are going through or how you feel. But what I do know, is we have come through a lot together. And with each child, you have taken care of them and taken care of me. I am very appreciative of your efforts to maintain a household and keep me happy. You warm me like the sun warms the earth on a bright summer's day." James touched her hand. "You nourish me like a flower nurtures a bee in the summertime. I take from you. You take from me. Our strength becomes one and there is no weakness among us. Sweetheart as long as we have each other, nothing can pull us apart. Our love is forever."

"James that was sweet. Where did you get that from?"

"At night, sometimes when you are sleeping, I tried to read those nursery rhymes, but I couldn't get into them. So I read some of your college books on poetry and English literature to the children. It puts them right to sleep. I may not have memorized the words exactly right, but sweetheart, just looking at you this very moment brought some of those words to my heart. I love you Theola. I think even more now."

"I love you too James." James leaned over and placed a small loving kiss upon her lips.

"Can I get you anything while I prepare dinner for the children?"

"No sweetheart. I just need to let my stomach settle right now, but thank you anyway."

While James prepared the dinner, he yelled from the kitchen. "Ok Marilyn, come and get it."

Marilyn walked into the kitchen.

"Wake your brother so he can eat too."

Marilyn did an about-face and went to get James Jr. While on her way, Theola came out of the bedroom. "What are you doing out of bed mother?"

"Marilyn I'm alright. I'll get your brother. I feel like I'm placing it all on your father."

Theola slowly walked into the children's room. Marilyn followed. Theola kissed James Jr. on the cheek, trying not to startle her three-year-old. James Jr. woke slowly, batting his eyes, trying to focus them. He reached for his mother. Theola still felt nauseous, but she picked him up from his crib and carried him toward the kitchen. Marilyn followed. James had his back to them. He was warming food on the stove. Theola placed James Jr. in a chair. Marilyn sat in her usual place. James turned. To his surprise, Theola was standing there.

"Honey I told you to get some rest. I have the children."

"It was no problem dear. I decided to save you the trouble of bringing me anything. I'll join my family for dinner."

"Ok… but I think the smell of this food might be a bit much."

"I'm alright dear."

James fixed James Jr. and Marilyn's plates of fried chicken, mashed potatoes and gravy with string beans. He placed it before them. They waited until their mother and father were seated before they ate. James went back to the stove and got his fried chicken and a beer from the refrigerator. He placed them on his placemat.

"What will my sweetheart have since she decided to join us?"

"Just give me crackers and water."

"The Chef Special." James smiled. "On its way babe."

James went to the cabinets to get the crackers and a glass of water. He placed them before Theola. When James was seated, Theola said grace.

"Thank you heavenly Father for the food we are about to eat and the nourishment it gives our bodies. In Jesus' name, we pray. Amen."

Both the children said, "Amen."

James did not part his lips. They all began eating. Marilyn broke the silence with a conversation.

"Mom, I was looking at Marcus Welby on television today. He saved this little girl who got hit by a car. She had lots of internal injuries to her body. She was well before the TV show was over. I think I would like to help people like that."

Theola and James laughed. Theola took a bite of cracker and a sip of water. "Oh honey, that's just television. Nobody gets well that fast. But sure, you can grow up to be a doctor if you want to."

"Me too," stated James Jr., copying his sister and placing mashed potatoes in his mouth.

Marilyn took two bites of chicken.

"Honey, someday when you become a doctor…" spoke Theola to Marilyn.

"Stop filling her head with false dreams," interfered James with a beer in one hand and a fork in the other. "And you got James Jr. saying something he doesn't even know what he's talking about."

"How is she going to believe she can achieve it, if I don't tell her that she can?" Theola sipped on her water and chewed on more crackers. These items seemed to ease her discomfort.

"She doesn't need to hear stuff like that now. She's only five."

"Now couldn't be a better time James. I can get her focused on establishing herself as a strong individual in society."

James' tone of voice rose slightly. "You are going to end up getting her killed. Do you think times are going to be any different for her than they are for us right now?"

"Yes, they can be if I try and do something about the way society is while I'm here on this earth."

"You're just one woman with one voice that will never be heard!"

"Got damn it James!" yelled Theola.

James was in shock at the language she used. The children stopped eating and gazed at their mother.

He turned to the children. "Eat," spoke James, motioning with his fork. He glanced back at Theola. "No cursing in front of the children, remember? Did you forget your own rule? And you're getting excited."

The children continued to eat and spoke not a word.

Theola lowered her voice. "Excuse me babies. You're not supposed to curse. Mommy is sorry."

The children began eating again.

"James laws will never change if they aren't challenged. Don't you want to emerge from the shadows of blackness and stand as a leader for your race, for injustice?"

"Honey, I don't want to eee-merge, sub-merge, anything. I leave that to the Martin Luther Kings and the Malcolm Xs. I'm not a leader. All I want is my wife, my children, my beer and my fried chicken, and I'm a happy man."

"But dear, we can't drink at the same water fountain as whites. We can't eat in public restaurants. Don't you want your children in an environment equal to their white peers?"

"Just my beer and fried chicken." James took another sip of beer. "Aaaaaa… that feels good going down."

Theola was agitated by his words. "Don't you want them to get the same education as whites?"

"Beer and fried chicken." James continued eating.

"Don't you want them to be able to compete for the same jobs? To stand toe-to-toe with anybody on intellectual issues, morals and values regardless of race?"

James slammed his fist to the table. He stood from his chair and pointed at Theola. His action startled the children and Theola. James Jr. dropped his fork. Marilyn revealed a distressed expression upon her face.

James spoke loudly. "Why are you busting my eardrums? You're the one trying to be the lawyer. You! You're trying to make a difference. See how far you get. You are a woman of a black-Indian heritage. Let me see you make a difference in a world full of racism. Every door you try to open will slam in your face. You're a Negro woman Theola. After all we have been through, you should understand by now that we don't have privileges or rights. So don't try to tell these children that they do too. Nothing will change by the time they are our age, nothing. Now let me finish my dinner in peace!"

James sat back in his chair. He took another bite of chicken and washed it down with his beer. The children had finished their supper while their parents traded words.

Annoyed by his words and actions, Theola rose from the table. "I will make a difference!"

Theola picked up James Jr. and Marilyn followed. They walked toward the children's bedroom as the shouting had disturbed the evening. "I will make a difference!" Theola shouted aloud, addressing no one.

Marilyn noticed tears in her mother's eyes. On their way to the bedroom Theola stopped. She knelt down on her knees and held Marilyn and James Jr. tightly.

"I apologize sweethearts. Sometimes Daddy and I get into disagreements and we raise our voices. Sometimes he makes me so mad I can just scream. But we still love each other, like I love you." She kissed Marilyn and James Jr. on their cheeks.

Theola rose from the floor. They continued to the bedroom. While they took their clothes off, Theola started to run their bath water. When Marilyn had James Jr. undressed, she stood by her mother's side as she knelt down to check the water temperature so they could get in.

Marilyn whispered to her mother. "Mommy don't cry. I want to make a difference too."

Theola hugged Marilyn again. James Jr. sat down on the floor and took his socks off, which were the last pieces of clothing to go. He jumped in the tub on his own. He thrashed and played with a little rubber ducky that squeaked when squeezed. Marilyn left the bathroom. Theola finished bathing James Jr. When Theola was done, she placed him in the crib. James Jr. pulled the blanket to his neck. Marilyn passed her mother the book James Jr. loved so much. Marilyn went to take her bath. Theola began reading. Not long after a few stories, James Jr. quietly went to sleep. Marilyn finished her bath, came into the bedroom and jumped into bed. Theola knelt down beside her daughter and pulled the covers to her cheek.

"Marilyn I will always tell you the truth and positive things to help you along in life. If everyone decided to be complacent with the rules of the land, then the rules would never change. If I have anything to do with the law, I will do everything in my power to see that you don't have to go through the same crap your father and I have had to deal with. I will teach you to reach for your dreams and let nothing or anyone deter you from your goal."

Theola kissed Marilyn on the cheek and they said their goodnight prayer. Theola began to sing. Marilyn just looked at her mommy. She didn't understand a word she had said, but the love was there. That's all Marilyn needed. She gave her mommy a big hug. Theola kissed Marilyn again. She continued to sing until Marilyn's eyes slowly closed and she was sound asleep. Theola tucked her sheets tightly underneath the mattress and turned out the lights. She went back into the living room. James approached her.

"Why does it always take you two hours to put the children down?"

"Why are you asking me that? You know Marilyn likes songs and James Jr. likes nursery rhymes. Are you drunk?"

"Not yet. I just began reading them books of yours to them and they went right to sleep within minutes. I do that because of you."

"Me?"

"Yeah you. My Dad, he would say, "Go to sleep and I better not hear a peep out of you, unless you want my foot up your…""

"Yeah I know." She was still angry from dinner. So she went to sit on the couch. James followed.

"Theola my daddy always told me I would never be nothing or amount to anything."

"So you have to prove your father was right. You have to believe what he tells you?"

"Look around you Theola. You're crying and whining because people call you names. On the same note, you expect these same people who are racist to help make you a lawyer. I know I won't amount to anything because it's the way society is. Negroes don't get the good jobs… face it! Neither will you."

"I won't face it James! I wasn't raised that way. My parents have tried to instill in me self-confidence my whole life. They applauded my efforts in school and rewarded me with special privileges when I exceeded their expectations of me. I intend to do the same for our children. My life was meant to stand for something. And I don't intend to sit by and accept my circumstances because they exist. I can change the way things are."

"But it's the law Theola."

"And the law can be changed James. You watch… it will change. I'm not the only Negro person that feels this way. We must try to live in this land as equals. The Constitution says liberty and justice for all, not just some."

"How are you going to change a nation that doesn't live by those rules? Negroes don't count."

"Do you know how to cross a lake in a boat? One stroke at a time. You start with a town, a city, a state and then the nation."

"Yeah, yeah, keep on dreaming Theola. I'll keep facing reality."

James turned his back on her and went to the kitchen. When he returned to the living room, he had a beer in his hand and a piece of leftover chicken.

"I got all I need right here." James raised his beer and a chicken leg to Theola. "I'm going to finish this and go to bed. I'm not going to argue with you anymore. I have to get up early. Keep dreaming sweetheart. Someday your dreams may come true. Goodnight."

James took three bites, finished his chicken, gulped his beer bottle dry and headed for the bedroom.

"I won't give up James. I'm going to be a lawyer!" Theola plopped down on the sofa in thought of their argument. Tears formed in her eyes. "I'm going to be a lawyer."

CHAPTER 54

Good Friends at the Right Time

Six months later. Their third child was born. James was just as proud of another son as he was of the first. All was going well for James and Theola so far. Sarah had brought over some food and clothing for the baby. Skip was congratulating James while Nikki played on the living room floor. Suddenly, Sarah screamed from the kitchen. James and Skip dashed into the kitchen area only to find Sarah bent over, holding her stomach.

"Not in here!" yelled James. "Wait until we get to the hospital."

"I'll get the car," cried Skip.

"I'll walk her to the door," spoke James.

James and Sarah slowly made their way to the front door just as Skip was leaving tire marks on the pavement, making his way to pick her up. James slowly helped Sarah into the car.

"Can you watch Nikki until I get Sarah to the hospital? I'll come back and get her when I get her grandmother to babysit for me."

"Sure Skip."

"Hurry!" Sarah grunted. Skip whizzed off like lightning on a cloudy day to get Sarah to the hospital.

James smiled when he went back inside to check on Theola and the children.

"Theola, what a coincidence that you and Sarah got pregnant around the same time. Skip and I must have been thinking alike?"

"Yeah, that's what our little secret was. Sarah was pregnant at that time."

James ignored her comment and continued his discussion. "Theola can we give up on classes for a while until we are sure that we won't have any more babies?"

"Yes James. I have to admit a five-year-old, a three-year-old and a baby would be a strain on you to watch while I tried to go to school at night."

"Thank you for being understanding. That's why I love you."

"Why is that honey?"

"For being rational."

They kissed each other and James went to attend to the children. James waited by the phone after he had put the children to sleep. Hours passed. James figured the mother-in-law must have gone to the hospital rather than wanting to babysit. James and Theola fell asleep on the couch, waiting for the phone to ring. At midnight, they got a call that Sarah had a baby boy. With great delight, Theola and James rested well.

Chapter 55

Another Plot Unfolds

While Theola and James relaxed with their children and Nikki, Frank and Lee Roy concentrated on James's dismissal late that night. They had to think of something clever and flawless.

Four months later, the packages arrived. Margaret alerted Frank that Sandy had received the packages. Sandy and Margaret knew they were not to speak a word to anyone of the arrival of the packages. Frank, Ed, and Lee Roy grabbed the packages and placed them in a room for janitorial supplies only.

"Frank how long are we going to leave these packages here?" asked Ed. Sandy signed for them today. James is here today.

"We don't want him to see them at all," stated Lee Roy.

"What do you mean?" asked Ed.

"Follow my lead. When James goes home tonight, we are going to follow him." Stated Frank.

"Why?" questioned Ed.

"You'll see," said Frank.

Sandy's time had run out for alerting James to the plan of the others. She sat all morning trying to decide what to do.

When the afternoon came, quitting hour for James, he headed home. Frank, Lee Roy and Ed followed James home. They waited until dark to make their move.

"Lee Roy find a sharp object and puncture one tire to make it look like he got a flat normally. Ed get up under the hood and loosen some wires or something so the car won't start."

"Loosen what wires. I don't know anything about cars," spoke Ed.

"Alright Lee Roy. You do it. Ed you flatten a tire," spoke Frank.

"Ok," stated Lee Roy.

"But Frank, he won't be able to come to work tomorrow," stated Ed.

"Precisely gentlemen. James will miss his most important day at work for the first time. Now we go back to the office and place the packages in James's area."

"When the boss comes in, he sees the packages in James's area…" spoke Lee Roy.

"I think I'm beginning to see the picture," interrupted Ed.

All three men headed back to the post office that night.

"How do we get in?" asked Lee Roy.

"I have a key," stated Frank.

"You never told me you had a key," stated Ed.

"I didn't. I had Margaret help me make a copy of the boss's key to the office building. When she does the payroll checks, Robert gives her the keys to the safe, but all the keys to each door are on his key ring. So for a brief period of time, until she finishes the payroll, she has access to all the rooms in the building. Robert goes to lunch. I go see Margaret, get the key to the door, make an extra copy and Wal-la. I have a key to the front door."

"Wow! Frank. You really thought this out." stated Ed.

"Enough chatter. Let's get those boxes moved into James's area."

The men worked quietly through the night until their mission was complete.

CHAPTER 56

The Plot Thickens

The next morning, James called into work claiming his car had malfunctioned and he would not be in that day. Robert came through to inform Joe Jansen, realizing that Joe doesn't get in until eight. He spotted Frank in his office.

"Frank this is a little early for you to be here, isn't it?" asked Robert. "You normally start at eight, right?"

"Yes sir. I had a few things I wanted to get done before everybody got in this morning."

"I was looking for Joe, but I forgot he is an eight o'clocker too. "I'll just wait until he gets in."

"Is this something I can help you with Mr. Hunter? Or can I let Joe know what it is, so you won't have to chase him down when he gets in this morning?"

"Frank, James won't be in today. Have Joe get someone to take his place."

"Yes Mr. Hunter and what about those boxes in James's area. I noticed they had special markings on them. Is that something I should make Joe aware of when he informs the substitute to handle James's area?"

"What! What are you talking about Frank?"

"Do those boxes need some kind of special handling? They looked important."

"Let's look in James's area." Frank and Robert walked to James's workstation briskly. Robert opened the door quickly. He looked in and could not believe his eyes. "How long have these boxes been here? They had to have come in yesterday."

"Yes sir. That looks like the invoice on top." Frank walked over and picked up the invoice from the box. "They came in yesterday at 9:00 a.m. Mr. Hunter."

"What! Yesterday! And they aren't out of here?" Robert was furious. "Frank you take care of this personally. These boxes are to go to specific areas in the city as soon as possible. Get the boxes and deliver them personally. I'm not trusting the job to anyone else. You! You take care of it, now!"

"Yes sir." stated Frank with vigor.

Robert walked out of James's area in disbelief that the boxes had sat for an entire day and James had not moved them. This was the straw that broke the camel's back. James was not going to mess up any more mail deliveries.

When James came into work the next morning, he expected it to be no different than any other day. Frank greeted James at the door.

"A little early for you today, isn't it Frank?" asked James.

"The boss would like to see you James."

James had a little concern on his face, but he figured whatever the issue, he would make it up on another day for whoever had to cover for him. James headed straight for Robert Hunter's office. Mr. Hunter was filling out some paperwork when James entered the office. James knocked on the door.

"Come in James and have a seat." Mr. Hunter's tone seemed distant and callous. James felt a little uneasy.

"Frank said you wanted to see me. Mr. Hunter?"

"Close the door and have a seat James." James did so quickly.

"Do you remember about six months ago, I spoke with you about some very important boxes that needed to be delivered once they arrived on the premises?"

"Yes sir. I do. I have been looking out for them. Sandy was going to let me know when they arrived."

"Well, they arrived."

"Oh no! Don't tell me they arrived yesterday when I wasn't here?"

"No. According to the invoice, they arrived the day before yesterday when you were here and you didn't take care of them!"

"Oh no. Mr. Hunter. Before I left on Tuesday, no mail was left in my area. Let's ask Sandy."

"Stop trying to weasel out of it James. Frank looked at the invoice yesterday and it was dated Tuesday. The day you were here."

"There has to be some mistake Mr. Hunter. I wouldn't have let you down like that."

"That's what I thought too James." Mr. Hunter bowed his head. He reached for some papers on his desk. "James I don't know what has happened to you over the past few months, but whatever it is the post office can't afford mistakes like this. I gave you the benefit of the doubt last time, but this! This is totally unacceptable."

"No! Mr. Hunter."

"Yes James. I'm letting you go. Your work performance has slipped considerably and I will not let the post office lose its integrity behind your mishaps. Take these papers to administration. You're fired."

"Mr. Hunter. Just give me a chance to get to the bottom of this."

"What bottom? All you had to do was deliver the packages when they came in and you failed to do that. No James. Here are your release papers. Give these papers to Margaret on your way out. We will mail you your check for the days you have worked. I'm sorry it had to be this way."

"But…"

Mr. Hunter extended his hand to give James his release papers. James accepted them. He stared at Mr. Hunter in disbelief.

"Goodbye James."

"Mr. Hunter…"

"Goodbye James."

James was almost tearful. Before he left, he needed to know what happened in the course of a day. He went hurriedly to the clerk's office.

"Sandy, you were to log these Special Delivery packages in and let me know when they arrived. I was here on Tuesday. Why didn't I receive those packages? You knew I was waiting for them."

Sandy stood from her desk. She glanced from the corner of her eye to see if Margaret was looking. "Why, James, I don't know what you are talking about. You didn't tell me you were looking for any special packages."

"How can you stand there and say that? When just about every day for the past few months I asked you so many times, that you told me to stop bugging you. That was just a couple of weeks ago. You said when they come in you would let me know."

"That was so long ago, I don't remember." Sandy put her forefinger to her forehead and thought. "Well dang. I can barely remember what I ate yesterday, let alone, what I said months ago or a week ago." James was perplexed. He looked toward Margaret. Margaret kept her head buried in files that were on her desk. James walked over toward Rosalind.

"Rosalind, don't you remember I used to come in here every day and ask Sandy if any packages with special markings come in, to please let me know?"

Rosalind glanced over at Sandy. Sandy's face was blank, with no emotional expressions.

"No James. I'm like Margaret and Sandy. It's hard to remember what was said days ago. I'm sorry James. I just don't remember."

James soon realized that he was alone on this one. Disheartened, he dropped the papers on Sandy's desk and walked out the door scratching his head. Now he had the difficult task of telling Theola he was fired and they had nothing in the bank to see them through the next month.

CHAPTER 57

Breaking the Bad News to Theola

*T*wo hours later, after driving around and trying to figure out what had just happened to him, James went home. Theola was preparing the baby's lunch in the kitchen when she heard the door slam. Theola dashed to the living room, thinking James was home early to give her some great news, perhaps another bonus.

"James what are you doing home so early? They didn't decide you were the greatest husband in the world and let you off work today, did they?" Theola smiled. James appeared extremely depressed. Her smile soon dissipated. "What is it honey? Did something go wrong at work today?"

"Sit down Theola."

"Oooooh, I don't like the tone of that." Theola grabbed Philip from the crib and sat down on the living room couch.

"What is it honey?"

"I was fired today."

"FIRED!" She jumped up from the couch with Phillip in her arms. "For what reason?" Her scream startled Phillip. He started to cry. Theola bounced Phillip up and down in her arms and paced the floor. Marilyn walked in. James Jr. waddled his way to the living room door, following his sister.

"There were some special packages I was to deliver upon their arrival at the post office."

"And what happened? They arrived on the day you were off?"

"No honey. They came on the day I was there. Sandy signed for the packages and never told me they had arrived. I had been questioning her about them until finally, she told me to stop bugging her. She said she would let me know when they arrived. But today, she denied everything we had talked about. To make things worse, Margaret and Rosalind heard our conversations on different days and they denied ever hearing me speak to Sandy about the packages."

"I see." Theola began to pace the floor faster while she patted Phillip on the butt.

"What do you see?"

"James… someone set you up to fail."

"But why Theola. I have done nothing to hurt or mess with anybody. What did I do?"

"It's not what you did. It's what you have accomplished in the short time you have been there." James was baffled by her comment. "Put the pieces together. You don't hinder, harm, hurt, or destroy. You keep to yourself for the most part and you do your work very well. This was an act of envy. You've been promoted faster than others. You've been rewarded in other ways for your accomplishments. People are jealous of that."

"If what you say is true, then Margaret, Sandy, and others are in on getting rid of me."

"That's right. You said the boxes came in on a day you were there. That means Margaret, Sandy or Rosalind told someone that the boxes had arrived. Since you were there that day, it would have been a possibility that you could have come to the administrative office and noticed the packages there. So they couldn't take that chance. Someone had to move the boxes as soon as they arrived."

"You're probably right. It had to be some of the guys. The women aren't allowed in the working areas. What are we saying Theola?" James paused in deep thought. That would mean the whole post office conspired to get me fired." James thought once more. "My boss, Mr. Hunter, isn't like that."

"Your boss may not have known anything about what has just happened to you."

"Theola this all seems too hard to believe."

At that moment, the phone rings. Theola handed Phillip to James and answered it.

"Hello."

"Tell James I am sooo sorry about what happened today."

"Who is this?" asked Theola.

The phone went silent.

"Who was it?" asked James.

"Someone who knew what was going on today, because all they said was, *'I'm sorry.'* Do you know who that would have been?"

"Was it a female or male?"

"Female."

"There are only three of them, but it could have been any one of them. I don't really know. They all acted distant when I questioned them about the packages."

"Well James, let's suit."

"Suit! Suit what! We don't even know what we are talking about. We are just speculating what could have happened to me."

"Obviously, there is someone out there who does know what happened to you."

"And you think they are going to risk their position to get me my job back. Suit! I can't believe you said that. You got too much law on the brain.

You're not a lawyer. The only ones who are, are all white. Now which white lawyer do you think is going up against another white lawyer to represent a Negro man?"

"James we have to do something. What are we going to do for money? The bills aren't going to stop coming in because you were fired. We have to make them pay."

"Theola just stop. We haven't got anything to stand on."

"Yes we do. If we can find the '*I'm sorry*' person, we could go to court."

"My best bet is to try and find another job."

"Who's going to hire you after they find out what occurred at the post office?"

"In that case, we'd better pack and move. If we fight back, we'll lose and maybe not just the case, but my life."

"Why are you so negative James?"

"Realistic, baby, realistic. Because we get branded as disruptive Negroes trying to shake up the system."

"That's right James. So let me talk to some lawyers from names I have heard around town. See what our options are. It doesn't hurt to ask."

"I don't know Theola. It might hurt."

"Please honey. Let's try."

James said no more. Theola's mind was made up. This gave her a small chance to play lawyer even if she wasn't one. That evening, Theola fed the children and James. Once the children were asleep, James passed out in front of the television. Theola set her sights on the phone book and looked up the names of individuals she had heard in conversation at the college, who said that these lawyers believed in equality for all.

Chapter 58

A Good Lawyer

The next day, Theola set out to find an attorney. She got a name from Mrs. Fenceroy, who lived across the hall. That same name had been spoken at the college as well. She found John H. Trick in the phone book. He had helped some Negroes once before in a lawsuit. He was pretty liberal for their rights. Theola called bright and early that morning. He agreed to see her. Theola wasted no time in getting dressed. She went to his office that day.

"What can I do for you Miss Taylor?" asked Mr. Trick.

"Mr. Trick my husband was fired from the post office for an act he did not commit."

"What was it he supposedly did?"

"Poor job performance."

Trick laughed. "Mrs. Taylor, I fire people for poor job performance. You have to do better than that."

"He was framed."

"How so, Mrs. Taylor?"

"Someone tampered with the mail he was supposed to be handling and he got fired for the mail not being delivered."

"Tampering with the mail is a federal offense. That sounds a little far-fetched. Can you prove any of this?"

"There was a person that called James yesterday, about three hours after he got fired and apologized."

"Do you know who this person is?"

"No sir. We don't."

"Do you have anything that can corroborate what you just told me about a conspiracy of some kind amongst the people in the post office?"

"No sir, we don't, but…"

"Mrs. Taylor, what are you doing here? I work with facts and witnesses. Without those two things or at least one of them, you have nothing. Do you want me to go court against the United States Postal Service with ahhhhh… '*I heard, or I think?*' Mrs. Taylor. I would look like the laughing stock of the law field. My suggestion to you is to tell your husband to find another job."

"If you start an inquisition, you might be able to get them on racism?"

"On what basis? All you have is '*I heard*.' Unless you can find that person to testify in your husband's behalf, there is nothing I can do." Theola appeared rejected. "Mrs. Taylor…go home and tell your husband what I said. Good day."

"I was hoping that with your professional expertise in law and clout among the citizens of this town, you would assist us in revealing who the individual who called us was."

"Good day! Mrs. Taylor."

Frustrated, Theola spoke her mind. "You are supposed to be a spokesman for our civil rights, those guaranteed by the 13th and 14th amendments to the Constitution and by acts of Congress!"

"Good day! Mrs. Taylor."

Theola stood up. Visibly disappointed. "He's a professional at what he does. There was no reason for him to be fired. I'll find the woman who called and bring her to you."

"You do that Mrs. Taylor. Good-bye."

Stunned by his behavior after all she had heard about his battle against injustice for minorities, Theola walked from his office with nothing more to go on than when she walked in.

As Theola drove home, she was bewildered by her conversation with Mr. Trick. She knew with his reputation and efforts that he could have discovered the person who made the phone call. But without the indulgence of a legitimate lawyer to solve their issue, her persistence in finding justice would be futile. However, the principle of the situation warranted some kind of perseverance to resolve the injustice. She decided she would discuss it further with James that evening.

As Trick watched Theola walk from his office, deep in his heart, he felt Theola was probably right about her assumption of the situation. He also knew he had to make a call to the gray-haired old white man that James met on his first bus trip a few years ago. If Bladwell found out that Theola had been in his office, practicing law in Chicago for him, it would become non-existent. He would have to leave town as quickly as Theola and James would after Bladwell had his talk with them.

CHAPTER 59

The Surprise Visit

When Theola arrived at home from her visit with Mr. Trick, she found James asleep with Phillip on his chest and Marilyn and James Jr. watching television. She quietly walked into the kitchen to begin lunch. As the hours passed, lunch was eaten, television was watched and there was playtime with the children. As the sun settled in the west and darkness had just begun to fall, Theola had dismissed the situation for the day as she prepared for the evening dinner. When suddenly, there came an unexpected knock on Taylor's door.

"I got it honey." James walked to the door. Placed his hand on the knob. "Who is it?"

"It's the lawyer," spoke a voice from the hall.

James slowly cracked the door to take a peek outside. The moment he did, he was overwhelmed by the force of three men. James was pushed back into the living room, falling upon the couch and held there by two white men. Bladwell walked in behind the two men with a weapon in his hand.

"Where is your wife?" spoke Bladwell.

"She's in the kitchen."

"Call her." Bladwell stared James in the face.

"Theola can you come here please?" James spoke softly, not to startle her or frighten the children with a frantic voice. James held his eyes down.

"Just a minute dear. Let me turn my pots down."

"Now please, Theola."

"Dear, if you could wait a few minutes, I'm just about to call you for dinner. And if you could get Marilyn and James Jr. to wash their hands, we'll be ready to eat in five minutes."

Bladwell put a bat to James's head. "Get in here now!"

Theola rushed into the living room, wiping her hands with a dishtowel. "Honey, why the urgen… cy?" Theola slowed her pace upon entering the living room.

To her surprise, a bat was at James's temple. Two men had both his shoulders pressed against the couch. Marilyn and James Jr. walked in at the same time Theola did. They raced to her side and wrapped their arms around her waist. Everyone saw the children frightened. But Theola's attention remained on the intruders in her house.

"Mommy why are these bad men in our house?" Spoke Marilyn.

"Shhhhh… baby girl and do as I say." She quickly gave a waving motion to Marilyn with her hand to go back into the bedroom. "Take James Jr. and go."

Theola's eyes stayed focused on these men that held her husband hostage in her own home. Marilyn grabbed James Jr. by the arm and went back into the bedroom.

"Come over here Mrs. Taylor." Theola walked slowly to Bladwell. He still held the bat to James's head. "Stand him up boys, against the wall."

The two men grabbed James by the armpits, slung him against the wall and pinned him there. Bladwell walked toward Theola and faced her eye to eye. "I found out what happened to your husband. I heard you went to see a lawyer today."

"Yes sir. I did." Theola didn't bat an eye.

"Well niggers don't have any rights in this town. My suggestion to you, if you love your husband and your children too, is that you leave this town and don't come back if you value life on this earth."

Theola's expression of disbelief, fury and hatred was apparent.

She thought, *"If I only had a weapon in my hand."* "Before you niggas got here, some niggers like yourselves tried to claim racism and injustice on their job too. Trick tried to help them. But I had to put Trick in his place and them niggers too. You see if we let niggers think they have rights, then they might get some idea that they got total control over things that go on in this town. I don't want that to happen. You understand me?"

Theola didn't respond. She was in a trance as she continued to observe the men that held James captivate, while Bladwell delivered his speech on the inequality of rights for Negroes. James was in awe of Theola's silence. Bladwell turned and raised the bat to James's head.

"You understand me woman!" yelled Bladwell at Theola.

His motion immediately caught Theola's eye. "Yes sir. I understand." Her voice was firm.

"Now I want you to say niggers don't have any rights here. Say that," spoke Bladwell.

Theola peeked at James from the corner of her eye. James closed his eyes. He knew how she felt about injustice. That moment of silence seemed like an eternity to James. Bladwell patted the bat on top of James's head softly.

Theola tried to bring herself to say the words. "Nig… Ahhh…Nig…"

"Say it! I won't repeat myself again." Bladwell positioned himself like a baseball player, ready to bat right at James's head.

Reluctantly, gritting her teeth, she spoke quickly, "Niggers don't have any rights here."

"Say it again, louder."

Theola paused and glanced at James, quivering. She yelled, "Niggers don't have rights here!"

"Good." Bladwell returned to a normal stance. "Now you understand. Now you get your black assess out of this town by the end of the week. I don't want to ever see you here in my town again, understand?" Theola nodded.

"Yes sir!" spoke James abruptly and loudly.

Bladwell took the bat and swung just above James's head, placing a dent in the wall.

"Don't have a desire to come back or you'll be leaving town, not by car, bus, or plane. We got a place for niggers like you. If you don't want to see it, I suspect you will be gone by Friday."

Intense visual eye contact flowed through the room.

"Come on boys. I think they got the message."

The two men released James. Pushed him toward Theola and walked out. Bladwell followed with one last comment. "You two have a good night now." He raised the bat once more to their faces. "Those some nice-looking children you have there. Sure hope you want to see them grow up." Bladwell closed the door behind him. James hurried and locked it.

"Are you crazy! You looked him straight in the eyes when he was talking to you. And what took you so long to respond to that man's questions? He was threatening to have batting practice with my head!"

"I was trying to show how I truly felt. You know I hate to be intimidated."

"See what you started by trying to get justice done. There is no justice if you're a Negro. Let's get the children and start packing."

"James...he said we had until Friday. Today is Tuesday."

"As far as I am concerned, tomorrow is Friday. I'm not waiting Theola. We'll pack tonight. In the morning, I will draw all the money we have from the bank, close our accounts, cancel the mail and tell the landlord goodbye. I am sure he will understand."

"James…"

"Don't James me. You and your lawyer crap! Look where the law has gotten us now. They could have hurt our children Theola. I'm not willing to risk my children for my pride, are you?" angrily spoken by James.

Theola sighed. "No James. You're right."

"You pack. I'll make a list of the things I need to get done tomorrow."

Theola was still furious. "Then we've been defeated James without any effort to resolve our situation."

"Your intolerance for injustice is going to get us all killed." James walked up to Theola. Placed both hands on her shoulders and gazed into her eyes. "How can we fight when our children are threatened too? We have to think of the children Theola."

"I don't want to leave without trying and let our children think that things are handled by running away."

"Theola our children aren't old enough to think. They barely know how old they are. They won't remember a thing. And besides, I would like to watch them grow up to be able to think, if that's ok with you?"

Discouraged, Theola frowned at James. "I'll start packing after we have had dinner." Theola marched off to the kitchen.

"Good."

Feeling humiliated and frightened, the Taylors ate quickly, packed and prepared to move, in that order.

Chapter 60

Sandy's Conscious

hile the Taylor family prepared for a speedy departure from Chicago, Illinois, Sandy was on her way to Robert Hunter's home. When she arrived, she had tears in her eyes.

She rang the doorbell at eight o'clock that night.

"Sandy, what are you doing here?"

"Please forgive me Mr. Hunter for coming over so late."

"Please come in." Sandy walked in with a handkerchief in one hand and a piece of paper in the other.

"What can I do for you?"

"Mr. Hunter, James didn't let you down. Frank, Lee Roy, Ed and Margaret all conspired to get rid of James."

"Ohhhh Sandy." Hunter sighed. "I should have known that James wouldn't have let me down. Why are you telling me this now? I can't reverse what I did yesterday. I would have nothing to base it on."

"Yes you would." Sandy presented the invoice from the office.

"This piece of paper is the invoice that actually came into the office. It shows the time of delivery. It was just after nine. James was in that day. But Frank and others hid the packages and I allowed it."

"Why didn't you warn James discreetly, if you didn't want to tell me about the conspiracy?"

"Because they are all racist and wanted to see James fired. If James found out, it would have been one of us who knew the plan that told. I didn't have the courage to let him know the packages were there." sniffled Sandy.

"Even so, what do you want me to do now?"

"You can give James his job back and tell the others you know what they did."

"And how do you think I would have found out the information? You would put your reputation on the line for James?"

"Yes Mr. Hunter. My conscience is tearing me apart. I couldn't think of anything else all day. I feel awful."

"Sandy you wouldn't be able to work in that office if they found out that you told me the truth. They would make your life unbearable. As much as I liked and respected James, the only thing we can do for him now is apologize. All I can suggest is to make your piece with James and let it go."

"You don't understand Mr. Hunter. I knew about the frame up six months ago and I said nothing for fear of my job and my reputation."

"Six months!" Hunter was shocked. "Why didn't you tell me then? Why didn't you alert James?" Sandy just bowed her head. "Then, I may have been able to prevent what has just taken place, but now… I'm sorry Sandy. There is nothing you or I can do at this point."

Sandy wiped her eyes with her handkerchief. "Is there nothing we can do Mr. Hunter?"

"Nothing Sandy. Call James tomorrow and apologize."

Sandy nodded slowly, walked out the front door and said nothing more. She drove home with tears streaming down her cheeks. Mr. Hunter's suspicions were now confirmed, but too little, too late. He watched Sandy drive away, only to know without a doubt that James was an innocent man.

Chapter 61

Where Will We Go?

James awoke early the next morning. He sat alone at the kitchen table, pondering his situation. Where would he lead his family now? How would he take care of them without a job and nowhere to turn? These were questions James had no answers to. He knew he had to just take whatever came his way. At that moment, he heard Phillip cry. Theola woke up. She noticed James wasn't beside her. She walked toward the children's room and noticed the light in the kitchen. With Phillip in her arms, she walked into the kitchen and noticed James with a beer in his hand and his head bowed.

"Honey, why are you up so early? The bank doesn't open for three or four hours?"

"I couldn't sleep."

"Why the beer?"

"It helps me think."

Theola didn't push the issue of the beer after what they had gone through. "Don't worry honey. I prayed before I went to sleep last night. God will provide a way for our survival."

"You keep on praying. I'll keep on worrying."

Theola took a bottle from the refrigerator to warm it up. "Honey, God has brought us this far."

"Yeah, yeah. I'm going to get dressed. I want to get some other things done and get to the bank before it opens and it gets crowded." James didn't want to hear it. Theola felt his pain, but there was nothing that James wanted to listen to that would ease the hurt. Theola fed Phillip, burped him and went back to bed. James got dressed, left the family asleep and drove out to Sarah and Skip's house. He found a piece of paper and a pen in the glove compartment and wrote them a note, thanking them for all they had done. He left the note in their mailbox. He drove around the countryside that morning, thinking of his dilemma until the bank opened. He retrieved his funds, bought tickets to Denver and came home. James found Theola fixing breakfast, but the children were still asleep.

"Honey our money bought us tickets to Denver, Colorado."

"I don't want to go to Denver."

James ignored the comment. "You feed the children. I'll pack the car with our bags and we'll be gone after breakfast. I've made arrangements with the landlord to have our furniture and things shipped when I call with a new address, since we still have two weeks before we actually have to be out of the apartment. Our mail is to be sent to Mrs. Fenceroy's address. I asked her this morning if she would be kind enough to hold it until we get settled. We will send her our new address so she can forward our mail. So I think I have covered everything? Ohhh, I gave the car to Mrs. Fenceroy. She said her grandson can use it to drive her to the store when she needs to go. She said she'll mail us fifty dollars for it when we let her know our address. Her grandson will pick it up at the station later today. I'm leaving the key under the visor."

Theola stood at the stove and cried. "I love it here."

"We'll make new friends Theola. Don't make this any harder than what it is."

Breakfast was eaten by all. Theola cleaned the kitchen and packed what was left of the dishes. They placed the children in the car and all sat quietly until they reached the train station. Their next stop, Denver Colorado.

CHAPTER 62

Sandy's Dilemma

S andy came by James's apartment later that morning. She knocked several times before Mrs. Fenceroy came to her door.

"You missed them by about two hours honey."

Sandy stepped from James's door and went to speak to the old lady. "Do you know where they went? I have a check for Mr. Taylor."

"Well I don't know for sure. But they promised when they got where they were going, they would give me their new address. You can leave that check with me. I will see that he gets it."

"Oh no ma'am. I must deliver it personally to him or I could be fired."

"If you want to wait, check with me in about a month or so. I should have an address."

"Yes ma'am."

Sandy walked away, depressed from not being able to explain to James what happened to him.

Chapter 63

Perseverance

Sandy's depression was nothing compared to what James was feeling. His family was now in uncharted territory. It was different when it was just the two of them with nowhere to go, but now they had children to consider.

They rode the rails for hours until they arrived at Denver's train station. Again, they were in a new city with no friends to think of. They got an apartment with the money James withdrew from the bank. James searched the city to find employment, day after day, for two weeks. It didn't matter how much a job paid, just as long as it paid. Soon, his diligence landed him work. He performed hard labor in a warehouse on the weekends and worked as a janitor in a grocery store during the week.

One night James came home early. Marilyn was there to greet him at the door.

"Daddy we don't get to see you as much."

James picked Marilyn up when he walked through the door. He gave her a huge kiss on her forehead and put her back on the floor.

"Honey, Daddy has to make sure his babies are well fed and that includes Mommy."

Marilyn and Theola both smiled.

"What's for dinner? I'm starved."

As Theola prepared supper, James grabbed a beer and sat at the kitchen table. "Babe you are working two jobs non-stop from Monday through Sunday." James took a swig of beer. "The stress of the work is going to take its toll on your body."

"And just what do you suggest I do Theola? We still have a child who needs baby clothes. I hear you, but if you have a better idea, let's hear it."

"What if we could secretly find out who the *I'm sorry* person is? Then we…"

"Drop it Theola! What part of *'I promised to kill you all'* did you not understand? That means the children too. So drop it."

Theola sat down. She rested her elbows on the kitchen table and intermingled her fingers. Lovingly, she said, "What if I get a job James?"

He gave an appearance of disbelief, "And do what with the children Theola? I rather feel comfortable with you taking care of them than some stranger."

Theola didn't argue. She leaned back in her chair. "Alright then, why don't you put in for a job at the post office? You have experience. There is no way they could find out what happened in Chicago."

James thought, "Perhaps you have a point. Two jobs are wearing me thin. I'll go tomorrow and get an application."

James got up early that next morning, reported to the grocery store. He asked to be released to run an errand. He went to the post office and filled out an application. James waited for thirty days. Feeling his efforts were futile, he had given up on the post office.

The very next day, Theola had a letter from the postal service. She stood at the door waiting for James to walk through on schedule. When he did, she opened the letter and to his surprise, he was accepted.

Theola was delighted. "See honey, I told you and I prayed very hard."

"Yes! I get to start in a week. I guess I'll turn the store job loose and keep the weekend warehouse job until we can get enough money to have a savings account."

"And I go back to college."

James sighed. "Yeah, but after we get a bigger apartment."

Theola agreed and was delighted James didn't try to discourage her.

Chapter 64

A Joyful Moment

For two years, all went well. James finally had a small savings account and they moved from a one-bedroom to a two-bedroom apartment. James worked well with the people at the post office. The job handed him incentive awards for outstanding performances of jobs well done.

"Theola I feel we are finally back on our feet again."

"God answered my prayer."

"Let's do something special tonight. Let's take the kids for an ice cream after dinner and a walk through the park."

"That sounds sweet. Let's do that."

All was well with the Taylors. Money was good. The family was happy. That evening, the children enjoyed an ice cream, had their bath and were sung to sleep. They were kissed, hugged and baby powdered. They fell asleep with ease.

"Hey, can I be tucked into bed tonight?" asked James.

"Anytime sweetheart, anytime."

James walked up to Theola and kissed her hand. He set the mood music with a little Barry White. They danced to a slow jam and embraced each other with loving care. They waltzed into the bedroom and rolled back the sheets. James leaped into bed and Theola gently eased under the covers.

"James I'm a little nervous."

"Nervous? Why Mrs. Taylor, I assure you I will be gentle."

"That's not what I mean?"

"What?"

"It's been two years and we haven't gotten pregnant."

"Let's keep it that way."

"Well don't you think we are due?"

"Stop talking about having more children, babe. We already have enough. Let's just have some fun."

James quieted Theola with sweet gentle kisses upon her cheeks and shoulders. She quickly surrendered her body and fell into his embrace. Soon all lights were out and the evening would be a memory.

Chapter 65

An Unexpected Visitor

That Saturday morning, Phillip had climbed from his crib only to crawl into bed with his parents. They felt the pressure of the added weight on their feet and they both looked to the bottom of the bed. There, Phillip laid with bright eyes, a thumb in his mouth and a smile on his face.

"I hungee mommy."

Theola reached for Phillip and placed him between them. She kissed Phillip on the forehead and laid him beside James.

"Let's feed your tummy sweetheart. Breakfast will be ready soon." Theola threw the covers back from her body and went to prepare breakfast.

At the table… "Honey, last night I felt something that felt like a knot on the side of your breast?"

"Which side honey?"

"The left side of your left breast."

Theola felt there. "You're right dear. It's just a little bump. It's nothing."

"You might want to check that out with the doctor. We do have insurance now."

Theola nodded. Nonchalant about the doctor, Theola had a deeper agenda on her mind. "Phillip is two years old dear. Our finances are back on the plus side."

"Soooo…" remarked James.

"Can I begin some college courses again?"

"Honey are you sitting at the same table where I'm sitting? Look around you." James stared at each one of the children. "They still need shoes, clothes and food. James Jr. is just four. He eats more than Marilyn and Phillip combined. No, honey. Not just yet. Let's see how our finances are in another year and then we'll talk again about college."

"But James, it's been two years since I have seen a college professor. I don't want to get out of the habit of studying and writing papers. Reading books on my own is not going to give me the challenge and experience of the professionals who have been in the courtroom."

"Theola I don't want you to lose sight of your goal, but I don't want to put us under a strain right now. True, our money situation is better. However, when I am able to give that warehouse job up on the weekends and our finances are better than they are now, then college will definitely be a consideration."

"Alright dear. I guess one more year won't hurt and Phillip will be three and out of diapers."

"That's my girl Theola. That's why I love you. You are so logical."

Theola gave a sarcastic smile.

At that moment, there was a knock on the door. "Are you expecting anyone this morning?" asked James.

"Not at eleven o'clock."

James got up from the table to answer the door. "Ohhhh my gosh!" He yelled.

"Who is it dear?"

"It's Sandy from Chicago. My old post office dear!" Sandy stood with her head bowed, holding a package in her hand. "Sandy what are you doing here? It's been a couple of years. I thought everybody hated me from back there."

Theola came from the kitchen to the living room. When she saw Sandy, she knew. "You're the person who said, *'I'm sorry'* on the phone. Aren't you?"

"How did you guess?" asked Sandy.

"There is no reason for you to travel the distance you did just to deliver our mail," stated Theola.

Sandy handed James the package. "Your back pay is in there."

"Come in. Have a seat. We were just finishing breakfast," insisted Theola.

"Thanks for the offer. But I don't want to disturb you. I am sorry it's taken me over two years to do this. I kept thinking you were going to hate me after you knew that I knew about the conspiracy against you and did nothing to prevent it. But my conscience got the better of me. I just came to apologize to you James and you, Mrs. Taylor for not being more help than I was. Mr. Hunter didn't know anything until after the fact. So that's all I have to say. I'm glad to see you are back on your feet."

"Well thank you Sandy. I appreciate you telling me this."

"I was afraid of what would happen to me if I tried to warn you James."

"Say no more," said Theola. "We understand. It's in the past now. Let's forgive and forget."

Sandy reached for Theola and hugged her. She also hugged James.

"I have to get back. No one knows I came up here, but Mr. Hunter. There is a letter in there from him. Good Luck to you all."

James opened the door. Sandy left with a load off her shoulders. "Well how about that honey? It was Sandy who called."

"Yes. It was very nice of her to deliver the mail in person. It must have been really troubling her for her to come this far."

James quickly opened the mail. "I didn't think they would have sent a check since I was railroaded out of there." He ripped the envelope that contained his back pay and a message from Mr. Hunter. James looked at the check and handed Theola the letter from Mr.Hunter. "Wow, honey, they actually gave me my full two weeks' pay. What did Mr. Hunter say?"

"It says..." Theola began to read.

> Dear James,
>
> I want you to know you are one of the best workers I ever had. Under the circumstances, I did to you what I would have done to any worker who was not performing up to standards. Unfortunately, I found out too late about your situation in order to prevent the outcome. Sandy explained what happened. I knew you were better than what appeared on the surface. But there was no evidence to disprove that your mishaps weren't your own fault. Unfortunately, we live in a society of jealousy and prejudice. The only thing I can say to you now is that I'm sorry and good luck.
>
> Sincerely, Robert Hunter."

"He sounds like a nice guy James."

"Theola he was every bit of a fair man. I'm sure that's why my check is correct."

"I wonder how Sandy found us."

"Good question honey. I was so surprised to see her, that I didn't think to ask. Let's let dead bugs lie."

They were both grateful they knew the truth. Now it was time to move forward.

CHAPTER 66

Can You Count?

The Taylor family's good fortune continued for another eight weeks. James came home from work one day only to find the children in front of the bathroom door. He heard moans of intense pain. As he made his way through the living room and squeezed through the barricade of children at the bathroom door, James saw an all too familiar sight.

James rubbed his eyes to focus on Theola. Then he sighed. "Tell me I'm dreaming baby." Theola was kneeling before the toilet. "Tell me it's the flu honey."

Theola raised her head. Sweat dripped from her brow. Her hair was everywhere. The armpits of her dress displayed extreme perspiration that had overwhelmed her body. "Ahhhh…"

"Tell me this isn't happening Theola."

Theola tried to push herself up from the floor. James grabbed her from behind and pulled her up to her feet. Unable to stand, James closed the toilet cover and let Theola sit down.

"Children leave us. Go into your room and play."

Marilyn led the way, James Jr. followed and Phillip waddled after him.

James got Theola a cool towel and placed it on her forehead. "Theola this will make our fourth child if this is not the flu."

Theola felt tension from James. She said not a word. She staggered into their bedroom and lay in the bed with her back against the headboard. Her head was drooped down against her chest. James had followed.

"Theola…"

She raised her head slightly from her chest. "James don't talk to me right now. Give me a little time to regroup. Then we will talk."

James sighed and went into the living room where the children were. They were playing quietly, rolling a little ball at each other. James smiled, went into the kitchen and grabbed a beer out of the refrigerator. He went back to the bedroom. Theola had quietly went to sleep. Hearing laughter, he went into the living room and sat down on the couch. He finished his beer while watching the children play. He soon joins them, rolling around on the floor. Finally, Theola slowly walked past them to the kitchen. James followed.

"Now can we talk?"

Theola's eyes were watery and red. She made every move in slow motion. "No. Not now." Theola rattled some pots and pans to make dinner.

James walked over to her and grabbed the pots and pans from her hands. "I'll fix some wieners and chili. You go and lay back down. I'll be in later and we'll talk."

Still feeling nauseous, Theola agreed. After dinner, he sent the children to the living room to watch television while he went to talk to mommy.

"Theola," James spoke softly. Theola sat up in the bed resting her back against the backboard. She had prepared herself for his harsh words. "Theola."

"Yes dear."

"I want you to go see the doctor tomorrow to confirm our suspicions."

"Ok."

"If you are pregnant…" James began.

Theola interrupted. "I don't want to hear you say anything about getting rid of this child. You're not hurting for cash right now. In fact, you just got a check from the old post office. And if you say anything negative about…"

James put his hand to her lips to quiet her. "Theola. I just want to say if you are pregnant, I couldn't be happier." Theola was shocked. "Don't look so surprised. While you were lying across the bed, I enjoyed the company of our three children. We played so beautifully together. I'm proud of our family. Having children with you has turned into a joy. I love you and with two sons and a daughter, all I want is a healthy baby."

Theola couldn't believe her ears. A smile came to her cheeks. She was ready for a fight. She had planned what she was going to say. But James's words made her forget the rest of her speech. "Ohhhh James. Do you really mean what you just said?"

"With all my heart. I love you woman and I love our children. I am indeed a lucky man."

Theola leaned to embrace James. She kissed him passionately.

"But of course, you know this means there will be no college courses until our newborn is at least two years old?"

"Of course darling."

Theola was happy and sad all at the same time. No college courses meant more time away from her own family she so dearly wanted to be reunited with, especially her father.

James went into the living room and got the children. He gave them baths and prepared them for bed while Theola rested. At midnight, Theola felt depressed about her college situation. She didn't want to lie down for the remainder of the night, just yet. When James went to sleep, Theola went into the living room and dialed her sister.

"Konee I'm pregnant. Now I have to wait again for my college career to get started."

Awakened from her sleep, Konee wasn't sure whom she was speaking to. "Do you know what time it is? Who is this?"

"I'm pregnant!" screamed Theola softly, not wanting to wake James or the children.

Konee soon realized she had the phone in her hand. "Theola? Is that you?" Konee, still groggy, "Theola are you sure you're pregnant. How many will this make?"

"Can you count? I have three already. What do you think about four?"

"Then the only thing I can say. He is a blessed child to have a mother like you, goodnight." Theola felt better after she hung up the phone and slept well.

The next morning, Theola and the children headed toward the doctor's office, where James escorted them. Their suspicions of pregnancy were true. While the Taylor Family celebrated their upcoming new birth, things were not quite as peaceful in Chicago.

Chapter 67

Where Is James?

One day, Sandy checked the phone book for Mrs. Fenceroy's phone number and wrote it on a notepad. Sandy called her. That day, Margaret overheard the conversation between Mrs. Fenceroy and Sandy on the phone that morning when she was coming back from lunch and hadn't quite made it to her desk. Margaret stood in the hallway and listened to the conversation. Margaret entered the room and pretended not to be disturbed by what she heard. When Sandy stepped away from her desk, Margaret extracted the phone number from the notepad. She wanted to immediately inform Frank, but he wasn't there that day. She hid the information in her purse and forgot to tell Frank.

Days later, one early morning, Rosalind asked Margaret for some lotion and she had to take everything out of her purse to find it. When she gave the lotion to Rosalind and started putting things back in her purse, she noticed the note. Immediately she buzzed Frank to her office.

"What is it Margaret? I'm busy."

"Frank, Sandy went to see James. That little bitch. I suspected she was a nigger lover."

"James has been gone for quite some time. How do you know that? How did she find out where he went?"

"James was having his mail forwarded to some woman named Fenceroy where he used to live."

"How do you know all this?"

"I overheard Sandy talking to the lady on the phone one day."

"But why would Sandy go and visit him?"

"Perhaps that's a question you should ask her. I overheard some of their conversation. Maybe she intends to help James in some way?"

"Not after two years have passed. There is nothing James can do now, even with Sandy's help."

"Do you want to take that chance?"

Frank pondered the question. "Perhaps not Margaret. See if you can find out from Sandy where James is living and what he is doing and I'll take it from there."

"Alright Frank honey. But it'll cost you."

"You just name it my love and it's yours."

"Let me find out the information for you and I'll think about what I want."

"You do that. But don't let Sandy realize what you are trying to do. I don't want her to alert James to the fact that we know where he is."

Margaret went back to her desk. She sat down and typed a letter to James's old address. She got Frank to stamp it in the post office as received. She held the letter in her hand to show Sandy when she got back from lunch.

"Sandy, I sure wish I knew where James went so I can forward his mail to him? That way I could make sure he got it?"

Puzzled at her comment, since she was a racist, Sandy didn't let her have James's address. "I'll just put it in the mail bin. It will get forwarded."

"Alright honey."

Margaret handed the letter to Sandy. Sandy scratched the old address off and placed Mrs. Fenceroy's address on the envelope. She took it down the hall and placed it in the mail carrier bag.

Margaret alerted Frank of Sandy's actions. Frank went down the hall to get the letter. He saw Mrs. Fenceroy's address. Frank took a large envelope that had bold letters Special Delivery on it and placed the letter inside. He drove to Mrs. Fenceroy's apartment. He knocked at her door. Mrs. Fenceroy saw Frank dressed in his mailman's uniform.

"Ma'am, I have a special delivery for James Paul Taylor."

He flashed the envelope before her eyes with the letters, Special Delivery on it. He handed her the envelope.

"Is he here?" She noticed it was addressed to James's old address.

"No he is not. He moved years ago. But I will take it for him." Mrs. Fenceroy turned to close the door and put the envelope away. Before she could make a complete turn, Frank pulled the envelope back from her hands.

"Ohhhh no ma'am. Special deliveries must be signed for by the individual that the package is addressed to."

She thought for a moment. This could be something important to them. "Hold on sonny, let me get my glasses and I'll write the address down for you so you can send it to him directly."

He stood at the door and waited. Moments later, Mrs. Fenceroy came back with a piece of paper that had the Taylor's new address on it. "Here you are young man."

Frank took the piece of paper and placed it in his pocket. "Thank you ma'am. Mr. Taylor will be most grateful for your assistance."

When he was outside the apartment building, he threw the special delivery package in the trash bin next to the building and walked to the mail truck with a smirk on his face.

Chapter 68

The Payback

rank didn't waste any time. When he arrived back at the post office, he went through his rolodex. He immediately called an old friend at the post office in Denver that same day.

"Dan, hey, you got a Negro man by the name of James Paul Taylor working for you?"

"Yeah buddy. I sure do. He's one of the best workers I have ever had and he is quick at delivering the mail. What about him?"

"I want you to fire him."

"What? What for?"

"We let him go down here because of poor work performance. Did he tell you he used to work for us?"

"Yes. I called your boss. He gave him great honors. So far, I have to say he has lived up to what your boss has told me."

"Well that is why he got fired down here, poor job performance. Our boss has a soft spot for niggers, but we don't, do we Dan?"

"Well Frank, he is doing a great job up here. I want to keep him."

"You don't get it Dan. I helped him get fired. Me and some of the other workers here wanted him out. He was getting better assignments and cash incentives, but the rest of us weren't. He was just one too many niggers in our organization."

"So you railroaded him out?"

"And I want you to do the same. Don't just fire him for any reason. His wife tried to get a lawyer and suit, but we had documented evidence of poor work performance."

"So you want me to help him along like you did?"

"Now you're getting the picture. Over the course of a year or so, his performance seems less than adequate. That way, he doesn't have anything to come back with you on and it looks like everything is his entire fault."

"Why should I do this Frank?"

Frank's tone of voice rose slightly, "Hey man, he is a nigger for one thing . That should be good enough. But if not, I don't like him and you will do me a favor. Plus, if you do this for me I will owe you one. Now keep me informed. Let me know when you have fired him."

Dan thought for a moment. "Alright Frank. But don't ever call me with something this shady again?"

"Ok buddy. You got it."

Reluctantly, Dan was contemplating some ways of discrediting James at the post office. Several months passed. Theola had their fourth child. A beautiful baby girl named Alesha Renee. James was excited. He let everyone at work know of his newborn. Dan found it even harder to pursue such wrongful actions.

Months passed. Frank called Dan to see how things were going.

"It's been a while since I spoke with you. Have you started the issues with James yet?"

"Not yet?"

"What are you waiting for? Get on with it Dan!"

"Yeah, yeah. I'll start tomorrow."

"That's what I want to hear." Frank hung up.

Dan had the mail delivered late by another worker to James. James had to start his route later than normal on that day. Daniel was working in his office and knew James would be leaving late. He saw James with his mailbag.

"James. Why are you leaving the post office late with your mail?"

"Sir, I…"

"Don't give me any excuses. Get out and get it done! This will be noted on your evaluation."

"But…"

"Now move! Before you're even later."

James hurried with his mail to make his deliveries. Dan's demeanor was a complete mystery to James. He pondered the whole incident while walking his mail route. Later that evening, he alerted Theola to Dan's impulsive actions when he came home that day.

"How was work honey?" Theola was sitting on the sofa, breastfeeding their newborn, Alesha.

"Something strange happened today at work."

"What dear?"

"The mail came to me late for the first time in over three years and Dan jumped all over me without letting me give him any explanation as to what happened. All he said was, this will be noted on your evaluation."

"That is strange for Dan, isn't it?"

"Yeah." James left Theola to get a beer from the kitchen. He came back to the living room and kissed the baby and Theola.

"Dan seemed so kind giving you a couple of Christmas bonuses and giving you praise for work well done." Theola thought for a moment. "Honey I would keep my eyes open if I were you."

"Why do you say that?" James swallowed a gulp of beer.

"Just remember what happened to you in Chicago. Each mishap that occurred at work was not your fault, yet you were blamed."

"True."

James sipped some more beer and placed his bottle on the end table. Theola passed Alesha to James so he could burp her.

"I'll go warm up dinner."

"Where are my other little precious angels?"

"They are in their room playing."

Theola walked toward the kitchen. They thought no more of what took place that day. After dinner, the kids were down. The evening was young. James started a Luther Vandross record, while Theola finished the dishes. James had just finished his fifth beer when Theola came to the living room. He grabbed her by the waist and they danced the evening away.

Chapter 69

The Boot

James had a wonderful evening with Theola. He slept well. When morning came, he dressed quietly. He kissed Theola on the cheek and woke her ever so gently.

"Honey last night I felt that knot again on the side of your breast. That lump wasn't that big a few months ago."

Sleepy and incoherent, "Yeah I know. I felt it too." Theola yawned. "I'll get it checked out."

James left and reported to work on another routine day. He had forgotten all about what had taken place yesterday, but Dan had a surprise waiting for him that morning.

"James I left this package for you to deliver to Mr. Fairbanks's house yesterday afternoon."

"Excuse me?" perplexed by Dan's actions. "Sir, I only saw you twice yesterday. Once in passing in the hall that morning and that evening when you asked me about the mail being late. I didn't see any package in my mailroom that didn't get delivered. I mailed everything."

"James now you are calling me a liar!"

"No sir." James was dismayed once again.

"James you're fired!"

"What! Wait a minute Mr. Dan. I have always done what you wanted me to do when you wanted it done. I do my very best to ensure things are correct and in order. Don't do this Mr. Dan. I have a little one that is just turning a year. She is still in diapers. I don't understand?"

"Understand this, fired! And tell your wife don't go searching for lawyers if she knows what is good for you and your family." James was speechless at the remark. "Pick up your paycheck for what's owed to you, next week."

James just shook his head. He realized that, somehow, Mr. Dan had prior knowledge of the incident in Chicago. On his way out the door, James replied, "Mr. Dan, this just isn't fair."

Dan's expression was stern but deep in his heart, he felt the pain. "Tell your wife to stop treading where she or you don't belong. I mean that honestly James, if you want to survive in this world." James nodded and left the building. He went home and gave Theola the news.

"Honey I got the boot."

"The boot? What does that mean?"

"I got kicked in the rear end again."

"What! You mean fired!" James nodded. "This time we are not going to take it lying down James! We do have some rights and I'm going to find out what they are!"

"Theola calm down."

"James, Marilyn likes her school here. I have good Christian friends and good neighbors here. They have beautiful surroundings and nature parks where I can take the children during the day. Our life is good James! Why is all of this happening?"

"I think our friends in Chicago had a little to do with this Theola."

"How do you know that James?"

"Let's just say I know."

"Well I'm going to find out what our rights are."

"Theola the last time you went to a lawyer, you know what happened and Dan warned me, to warn you, not to do that."

"So that's how they know. Someone in Chicago got to Dan." Theola sighed and paced the floor. A terrifying expression creped upon her face, almost like she wanted to hurt someone. "James do you think it was Sandy?"

"Oh no, not at all. You remember her expression of regret. Not Sandy."

"Then who?"

"It doesn't really matter now Theola. Even if we knew who, there's nothing we could do about it now."

"What are we supposed to do?"

"Move on sweetheart, move on."

Theola was furious as tear drops lined her cheeks. "Where? Where James? Just where are we supposed to move to?"

"I don't know Theola, but we survived the first move. We can survive another one. And besides, we are a little better off than last time. Our money situation isn't quite as bad as it was when we left Illinois."

Theola shook her head. "We are just supposed to keep taking the abuse and move on, huh?" Theola sniffled and wiped the tears from her eyes. "If I were just a little bit of a lawyer, I would…" mumbled Theola, walking away from James.

James spoke not another word. He knew if he continued to answer, her anger would only escalate. He walked away from her and began making a list of the things that needed to be done. James waited on his check from the post office and alerted the landlord of their need to depart in a month. He sold what furniture they had. After several days had passed, they packed the car with luggage and placed the children in the back seat. They sat in the car for a moment with blank expressions upon their faces.

"Where are we headed?" asked Theola.

"I've seen magazines about California. Why don't we head there? It's far away from Denver and nobody will ever find our new address unless we give it to them."

"Not even my sisters?" Theola kissed Alesha as she held her in her arms.

"Not even my parents Theola. Not for a little while. Not until we are settled and a little money under our belts. I'm not going through someone tracking us down and turning a good situation into a bad one again."

Theola took a deep breath, but she didn't disagree. "You're driving dear."

James started the engine and again, they were headed for uncharted territories.

Chapter 70

Over Worked

hen they reached California, James could only afford a one-bedroom apartment. The children camped out on the floor. James and Theola had the bedroom along with Alesha.

"Will the money we have see us through, until you find a new job?"

"Theola that's why I only got a one-bedroom. We have enough to last us through two months. After that, I had better find a job or we will be out in the streets."

"Why don't you go for another postal job?"

"Oooh no. Me and the postal service have seen the last of each other. If they have a connection to reach from Illinois to Denver, then from Denver to California is probably no different. I need something different where I can't be looked up or found out."

"Alright James."

James went out into the city of Los Angeles and went from store to store and restaurant to restaurant. When he came home, Theola was changing Phillip.

"How was it out there dear?"

"You're not going to like it, but until something better comes along, it's the best I can do."

"And what is that?"

"I got a job stocking a store and cleaning it during the day and I took a job waiting tables and cleaning a restaurant at night."

"What time will you be home?"

"I'll be home by eleven every night. Wednesday is my early night. I'll be home by nine."

"But you're home on the weekends?"

"Not exactly. The restaurant will pay me overtime if I work Saturdays and Sundays."

"Honey when will the family see you? The children need to see their father too."

"Honey it's just like Denver. I did the same thing until something better came along. Bear with me. I'm doing the best I can."

"I know you are. I'll keep on praying."

"There you go honey." James smiled. "You pray for all of us. I'll stick to the reality of life."

"One of these days James, you will recognize God as your Father. He will bring you to Him."

"Yeah, yeah. He better send a team of horses, because I'm a little hard to pull."

Theola ignored his comment. She prepared the apartment to look like home, while James worked diligently for six months. The family barely saw him during the day and Theola only knew him at night.

Marilyn was only six years old. Even though she hated when her father read poetry to put them to sleep, she loved her big hugs and kisses on the cheek.

"Mommy why don't we see daddy anymore?" asked Marilyn.

"He is working honey."

"Can I call him to say goodnight?"

"Of course you can." Marilyn dialed the number to the restaurant. An employee answered the phone.

"James it's for you!" Theola heard as the young man yelled.

James dropped the mop and raced to the phone. "Hello."

"Hey babe, your daughter just wanted to tell you something."

James was relieved there was nothing seriously wrong at home.

"Okay."

Theola handed Marilyn the phone.

"Hi Daddy. I miss you. Can I get another big kiss from you, even if I am asleep?"

"I miss you too sweetheart and you most certainly can get a big kiss."

"Can you hurry home? I miss you soo much that the daddy side of my heart is hurting."

"The daddy side of your heart?"

"Yes, because I love you and mommy. You both share my heart. Since you are not here, the daddy side is aching for you to be home."

"Oh sweetheart, Daddy will hurry home soon and whether you are asleep or not, I will give you the biggest kiss any father could ever want to give his daughter when I get home. Daddy promises."

Marilyn smiled. "I love you daddy." Theola took the phone.

"Hurry home dear. I miss you too."

"As fast as I can sweetheart." James hung up the phone.

Theola put Marilyn to bed. James got home at about two in the morning. All were asleep. Theola heard James when he entered the house. She met him in the living room. James did as he promised and kissed Marilyn lovingly upon her forehead, trying not to wake her.

Theola smiled, waited for her kiss and they strolled to the bedroom.

Chapter 71

Surprise!

James worked steadily and hard for weeks, until one evening, he came home. When he turned the key to the door, he heard Phillip crying as loud as he could. James quickly opened the front door only to find the children gathered at the bathroom door. James hurried to see what was ohhh so familiar to him.

"Move children. Marilyn take your brothers and sister to the living room. Go on now."

Marilyn did as daddy instructed. James assisted Theola up off the floor.

"Theola when I lifted you, I could feel that same lump on the side of your breast. It felt bigger than the last time. Did you go to the doctor's and have that checked before we lost our insurance in Chicago?"

"No I didn't. Don't worry, whatever it is, it will go away."

"Honey it's been a little over six weeks since we made love."

"That's what happens when you do that. I believe six weeks is about right James. That was the last time we made love."

"I don't have any medical insurance this time. I can't take you to the doctor and have you checked out without it coming from the food or house money."

Theola, weak from her ordeal, sat on the side of the bathtub. "That's ok honey. I think we have had enough children to already know we are about to have our fifth child."

"Theola we are barely getting along. A fifth child? This is a big surprise."

"He is going to be a blessing as they all are."

James wasn't going to argue. James leaned down and kissed Theola on the cheek. "You are a strong woman Theola Delsin. No one can ever take that away from you. Let me help you to the bed so you can rest." James pulled Theola by one arm and placed it around his neck. She slowly walked to the bed, leaning on James.

"Theola I have got to find a job now that will pay for health insurance. Otherwise, the baby will have to be born here at home. I don't want to take that chance of having anything go wrong."

"I appreciate that dear. I know you will do your best. But for right now, I'm extremely tired and would like to rest. If you could please just watch the children for a couple of hours."

"I'll feed them. You get some rest."

No sooner than Theola's head struck the pillow, she was fast asleep. James stared at his wife of almost ten years. She looked just as beautiful as the day he had met her. Their lives had changed so much since that day they first made love at the schoolhouse. He left Theola and went to the kitchen to feed the children. But before he did, he pulled a beer from the refrigerator and pondered the birth of their fifth child. For the next two months, James took it all in stride. He worked hard and paid the bills. Theola prayed every night for a way to see themselves clear of their financial burden and for a healthy baby.

James tried to find employment that paid health insurance, but to no avail. Time was running out. It seemed the harder James worked, the more Theola's health declined.

"Honey are you eating and keeping up your strength? You look a lot thinner than you did two months ago."

"Dear, I just don't have an appetite."

"You're pregnant Theola. You have always had an appetite. You need to see a doctor for your health and the baby's sake too."

"On what health insurance James? It would cost you a fortune. You are already working three jobs just to keep the family sheltered and fed."

"But I'm worried about you. You seem to be getting skinner instead of bigger for a pregnant woman."

"Oh James, it's just the other four children. They keep me moving so much that sometimes I don't know whether I'm coming or going. Sometimes I even forget to eat." Theola gave a half smile.

"Alright honey, but please try to keep your strength up. The baby needs nourishment."

"Yes Mommy," spoke Theola sarcastically.

James went to bed a little concerned over Theola's health.

James watched Theola week by week until a couple of months had passed. She only seemed to be getting worse. James repeatedly begged her to get medical attention regardless of their financial circumstances. Theola refused. One day, while James was at work, Marilyn was watching television in the living room and James Jr. was trying to change Alesha's diaper. Phillip was following Theola around the house as she dusted and vacuumed the floors. Suddenly, Theola grabbed her chest and fell to the floor.

"Ahhhhhh, Mommy!" Phillip screamed.

Theola reached for the arm of the living room sofa. Marilyn leaped from the floor and ran to her mother's side. James Jr. dropped the diaper and ran toward the sound. Alesha waddled behind James Jr. with no diaper on.

"Mother what is it?" asked Marilyn.

"Marilyn I just felt a pain in my chest like I have never felt before."

"Let's call daddy. He'll know what to do," stated Marilyn.

"No honey. Let's not worry daddy while he's at work." Theola pulled herself up by the sofa arm and sat there for a few moments to regroup. Marilyn sat beside her. Theola took deep breaths. All the children watched curiously and quietly. "Honey I need you to take your brothers and your sister into the kitchen and I will come and fix some lunch. Do that for me while I catch my breath. And make sure they are not into mischief until I get there. Before you do that, fix Alesha's diaper, please."

"Yes ma'am. Come on. Let's go into the kitchen like Mother said." Marilyn did as her mother instructed. The children followed Marilyn. Theola stood from the sofa. She walked toward the bathroom. Once there, Theola closed the door, took off the blouse and unfastened her bra. To Theola's surprise, the lump had become a small sore and slightly painful. She washed it, placed two small Band-Aids over it and continued with her household responsibilities.

Chapter 72

Missing Person

eeks passed, and Konee and Deborah felt a need to get in touch with their sister. They did not get their usual once-a-month check-in phone call from Theola.

At the Taylor house, Henrietta heard the phone ring.

"Hello."

"Mrs. Taylor, this is Konee."

"Yes my dear. What can I do for you?"

"We haven't heard from our sister in a few months. We called the old number that we had. The operator told us that that number had been disconnected. We were wondering if you have heard from them."

"No, as a matter of fact, James normally calls me every three or four months. So this is not unusual for him."

"Yes Mrs. Taylor, but we keep closer contact with our sister. Either she calls us or we call her no less than once a month. And we haven't heard from Theola in over five months."

"I don't know what to say. If you leave me your number and when they call, I will be happy to call and let you have their new number."

"Yes ma'am. We would greatly appreciate that. Our number is…"

Chapter 73

The Agony of Pain

As the weeks passed, Theola was enduring more agonizing pain. The throbbing aches tormented her body as she tried to rest at night and nap during the day. Theola was grateful that James was so tired when he came home at night, that he didn't notice her discomfort when he lay next to her in bed. But the once small sore had turned into the circumference of a golf ball. This morning, Theola fixed breakfast for the children and prepared lunch as she normally does on any given day. When suddenly, she crouched over the kitchen sink, gripping her chest.

"Mommy what's wrong? How can I help you?"

"Marilyn help me to the sofa."

Marilyn took her mother's arm and pulled her along until they reached the living room couch. Sweat dripped from Theola's brow as she lay on the sofa.

Marilyn touched her forehead. "Mommy you are very hot."

"Marilyn just let me rest for a...moment." Theola's throat and lips were dry. She spoke quietly to Marilyn, trying not to alarm her. "Watch your brothers and sister for me while I rest. I promise I will do better by taking you to the park and playing games with my lovely children." Theola smiled and licked her lips. She tried to reassure Marilyn everything would be alright.

"Oh Mommy. I love helping you. You can take us to the park whenever you feel like it."

Theola hugged her daughter, but Marilyn sensed something deeply wrong.

"Get me my face towel from the bathroom, wet it with some cool water and place it on my forehead."

Marilyn raced to the bathroom and performed the actions necessary to help her mother. When she arrived back at Theola, she was sound asleep. Marilyn placed the cool cloth on her head. Marilyn had a sincere concern about her mother. It was not like her to fall asleep in the middle of the day when she had promised a walk in the park. Marilyn knew what she had to do in order to help her mother to rest. She went to find her two younger brothers and baby sister and kept them quiet while their mother rested. Theola slept for two hours before Phillip woke her, crying from hunger. Theola awoke to see Phillip staring her in the face, knowing that Marilyn would not have let him wake her unless something was wrong. Panic struck her heart. She cried out.

"Marilyn! James! Alesha! Where are you?"

"I'm in the bathroom Mommy!" shouted Marilyn.

James was playing with his toy soldiers behind the sofa. He walked around the sofa. "Where is Alesha James Jr.?"

"Marilyn laid her down for a nap a while ago in your bed."

Theola was relieved. She picked Phillip up with pain lingering upon her chest. She carried him to the kitchen. The pain was dull, but still active. She turned toward James Jr.

"Are you hungry too sweetheart?"

"Yes ma'am."

After making peanut butter and jelly sandwiches for a snack until dinner was done, Theola toiled about the house. The pain continued to pound her body. Before long, the throbbing was too stressful to ignore. Theola gathered the children and went to the local grocery store to try and find something that might help ease the pain. She gripped her chest from time to time to fight back the stressful discomfort.

While she observed all types of pain relievers at the store, a man noticed her lingering in the drug section. He noticed the anguish on her face. Theola noticed him out of the corner of her eye. He was a medium-height white male. He was dressed in drab clothing, dark gray pants, and a black shirt. His shoes were black and appeared heavily worn. He had on a long, thin black coat, frayed at the ends of the sleeves, with the pockets bulged slightly. He approached her. Marilyn was holding Phillip's hand and James and Alesha were holding each other's hands.

"What beautiful children you have?" stated the man.

"Why thank you," replied Theola. Theola frowned a little bit.

"Are you in some kind of pain," asked the man.

"Yes. I'm trying to find some medication to relieve it."

The man looked around the store to see who might be watching them, then he reached into his pocket.

"I have just the thing for you ma'am."

"That bottle looks like it came straight from a hospital. What is it?"

"It's morphine. I guarantee it will take your pain away."

"But how did you ...."

Before Theola finished the sentence, the man interrupted.

"You don't ask questions. Do you want the relief or not?"

Another pain struck Theola at the moment. Marilyn and the children were silent, but they observed every action.

"I'll take it."

"It's going to cost you," stated the strange man.

"How much?"

"One hundred dollars."

"A hundred dollars?" The pain struck again, even harder this time. "I don't have a hundred dollars on me. But if you let me have it now, I will meet you here the first of the month and give it to you."

"Lady do I look like some kind of charity? Now or not at all."

"Do I look like I am rich?" The man looked into the faces of the children. "Sir, I have twenty-five in my purse. I can pay you on the first of the month. You can ask the storekeeper if I pay my debts."

"Alright Lady. I can find out where you live and if you don't show on the first with the money… Well, let's just say it won't be pleasant for you or the children." The man gave Theola the bottle of morphine, a needle, and a syringe. "Do you know how to use the syringe?" The man again glanced around the store to make sure no one was watching. He demonstrated briefly the actions Theola should take. Then he took the twenty-five dollars and left.

"Come on children. We need to take my medicine home."

Theola grimaced again and quickly walked from the store. The children followed their mother with hast. When Theola got home, she took the bottle and injected herself at different times of the evening with small doses of morphine to ease the pain. A bottle would last her a month, she thought.

Theola met this man for the next three months to receive the morphine until the day finally came when just a bottle of morphine wasn't enough to fight the hurt. Soon, one bottle became two. At two hundred a month, Theola realized she could see a doctor for what she was putting out in drug money. Theola was now eight and a half months pregnant. She paid her last debt to the man at the store. Theola tried to withstand her pain. But without the drug she had become sooo dependent on over the last few months, the pain became almost unbearable.

One morning, right after James left the house for work, Marilyn came into her mother's bedroom and stood by her bedside. Marilyn knew that she always got up after daddy left to fix breakfast before they woke up. This morning, Theola did not move.

In agony, Theola slightly opened her eyes and spoke softly. "Come closer." Marilyn walked closer. "You know, at nine years old, you're a big girl now."

"I know Mommy." Marilyn smiled, a little bit concerned about her mother.

"I want you to do something for me sweetheart."

"Yes ma'am."

"If I am not awake when your father gets home, tell him mommy is very sick and needs to get to the hospital."

"But Mommy, what's wrong?"

The way her mom talked really worried Marilyn. She had seen her sick many times, but she never talked like this before.

"The pain is extreme. The medicine is no longer working. The sore on my breast has gotten worse, see." Theola pulled the cover back and showed Marilyn the area where cancer had eaten a small part of her breast away.

"My goodness! Mommy. That looks nasty. Why have you waited this long to do something about it?"

"Baby girl. You see, Daddy is working three jobs to keep a roof over our heads and food in our mouths. He can't afford any hospital bills."

"But mommy…"

"Listen carefully to me baby girl. I'm very tired. Your brother and sister will be waking up soon. I need you to feed them some cereal and watch them for me. I don't think I have the strength to get out of bed."

"Mommy, Daddy just left. Let me try to catch him?"

"No sweetheart. I might feel better if I just get some rest." Theola laid her head back on the pillow. Soon, she fell asleep.

Marilyn went to the kitchen, took a chair from the dining room table and got the cereal down and some bowls to set the table for her brothers and sister when they awoke. When she had finished, she went into the living room to watch her favorite cartoon, Mighty Mouse. A few moments later, Phillip and James Jr. came into the living room.

"Where's Momma?" asked James Jr.

"She is still asleep and doesn't feel well. So we have to be quiet so she can rest. You two hungry?"

"Yes," replied James Jr. and Phillip nodded his head.

Marilyn took them to the kitchen. They all ate. After they had eaten, there came a cry from Alesha's crib. Marilyn raced to her bedroom, pulled her stool to the crib and leaned over the side to help Alesha get out of the crib. Marilyn changed her diaper, picked her up to her shoulder and carried her to the kitchen.

"Come on baby girl. Let's get something to eat." She got a chair. Stood in it, picked Alesha up and placed her in her high chair. Marilyn fixed her baby sister's cereal and fed her with a spoon.

Morning passed into afternoon. Theola still had not gotten up. Marilyn was concerned and went to check on her mother. Theola was still sound asleep, so Marilyn shook her.

"Mother! Mother! Are you alright?"

Delirious and in pain, Theola focused her eyes on her daughter.

"Marilyn come close to me." Her voice was weary. Theola reached her hand to pull Marilyn closer to her.

Marilyn touched her mother's hand. She leaned closer to listen carefully. "Marilyn I want you to call your father. I am having a hard time dealing with the pain. I need to see a doctor."

"Yes Mother." Marilyn started to dash into the kitchen, but Theola still held her hand snug to her body.

"Wait sweetheart."

"Yes ma'am."

"Check on your brothers and sister to make sure they are alright."

"Yes ma'am."

Theola released Marilyn's hand. Marilyn did as her mother directed. The children were watching television quietly in the living room. Marilyn got the work number of her father which was taped on the refrigerator door in case of emergencies. She dialed immediately. An hour later, Marilyn heard a key at the front door. James walked into the house. He saw Marilyn standing in the doorway. Her eyes were sad.

"Hurry Daddy!" Marilyn pointed to the bedroom. James rushed past Marilyn and went to the bedroom. He swept Theola into his arms and carried her to the car.

"Marilyn watch the children. I will be right back as soon as I take care of your mother. Be sure and lock the door behind me."

Marilyn nodded. She closed the door behind her father and held her head down in prayer for her mother.

Chapter 74

Hospital Stay

James rushed Theola to the emergency room of the hospital. He stood in the hallway holding Theola in his arms, unconscious.

"What seems to be the problem?" asked the nurse on duty, waving for the orderly to bring a gurney.

"She is almost nine months pregnant. I came home a little while ago and she was in bed just as you see her right now. Please do something."

"Lay her here, on this gurney." James did as the nurse instructed.

"Who is her doctor?" asked the nurse. "We need to call him."

James started to slowly back out the same way he came in. The nurse followed him. "We don't have a doctor. But I will pay whatever it takes to make her better, please." James was fumbling in his back pocket for his wallet. "Here is my social security card and her name is Theola, Theola Taylor." The nurse took the card. James continued to walk backward.

"Wait! You just can't leave her here! Where are you going?"

"I have to leave." James was now pushing on the emergency doors that led to the street.

"Are you sure you can pay for this?"

"I'll pay. Just take care of her, please." James continued his way out.

"Don't leave!" James stood at the emergency doors. "We will need some more information!"

"I have to leave now. I have four children at home. I need to find someone to take care of them until I can get back here."

"Very well, leave your phone number and hurry back." The nurse looked at the social security card.

"It's 661-349-9980!"

The nurse watched as the doors closed. She turned to the gurney. Theola was still unconscious. "We will take care of Mrs. Taylor," spoke the nurse silently to herself with sympathy as she gazed upon this seemingly lifeless woman with child. The nurse immediately called for the doctor on duty.

Chapter 75

Emergency/Help!

James rushed back home to take care of his four children and relieve his nine-year-old daughter of babysitting duties. Marilyn greeted him at the door. James Jr. looked at him. Phillip and Alesha were in front of the television.

"They are taking good care of your mother sweetheart."

He passed them quickly and started searching through the house. Marilyn watched as James went from room to room. He searched the bedroom drawers, the kitchen drawers and the living room drawers, throwing paper out of the drawers.

"What are you trying to find Daddy?" asked Marilyn.

"I'm looking for your grandmother's phone number. You'd think I'd remember my own phone number after years of living there, but with so much on my mind... We haven't called her since we've been in California. I don't know if I can find her number."

"I know it by heart Daddy."

James smiled. "How?"

"When in school, I had a hard time remembering how to spell words and remembering my timetables. Mommy taught me how to remember numbers when I see them. She said to divide a number or word by section and..."

James interrupted, "Never mind all that honey. Just give me your grandmother's phone number."

"It's 318-728-1343."

"You're sure?"

"Yes Daddy. Mom used to let me call her all the time in Denver and I never forgot."

He immediately got on the phone to call his mother. The phone rang several times. James danced with anticipation and mumbled words to himself. "Please be there." Seconds later, a soft voice answered the phone.

"Hello."

"Mom…" exclaimed James, grateful to hear her voice.

"James, how wonderful it is to hear from you."

"Mom…"

"What is it honey? You sound upset."

James raced to get his words out. "Theola is in the hospital. I think it's very serious. She's pregnant with our fifth child. I need you to come here and take care of the children until I can make sure Theola is alright."

"Hold on. Slow down. What's wrong with Theola?"

"I don't know. I took her to the hospital an hour ago. I need you to come here and watch the children while I see about her."

"I would be more than happy to help you if you tell me where *here* is?"

"Forgive me. I'm in Bakersfield, California."

"California! Oh honey, you know I don't fly. Even if I could, your father would never pay for a plane ticket for me to come and help you. But don't threat now. Give me your address, phone number at home and the hospital number. I will call Theola's sisters and have them call you. They have been asking about her."

"Ok. Mom. That would be great. My home phone number is 661-349-9980. I'm not sure what the hospital number is, but I will find out before they call. My address is 3332 Allenton Court, Apt 222."

"Alright honey. You hang in there. Believe in God. He will make everything alright. Bye now."

James hung up the phone, muttering to himself, "Believe in God, Ha! Where is He now that Theola is in the hospital and she believes in Him?" James went to check on the children in the living room.

"Are you all hungry?" James Jr. nodded. Marilyn was tearful. She nodded. Phillip ran to hug his daddy's leg. In the process, he stepped on his foot. Alesha was asleep in the children's bedroom.

"Well let me go to the kitchen and see what I can find." James started toward the kitchen. Phillip continued to hold his leg. James was too occupied to realize that Phillip was still hanging on to his leg as he walked to the kitchen. He didn't know why daddy was home, but he knew something was wrong. When James knelt down to get a pot from the cabinet, he struck Phillip in the head with his hand. Phillip whimpered.

"Oooops, I'm sorry son. I didn't realize you were there. You got to let go of my leg, son, if you want me to fix some food." Phillip immediately let go. James pulled pots and pans from the cabinets and began a task he occasionally did when Theola wasn't feeling well. James began to make sandwiches and boil soup with tears in his eyes. He tried not to let his children see him cry as he warmed soup for dinner.

While James fed the children, his thoughts were still back at the hospital. There, the doctor removed Theola's nightgown. He was shocked and dismayed that a hole the size of a golf ball hadn't taken her life sooner. They checked her vital signs. They were faint but steady. But from physical observation, they realized she probably fainted from the agonizing pain of cancer that had eaten away at her body.

"We will have to take the baby soon." The doctor told his staff. "There is no telling how far the cancer has spread. This woman's days are numbered."

They stabilized Theola and gave her as much medication as they could to relieve the pain and not harm the child. They left her to rest for a few hours. They needed James badly in order to complete any examination or perform any necessary procedures.

"Nurse. Get the husband back here. Now!"

The nurse scampered away to call James immediately.

Chapter 76

Desperation

est was something that James found hard to do after the children were fed. He sat down on the couch to catch his breath. The phone rang.

Quickly, James picked up the phone. "Hello…"

"What are you doing in Bakersfield? The last time we talked to Theola, you were in Denver. We have been trying to get in touch with you two for the last eight months. No one knew where you were. Why all the secrecy?" spoke Konee.

Anxious to get a word in… "If you stop with the 90 questions, I will answer one of them. I have some bad news about your sister."

"Is Theola sick?" Konee became silent and waited for an answer.

"Theola is very sick. I don't know what is wrong with her. I haven't been able to be with her at the hospital. I need someone to watch the children while I spend time with her to find out exactly what is wrong."

"He done poisoned our sister," spoke Deborah to Konee while she was still on the phone.

"Shhhhh," stated Konee. "Alright James. Deborah and I will be out on the first plane in the air. Where are you located?"

"Fly into Bakersfield, California Airport. I can pick you up."

"Know we will get transportation to you. Just give me your address and we will be there as soon as possible."

"My address is 3332 Allenton Court, Apartment 222, Bakersfield. We are at Bakersfield Medical Hospital. The address is…"

"Never mind. We'll find it." Puzzled by their new location. "You were in Colorado, why are you in…" Konee broke her statement. "Never mind, you can explain when we get there." She hung up abruptly.

"What are they doing in California? If James has hurt our sister, I will never forgive him," spoke Deborah.

"Let's let Keshna know and see if she wants to fly with us and let's not jump to conclusions. We will find out more when we get there," spoke Konee.

Deborah got right back on the phone to call Keshna and make reservations for two, possibly three. They all got on the first plane headed west.

CHAPTER 77

Sisters to the Rescue

As James waited for Theola's sisters to arrive, he tried to get a neighbor to watch the children while he went back to the hospital. None would help him, not with four children. Meanwhile, Theola was stabilized as the doctors examined her. The nurse had followed doctors' orders. The phone rang.

"Hello."

"This is Nurse Wanda. We need you here. Now!"

"Yes ma'am."

James hung up the phone and paced the floor. Does he leave the children? Does he take them with him? James got the children and drove back to the hospital that night. James answered all questions while Marilyn watched the children in the lobby.

James and the children left the hospital the next morning with the expression of deep sadness on their faces. He got a call later that morning from Theola's sisters. James took the children with him to pick them up. The sisters followed James in their rental. No one wanted to ride with him.

Meanwhile, the doctor returned to Theola's room with the nurse to check her vital signs and update her chart. Theola was conscious.

"Your husband is waiting in the lobby with three of your sisters and your children. But I told him no children were allowed. At least not until you are strong enough to talk."

"Yes Doctor Jansen."

"How did you know my..." He looked at the name tag on his medical jacket.

"My children are here too?" Theola was groggy from the medication but excited to know that her family was there to see her.

"Yes, but I told him that children were not allowed in the hospital rooms."

"I know doctor, but I beg of you to please make an exception in this case for my oldest daughter. Let her stay. I beg you, please."

"Alright, but she can only come in for a few minutes."

"Thank you so much, thank you."

"If I may ask Mrs. Taylor, why have you taken so long to see a doctor? You are eight months pregnant. Haven't you been seeing a doctor for prenatal care?"

"No doctor. We couldn't afford it. This is the first time I have seen a doctor since I was pregnant with this child."

"My God! Woman...how have you taken the pain for this long?"

"I have been taking some morphine on the side."

"How? Morphine is a prescribed drug."

"A friend," Theola said nothing more. She turned her head away from answering any more questions.

"Alright, I understand. I'm glad you told me. I will look for any miscues with the baby."

"Will he be alright?"

"That's what I am going to make sure of. I hate to be the bearer of bad news, but we are going to take the baby and x-ray you just to see how far the cancer has spread. If there is anything at this point that we can do for you 'to prevent further spreading, we will if it hasn't spread too far.

"Do what you must doctor. I'm just praying for a healthy child."

The doctor turned to the nurse. "Prep her for surgery."

"Yes doctor."

The doctor headed toward the door. Theola made one more request. "Could I see my sisters before I get prep?"

"It will take us a few minutes to get the materials I need," spoke the nurse.

"They can have just a few minutes while we prepare, but only a few minutes."

"Thank you doctor." smiled Theola.

"Nurse Blancher, please send in Mrs. Taylor's sisters. Tell them they only have ten minutes."

"Yes doctor."

Theola was delighted. The nurse immediately went to the lobby to inform Theola's sisters that they may come in to see her. When Nurse Blancher made it to the lobby, she interrupted a dispute in the middle of the floor between James, Deborah and Konee. Keshna sat in the lobby chair with the children.

"If you hadn't dragged my sister away from home, none of this would have happened!" screamed Deborah.

"I love your sister and no one can drag her anywhere without her wanting to go!" yelled James.

"Excuse me!" exclaimed Nurse Blancher. All eyes focused on her. "Now is not the time to be arguing amongst yourselves when the children sitting there need your support and so does Mrs. Taylor. This is a hospital, not the streets. Let's act like it!"

Everyone was quiet. James went to sit with Marilyn on the couch.

"Theola will see her sisters now. You must be brief. We will be prepping her soon."

"What does that mean?" asked Keshna. She had Phillip, James Jr. and Alesha sitting by her.

"The doctor will be out shortly to explain everything. Just be patient. Mrs. Taylor's room is 313, down the hall to the right."

"You two go. I will take the children back home and babysit them there. I don't think I can take seeing her in a hospital bed," stated Keshna.

"Very well," spoke Nurse Blancher. "Ms. Taylor wanted to see her daughter as well, but not right now."

"Marilyn will stay here with me." Remarked James.

Konee and Deborah walked away, staring at James. James stared back. Nurse Blancher followed the sisters out. James gave Keshna money and his address. Keshna left with the other children in a cab and went back to James's apartment. When they were gone, James sat down beside Marilyn.

"Baby girl, your aunties have been chewing on my leg since they got here. I don't think you should try to get to know them. They won't be seeing very much of you if I can help it."

"Daddy you always said you never did like them."

"Yeah, yeah. Now I remember why."

James kissed Marilyn on the forehead and wrapped his arms around her shoulders. Everything will be alright baby girl." James held her tight. They leaned back on the couch and waited for the nurse to return.

Marilyn smiled and looked into her father's eyes. She felt everything would be alright.

CHAPTER 78

Our Love for You Theola

By this time, Konee and Deborah had reached Theola's room. They took a long look at their sister, whom they had seen only a couple of years ago, healthy and full of life. Now Theola lay there with tubs in her arms and nose. She appeared tired and feeble, as if each breath was a strain to take. Theola reached out her arms to both of them. She tried to place a smile on her face. In awe of her appearance, frail and pale, they didn't let their feelings be known right away. They smiled back at her.

"My sisters, it is so good to see you both." Each sister grabbed a hand, each on one side of the bed. They squeezed her hand and leaned over to give Theola a kiss on her cheeks. They tried to maintain their smiles.

"It's good to see you too," spoke Konee.

"But not under these circumstances," spoke Deborah.

Theola was saddened by the remark. Tears formed in her eyes. She began to sob heavily. She paused for a long time, trying to regain her composure. She released their hands and tried to wipe her tears away with her fingers. Konee grabbed a tissue from Theola's bedside to dry her eyes.

Theola took the tissue and finished the action. "Konee and Deborah what have I done with my life? I have failed my parents. I have failed at being a big sister to you, Keshna and my brothers. I have failed my family and now I am leaving them with a bunch of shattered dreams and broken promises. Where did I go sooo terribly wrong?" Tears trickled down Theola's cheeks again.

Konee and Deborah both had tears in their eyes too. They sympathized. "Theola you are and always will be a loved sister. You haven't failed at anything. It's not your nature to fail. The only thing that happened is you ran into a roadblock. Once this obstacle is out of your way, you will be back on track. All your goals will be accomplished and all of the promises will be kept," said Konee.

"That's right. If you hadn't let James ruin your life and get you pregnant, none of this would have ever happened."

"Deborah. Not now!" cried Konee.

With tears still streaming down her cheeks, Theola dapped them with her tissue. "Ohhhh my sisters, please don't blame James for my failures. You can say if I hadn't disobeyed our parents, if I hadn't gotten pregnant, if I hadn't run away from home… out of all those *ifs*, I made the choice of what to do. James didn't twist my arm or coerce me in any way. As a matter of fact, he tried to get me to come back home when we were running away. So please, please don't blame my misfortune on James."

"Theola we met the doctor briefly just before we came in to see you. He said the cancer has probably spread throughout your entire body from the looks of your wound. He also said this was over some years. How could James not know?" questioned Deborah.

"No one knew. James works nights and days to keep food on the table, the children in clothes and shelter over our heads. None of the jobs paid health insurance because the pay was so small."

"He found time to have babies," said Deborah.

"Don't be so critical of someone else until you have walked in their shoes. He has shown his family love and affection whenever he got the chance. Most of the time that was on the weekend. We barely saw him during the week. He only came home to sleep and sometimes, he was just too tired to eat. He seldom made it to the bed. He would sleep on the couch when he entered the house, too exhausted to reach the bedroom. Sometimes, he would stay on the couch until the next morning."

"Soooo?" said Deborah, sounding non-sympathetic.

"Soooo. What I'm saying is for the past two years, he has just been too physically drained to notice and I didn't take the time to tell him. I didn't realize what it was until it was too late. I just thought it was a bad sore that just got worse."

"He hasn't touched you in two years?" asked Konee.

"He touched something to get another baby here."

"Deborah please." stated Konee.

"Not passionately, not lovingly. He worked late nights every weekend too. His physical exhaustion from work left him too drained to notice. I hid it from him too. So please, don't be so quick to judge." Theola wiped the tears from her cheeks with the little tissue in her hand. Deborah nor Konee spoke another word about James. "Who's watching the children with you two here and James here?"

"Keshna has them at your apartment," said Konee.

"Bless her little sweetheart," said Theola.

"She's not so little anymore. Keshna stands five-eight and weighs a hundred and seventy pounds. She missed you a great deal when you left, especially at night. She tried to get me to read those bedtime fairy tale stories to her. But I couldn't put the emotional flare into them the way you did, so after a while, she quit asking me to read to her."

Theola smiled.

"Keshna didn't want to come to your room. She said she wanted to remember you as you were years ago. She couldn't bear to come and see you in this condition. She volunteered to stay with the children while we came to visit you." Tearfully spoke Konee.

Tears fell heavily again from Theola's eyes. "If I hurt Keshna that much, what do Mom, Dad and my brothers think of me?"

"Mom and Dad don't know that you are in the hospital and very sick. We never let them know that we were keeping in touch with you," said Konee.

"Yes Theola," spoke Deborah. "Our parents wrote you off the day you walked away. Daddy moved the entire family to Sabine Parish not long after you left. The questions from the community were too embarrassing for him to answer with the truth."

"He resigned from being the pastor of the church. Our mother got another teaching job in Sabine. Mom just never spoke your name, but we knew she was hurting inside. Ronnie, Larry, Bobby and Carl are in the military overseas. We haven't told them yet." Added Konee.

"My God, what chaos I caused the whole family. I guess Mom and Dad will be shocked when they hear the news."

"No Theola. We aren't going to tell them. We aren't telling our brothers either. Dad and Mom got you out of their hearts years ago. This would devastate them to know you left and they didn't have a chance to say goodbye. This would eat Mother up. It's better that they never know."

"You're right." Theola sniffled. "I guess it is better this way."

"Yes. We think it best Theola," spoke Deborah.

Theola thought for a moment. "My sisters I hate to ask this of you, but James is going to need help financially. He cannot pay for this hospital bill and support the children too. Is there any way you can help him out?"

"Theola we live together in a two-bedroom apartment in Shreveport. We save the money we have left over so we can move into our own apartment one day." Konee paused. She glanced over at Deborah. "I guess we could take that money and pay the hospital, but it will take a little longer before we move into our own places. Right Deborah?"

"Speak for yourself. I don't want anything to do with James."

"Please," begged Theola.

Konee looked at Deborah. "Deborah come on." Deborah thought. "It's not just James. It's for the children too and Theola."

Deborah still paused. Moments later, she responded, "Ok."

"Thank you," sighed Theola.

"We could take a couple of the children off his hands as well," stated Deborah. "But with a couple of kids on our hands, our pocketbooks could be stretched to the limit."

"It's just until you are back on your feet." Added Konee.

"Ohhhhh no!" cried Theola. "I don't want you to take the children. I would appreciate it if you could help him with the hospital bill. The children stay together."

"But Theola, James can't handle a newborn and four little children and work too." Deborah said.

"He will. They are his responsibility. If you want to help James with the children, take them all or none at all. If they are separated, they might never get to know each other as brothers and sisters."

"Stop talking like you're not going to get through this." Konee smiled.

"It's not that Theola, we don't care to be associated with James after what has happened to you," said Deborah.

"I know you are not that fond of James, but it's not James's fault. He was every bit of the man he was supposed to be for the children and for me. Don't separate the children, please."

Deborah and Konee didn't argue.

"Alright Theola. We will pay the hospital bill. That is all we will do. We couldn't support five children at this time with our schedule of work and activities anyway," said Deborah.

"Trust me, my sisters. Paying the bill will lift a heavy burden from his shoulders. Thank you so very much. James wouldn't agree with you taking the children anyway." Theola flinched from agony.

"Should we call the nurse?" asked Konee.

"No! It will pass."

Theola stiffened. The girls watched her in grief, feeling powerless to stop her pain.

Theola soon relaxed her body and took a deep breath. "I'm better." But signs of anguish still remained on her face. The girls continued their conversation, trying not to focus on Theola's suffering.

"Are you sure James is ready for the responsibility of five children on his own for a while?" Asked Konee.

The nurse came in at that very moment. "Are you in pain Ms. Taylor?"

"Yes." spoke Konee quickly, happy to see the nurse.

"You are about to be prep for surgery. You ladies must leave now. We will take care of her."

"What are you about to do?" asked Deborah.

"We must prep Mrs. Taylor for a C-section."

As Deborah and Konee kissed their sister on the cheek, Theola whispered softly, "Yes, yes, James is ready. Could you ask the doctor to send Marilyn in alone, please?"

The nurse overheard what Theola had spoken. "No. Don't do that, ladies." Nurse Blancher turned to Theola. "We must get you ready for surgery. The doctor may grant your request later." The girls blew a kiss to Theola. She smiled. The nurse pushed Theola's bed to the operating room.

As the nurse left with Theola, Konee and Deborah found the doctor in the lobby with James and Marilyn. Marilyn was sitting on the couch. James was speaking with the doctor. When the two sisters walked into the lobby, they approached the doctor. They begged the doctor to let Marilyn visit her mother for a few minutes alone. Marilyn stood from her seat in anticipation of the doctor's permission to visit her mother.

"Her wish may be granted, but after we see how well she is recouping from her surgery," spoke the doctor. He started to leave to prepare for the operation. Marilyn sat back down. But before the doctor was out of the room, Deborah lit into James.

"This is your entire fault!" yelled Deborah.

"Yeah!" said Konee.

Marilyn leaned forward on the couch and placed her hands over her ears. The doctor noticed the discomfort of the little girl. He addressed the sisters before leaving the lobby.

"The best thing you can do for your sister right now is pray for a healthy baby, a healthy Theola and stop the bickering."

The sisters and James agreed. Konee and Deborah went to one corner of the lobby and silence engulfed the room. Marilyn bowed her head and leaned back on the couch. James joined his daughter. He placed his arms around her shoulder and held her tightly once again. Marilyn leaned into her father's arms and rested until the doctor's return.

Chapter 79

Doctor's Diagnosis

bout an hour later, Theola was wheeled from the operating room to her room. The doctor entered the lobby. Everyone stood, even Marilyn.

"You have a bouncing baby girl Mr. Taylor. She is doing just fine."

James smiled. "How is Theola?"

"While I was in there, I took a peek around. It appeared the cancer had not spread to the abdominal area yet. But we x-rayed to find out just how far the cancer had gone. Those results will be available to me later."

"What do you think her chances are?" asked James.

The doctor looked into Marilyn's eyes. Theola's sisters stared at him intensely.

"It's hard to say without further examination and the results of the x-rays." The doctor started to walk away. "Ohhh, you may go and see your baby girl in the nursery room, four doors down the corridor to the left."

Marilyn spoke softly, "When may I go see my mother?"

The doctor smiled at Marilyn. "Later my child. She is resting. Why not try in about four hours." The doctor walked out. James sat back down. The sisters got up and left without saying a word.

Chapter 80

James's Dilemma

Later that afternoon, after Theola had some lunch and a chance to rest, the doctor went to see the family in the lobby. Marilyn was sleeping on the couch in her father's lap. The sisters were on the opposite side of the room.

Konee rose from her seat when she saw the doctor enter. "What were the results doctor?"

Dr. Jansen noticed Marilyn was asleep. He looked into the eyes of the sisters and glanced over at James. He whispered to them to join him in the corridor. He didn't want to wake Marilyn. James gently laid Marilyn on the couch so as not to wake her. The sister immediately followed the doctor out of the waiting room. James met them in the hall.

"Her chest is completely infected with cancer. If it had been noticed in time, it could have been prevented. We will have to remove her breast to try and save her life."

The sisters stared at James.

"Will the surgery save her doctor?" asked Konee.

"That is our best option right now. We are doing all we can. It's just a waiting period after that operation."

The sisters turned their heads. Tears streamed freely. "I promised Theola something. If you will excuse me." said the doctor.

The doctor granted Theola's request. The doctor went into the lobby. He kneeled down and touched Marilyn on her shoulder. She awoke to the doctor's smile.

"Want to go see your mommy now?" Marilyn smiled at Doctor Jansen. He reached his hand out toward her. Marilyn arose from the couch. She grabbed his hand delightfully. The doctor and Marilyn passed Konee, Deborah and James in the corridor. The sisters were not done with James yet.

"James…"

James interrupted before Konee finished her sentence.

"I'm sooo sorry we have never been properly introduced. When you visited a couple of years ago, I was away working in another post office as a substitute. And now we meet under such circumstances as these." James reached out his hand to shake one of theirs. Neither sister extended their hand.

"You murderer!" screamed Deborah.

"Murderer?" James was puzzled by the remark.

"You murdered our sister. You good for nothing…"

"Deborah now is not the time." Stated Konee.

"I love your sister very much."

"That's why you let her exist for years with cancer eating away her body," said Deborah.

"I didn't know." James was almost tearful.

"Yeah… Theola told us you work three jobs every day," said Konee.

"And weekends too. That's right, I do."

"You're a sorry excuse for a man. How can you go for years and not notice? I don't care if you worked twenty-two hours a day. The other two hours you should have noticed your wife and family. There should have been something different about Theola that would have told you things weren't quite right," said Deborah.

James paused and bowed his head briefly, then, with watery eyes, addressed both sisters once again. "Perhaps you're right, but I was too concerned with the way I was feeling, being tired and not noticing what was going on with Theola."

"You're damn right!" spoke Deborah.

"Deborah don't curse this man."

"Konee, Deborah, I would gladly give my life to Theola right now. She is a beautiful woman. She does not deserve what she is going through."

"You're darn right she doesn't. I blame you James. The doctor says we have to hope that she pulls through. You heard the doctor after he reviewed the X-rays. If they could have caught it in time, they may have been able to prevent this from going this far," spoke Konee harshly.

"Konee I didn't know. Theola is strong. She will pull through this."

"I know you didn't. You didn't try to know. Is that all you can say? You sorry bastard!"

"Enough Deborah!" yelled Konee. "We weren't raised to speak ill of our enemies. Let's do what Theola asked and be on our way."

Deborah was silent and stared at James. "James we have a few things to discuss with you." Spoke Konee.

"You think of me as the enemy?" James paused, he got no response. "And what is it you want to discuss with me?"

"The hospital bill. We will pay for it." Spoke Konee.

"I can pay my own bills."

"Not working three jobs, you good for nothing…" began Deborah.

"Deborah stop. Just be quiet. I will do the talking. James let us pay the hospital bill. We will also take care of Theola if she doesn't pull through this as much as it pains me to say something like that."

"No! I'll take care of my wife."

"With what money? You are working three jobs now to pay the rent, to feed the children, to pay the car note… Please, let us help." Konee pleaded. "For the sake of the children."

"Yeah! You sorry son of a…"

"Deborah. Enough! Go in the lobby and wait for us. We are making too much noise in this hallway." Deborah didn't move. Konee directed her attention back at James. "Let us help James?"

He thought for a moment while pacing the floor. "I don't know."

"Let us take the children too. Working three jobs, how do you intend to watch the children and work at the same time? You son of a bitch." asked Deborah. James said nothing. "What are you hesitating for? You can't even see a gift right in your face. No wonder you didn't see Theola's illness. You're stupid."

"That's enough! I told you to go to the lobby." Konee turned to James. "Pay no attention to Deborah. She's just upset. You and I, let's go to the lobby."

"Ladies, I hate speaking of my wife in this manner." Tears trickled from James's eyes.

"It's a reality now James. She wanted us to discuss these things with you." stated Konee.

James thought briefly of their proposal. He knew he didn't have the finances to take care of the bills and anything else that might come along right now.

"Alright. I will let you handle everything under one condition."

"And that is…"

"That I am with you through everything."

"Alright James," said Konee.

"Oh, hell no! I don't want to ever see him again after today."

"Deborah please." Konee grabbed James by the arm and went to the lobby. Deborah followed.

"What about the children James?" asked Konee.

"The children will stay with me. I will work something out."

At that moment, the doctor entered the lobby. "Mr. Taylor, your wife would like to see you now."

"Yes doctor."

The doctor left the lobby.

"Alright then, it's settled. We will take care of the hospital bill and the arrangements for Theola, if necessary. Agreed?" asked Konee.

"Yes." James pulled his handkerchief from his back pocket to wipe tears from his eyes.

"Alright. Let's go Deborah."

Deborah stared at James the whole time Konee was talking to him and she continued to stare.

"Let's go Deborah," Konee spoke once again.

James also noticed her glaring eyes. He put the handkerchief back in his pocket. At that moment, Deborah walked close to James. She looked into his eyes and without warning, slapped him across the cheek so hard that the blow turned his cheek to one side. James held his composure and acknowledged her anger.

"Would you like the other cheek too?" Deborah raised her hand and clenched her fingers into a fist. She reared back so far that James saw the blow coming, caught her by the wrist and held it tightly. He pulled her close to his chest, still gripping her arm. "I only let you get away with the first one because I understand your pain. But there is no need for the second, because I love her too. You just don't know how much. And if I were in your shoes, I would probably feel the same way. Now if you ladies will excuse me, I'm going to see my wife and get my daughter." James released Deborah's wrist. "She will pull through this thing. God has her back. She will pull through."

He left the sisters standing in the lobby.

"Murderer!" yelled Deborah.

James ignored the comment and continued down the corridor. Konee and Deborah watched him walk away. They left the hospital to talk with Keshna about the arrangements they made with James. They felt deep in their hearts that they may lose their sister. James was still clinging to Theola's belief in God and her strong, aggressive attitude to fight through difficult situations.

Chapter 81

Remember Our Love

James was on his way to speak with Theola. He was hurting severely over her illness and hating himself for her condition. While James slowly took his walk down the corridor, Marilyn still conversed with her mother.

"If I don't come out of the hospital with your father…"

Marilyn interrupted. "When you go to the hospital, you always come back. It's just the baby making you a little sicker than normal. You always come home Mommy, always."

"Yes dear, but it's not the baby this time. The doctor has the baby girl now, in another room. Something else is wrong with me. If I don't come home with you this time, Daddy is going to need you more than ever to help with your brothers and sisters. You know how you helped me?"

"Yes Mommy. Another sister, that's great Mommy. Now the girls outnumber the boys." smiled Marilyn.

"That's right sweetheart." Theola slightly smiled. "But Marilyn, please, hear me. Now you must help Daddy more than ever."

"I will try to always be there for Daddy, Mommy."

"And I want you to pray, even if Daddy doesn't."

"But Mommy, I am sooo small. I pray for small things and Daddy is sooo big. I would have to pray for big things. There are so many people in the world who are big. My voice is sooo tiny Mommy. How will Jesus hear me among all the other big voices in the world? Will God hear my prayer?"

Theola smiled even more. She forgot her pain for a brief moment. "Ohhhh sweetheart, God may hear your prayer before he hears any big person's prayer. But He hears all of our prayers no matter how small or how big we are."

"Then why can't I pray right now for you to feel much better?"

"Ohhhh sweetheart, you can. But our lives are in God's Hands. If it is God's will for me to get better, then it will be so. But continue to pray and thank God, no matter how bad things are. God always comes through. Promise me you will pray, always."

Theola's words frightened Marilyn. Her mother sounded as if she would now be doing things on her own. But Marilyn loved her mother soo much that she would never let her down, no matter how afraid she felt.

"I will Mommy, I will." Tears began to form in Marilyn's eyes. "But I don't want to lose you Mommy. I'm afraid of being without you. Please don't leave Mommy, please."

Theola raised her hand to gently touch Marilyn's face. Theola stared into her watery brown eyes. "I'm not leaving you sweetheart. Whenever you want me, just close your eyes and remember the love that I have for you and the things I have tried to teach you. If you remember the love we've shared and the words we've spoken, then we will always be together." Theola's hand dropped from Marilyn's face. Her body went limp.

"No Mommy, no Mommy." Marilyn shook her mother's hand over and over again. She heard the hospital door push open. Marilyn turned to see who it was. "Daddy's coming Mommy. Pleassse hold on." Marilyn held her mother's hand until James was completely in the room.

James saw Marilyn on her knees and Theola lying unconscious in bed. He immediately swept Marilyn up from her mother's bedside and held her in his arms. James went to the door and yelled. "Doctor!"

A nurse immediately entered the room. She raced past James and Marilyn. Marilyn watched the nurse intensely.

"I'm afraid you both have to leave now," spoke the nurse.

James walked out the door, holding Marilyn in his arms. He stood by the door to see what the nurse was doing.

"Honey," James spoke to Marilyn as he kissed her on the cheek, rocking her in his arms. "I'm going to take you back home. I want you to watch your brothers and sister until I get back from the hospital. Your Aunt Keshna will be there to help you. You keep your brothers and sister in order and let your aunt know where everything is. Be a good girl for daddy."

A doctor walked briskly past them into Theola's room. Marilyn just stared in the direction of her mother as the doctor slowly closed the door behind him. James knew Marilyn didn't need to see what they were doing. He left from the doorway. Marilyn spoke out loud while her father carried her down the corridor.

"I'll remember mommy. I'll remember the love we shared and the words we spoke. I'll remember. I won't ever forget."

Tears streamed heavily from Marilyn's eyes as she watched the hospital door shut tightly to her mother's room. Marilyn felt in her heart that she had spoken to her mother for the last time. She closed her teary eyes and squeezed her father's neck tightly. James took her straight home. He drove slowly and glanced at his daughter with her head down as tears fell rapidly on her dress into her lap. He searched his heart for the right words to say to Marilyn. But the words never came.

James continued to drive silently and slowly until he finally reached the parking lot. He picked Marilyn up once again in his arms and carried her to the apartment.

Keshna greeted him at the door. "James the children are down for the night. I will be back tomorrow."

"No Keshna. If you could spend the night, I would greatly appreciate it. I'm going back to the hospital right now. I just brought Marilyn back to get some rest.

Keshna felt animosity toward James, but she loved children. Her passion for her nieces and nephews outweighed her hatred for James. "Alright James. I'll stay."

"Thank you so much."

Keshna closed the door behind him and took Marilyn from his arms to the bedroom.

Chapter 82

Love of My Life, Forever

James returned to the hospital to spend the night with Theola. When he entered her room, she appeared weak and sleepy. Theola noticed James when he walked in. She managed a smile and reached her hand out to James. He took her hand and sat on the side of the bed. He kissed her forehead.

"I hope my sisters were kind?"

"Ohhh yeah. They were as gentle as bobcats that hadn't eaten in two days and just had a fresh kill before them."

"They just don't know you like I know you. I love you James. Always and forever."

At that moment, Theola drifted into a deep slumber. They gave her some medicine and she was happy James was by her side before she fell asleep. James laid her hand upon her chest. He kneeled down next to her bed and placed both his hands together. He began to pray.

"Dear God, I know I have not recognized you as my Lord and Savior. I know, I don't know how to pray. But I am on my knees now, begging for the life of this beautiful woman I have had the pleasure of loving for the past ten years. She is the love of my life. The mother of our children. I need her to be by my side to make our family whole. Please spare her from death. She loves and believes in You so much, dear God. She doesn't deserve an ending like this. I know. Who am I to be asking a favor, when I have doubted? But Lord, Theola has never doubted you. She has gone to church every Sunday morning. She made the kids say their prayers every night. She loves You, Lord. How will I make it without her? So love her now. Please spare her life. Please. Amen."

www.ingramcontent.com/pod-product-compliance
Lightning Source LLC
Chambersburg PA
CBHW060549080526
44585CB00013B/494